UNDERSTANDING THE TEACHER UNION CONTRACT

SOCIAL PHILOSOPHY AND
POLICY FOUNDATION

UNDERSTANDING THE TEACHER UNION CONTRACT

A Citizen's Handbook

Myron Lieberman

transaction

Transaction Publishers
New Brunswick (USA) and London (UK)

Published by the Social Philosophy and Policy Foundation and by Transaction Publishers 2000

Library of Congress Cataloging-in-Publication Data

Lieberman, Myron, 1919–
    Understanding the teacher union contract : a citizen's handbook / Myron Lieberman.
        p.   cm. — (New studies in social policy ; 1)
    Includes bibliographical references (p.) and index.
    ISBN 0-7658-0014-4 (cloth). — ISBN 0-7658-0681-9 (pbk.)
    1. Teachers' contracts—United States.   I. Title.   II. Series.
    KF3409.T4L54 2000
    344.73'078—dc21   99-31392
                                                    CIP

Cover Design: Kathy Horn
Cover Image copyright © TSM/William Whitehurst, 2000

Series Editor: Ellen Frankel Paul
Series Managing Editor: Matthew Buckley

The Social Philosophy and Policy Foundation, an independent 501(c)(3) tax-exempt corporation, was established in 1985 to promote advanced research in political philosophy and in the philosophical analysis of public policy questions.

Contents

Acknowledgments

I am deeply indebted to the Scaife Family Foundation and the Donner Foundation for the financial support that culminated in this handbook. I am especially grateful for their patience as I struggled to find the most effective format for a discussion of school board/union relations. I am also grateful to the Social Philosophy and Policy Center, Bowling Green State University, Ohio, which provided the editorial and other support that made it possible to complete the research and publish the results.

I am also indebted to the New Jersey School Boards Association for permission to paraphrase materials from *The Negotiations Advisor,* its outstanding annual review of school board/union relations in New Jersey. Of course, I am solely responsible for the content of this handbook.

Preface

In the fall of 1961, I was a participant in the representation election to choose a bargaining agent for New York City's teachers. In this first significant representation election in public education, the American Federation of Teachers (AFT) affiliate in New York City, the United Federation of Teachers, won an overwhelming victory that triggered basic changes in virtually every phase of K–12 education in the United States. Within ten years, more than half the nation's elementary and secondary teachers were employed pursuant to collective agreements between teacher unions and boards of education; under the previous practice, teachers had been employed pursuant to contracts drafted by school boards and submitted to teachers individually on a "take it or leave it" basis.

Today, it is clear that teacher unionization has generated basic changes in the politics, economics, and management of education. Nevertheless, this handbook is partly the result of my conviction—as someone who was present at the creation, as it were—that there is still pervasive, widespread failure to come to terms with the implications of the bargaining revolution in education. This failure is partly the result of a failure to understand the dynamics of school board/union relations.

An understanding of these dynamics is essential for anyone who seeks to play a constructive role in education. This point is just as applicable to teachers and union representatives as it is to school board members, school administrators, legislators, and education activists. Understanding these dynamics requires an appreciation of the perspectives of all the parties in collective bargaining. In collective bargaining terminology, the parties at the table are "management" and "union." In public education, however, "management" is the school board, the party that is theoretically and legally responsible to the electorate for representing the public interest. The use of collective bargaining terminology should not obscure this critical fact; otherwise, taking sides on behalf of the public interest will be interpreted as no different from taking sides between labor and management in a private sector labor dispute. To put it in different terms, neutrality between management and unions in the private sector is very different from neutrality in the public sector, when one of the parties at the table represents the public interest.

This does not mean that the actual school board positions at the table are always in the public interest. It means only that in espousing a "management" position in this handbook, I am espousing the public interest (as I see it, of course) in a way that would not be the case if this handbook were devoted to union/management relations in the private sector.

It is not my intention to encourage school boards to adopt a "one size fits all" approach to teacher union contracts. Nevertheless, almost forty years after the bargaining revolution began, school boards are characterized by dramatically different approaches to teacher unionization and teacher bargaining. My purpose in this handbook is to analyze these differences in ways which will be useful to parties who play a role, or aspire to play a role, in school district policy-making and governance. For instance, one frequently encounters political leaders who recommend tying teacher pay to student achievement. Apart from the tremendous technical problems involved, there is virtually no recognition of the fact that such changes will have to await the expiration of collective bargaining contracts, and will have to overcome the deep-seated union objections to the change. Indeed, one reason so many education reforms never materialize is the failure to understand how they would affect, and would be affected by, teacher unionization. Because this failure is so pervasive, this handbook is intended for use by:

- School board members
- Candidates for school boards
- School administrators
- State legislators and state education agencies
- Teacher representatives
- Parents and taxpayers
- Media personnel who report on education

Of course, many people in each of these groups will, or may, disagree with the conclusions and/or recommendations this handbook sets forth. Nevertheless, the disagreements will be easier to resolve if there is better understanding of the rationale(s) for conflicting positions. This handbook will not eliminate disagreement, but my hope is that it will facilitate better understanding among all the parties interested in school board/union relations and teacher union bargaining.

1

Introduction

This handbook is about school board/union relations, especially as embodied in collective bargaining agreements. It does not discuss all of the issues in collective bargaining with teacher unions; instead, it is intended to provide an overview of school board/union relations as they are found in contracts with teacher unions and/or affected by the bargaining process.

One reason for this handbook is that school boards often do not evaluate their relationships with teacher unions as a whole. Typically, school boards consider each union issue discretely, but boards and administrators also need a comprehensive approach to school board/union relationships. This is essential to assess the work of their representatives at the bargaining table and to guide negotiations in the future.

Although my main focus will be on contractual language, most of the discussion will also be relevant to school districts that do not bargain collectively. Many school districts that do not bargain collectively have adopted policies that are the same or similar to policies in collective bargaining contracts. Contractual provisions are board policies in this respect; they differ from noncontractual policies only in their duration and manner of enforcement. These can be important differences, but the policies themselves are important, whether or not they are embodied in a collective bargaining contract. For this reason, the discussion should be useful in districts that do not bargain collectively.

I. Strategic and Tactical Considerations

School board candidates and incumbents are frequently unaware of the implications of contractual language; quite often, neither group includes experienced school district negotiators. The questions that I will raise regarding the items in a contract are intended to draw out these implications. For example, if a school district has experienced a high number of grievances, the board may be remiss in having agreed to vague language in the contract. Alert board members or candidates for the board should review the contract to ascertain whether it includes language that is conducive to grievances.

Although this handbook is designed to help readers identify contractual deficiencies, it must be used carefully to avoid being misapplied. It might be very unfair to impute responsibility for a poor contract to a particular school board member. The member may have opposed the agreement or the parts of it which are objectionable, or the agreement may have been negotiated before the board member was elected, which would make holding the member accountable for the agreement unfair. Furthermore, comparability among school districts is very important. If every school district except one has made a certain concession, it is extremely difficult for the exception to refuse to make the concession, even if the concession is undesirable from a public policy point of view.

The discussion which follows does not make any assumptions about the period of time in which items have been included in contracts, however, this can be an important consideration. Most teacher contracts have been in place for several years. In a well-run district, only a few contractual provisions change very much in a few years. The contract sets forth the rules governing the workplace; if these rules are well thought out, wholesale or frequent change should not be necessary.

Although I will frequently identify board policies that should be changed, I do not assume that such change is easily negotiated; usually it is not, especially if the change requires taking away or reducing a union advantage. To justify a potentially troublesome change in a contractual provision, school management often finds itself in a dilemma. Leaving a provision in the contract may be risky, but trying to negotiate it out of the contract may alert the union to the provision's strategic value.

The judgments about what to do in these situations can be difficult to make, and the right decision often depends on the negotiating climate when the danger is recognized. There is a strong tendency in bargaining to underestimate the risks of potentially dangerous provisions, and to assume that everything will turn out well if unpleasant issues are avoided. Sometimes troublesome issues must be raised, but in general, school board negotiators should not raise them unless they are prepared to insist that the risky provisions be removed. Sometimes potentially troublesome provisions remain in contracts for years, and it is not until they are triggered that school boards discover their undesirable implications. Of course, by then, the board cannot remedy the problem until the next set of contract negotiations, and at that point the remedies may be very expensive.

Although I will discuss bargaining strategy and tactics from time to time, this handbook is not a manual on these subjects; readers interested in a more extensive discussion of bargaining strategy and tactics should consult the references listed in Appendix B. There are, nevertheless, some important strategic and tactical considerations that readers might find useful to keep in mind while reading this handbook. The fact that a contractual item is undesirable from a management perspective does not necessarily mean that an effort should be made to remove it. A great deal depends upon situational factors such as the following:

- What is the actual and/or potential harm resulting from the item?
- How important is the item to the union?
- What inducements can be offered to the union to delete or amend the item?
- Are the union negotiators sensitive to management needs, and are they capable of persuading the union to accept the change that is needed?
- How long has the item been in the contract?
- What is the duration of the contract being negotiated?

In districts where relationships are less adversarial, a different concern may arise: Is it worthwhile to introduce a proposal that may compromise the amicable atmosphere by generating adamant union opposition? The answer is that sometimes it is—and sometimes it is not. This is the kind of decision that must be made locally. It is seldom easy to take away negotiated benefits, but boards should not assume that it is impossible or that the skies will fall if the effort is made. Generally speaking, the issue is usually not whether the union can be persuaded to forgo a union benefit, but rather what the quid pro quo will be: What price, in terms of management concessions, must the board pay to "take away" benefits? The "price" cannot always be predicted accurately, but sometimes the change is worth it, and sometimes it is not.

Generally speaking, board members tend to underestimate the negative consequences of potentially harmful items in the contract. It is a human trait to overestimate the likelihood of favorable outcomes, and to underestimate the likelihood of negative consequences. As Samuel Johnson said about marriage, it is "the triumph of hope over experience."

Board members often fail to grasp the implications of a point that is frequently emphasized by the teacher unions. Board/union relations may be very cooperative, but the union will continue to insist upon contractual protections against abuses of discretion by the board. The union argument is that board membership changes; today's "nice guys" might retire, or lose their reelection campaigns, or leave the board for various other reasons. Given the potential for such changes, the union argues, board/union relations should not be dependent upon the relationships between people whose status at the bargaining table may change for many reasons without fault on anyone's part.

This argument is just as applicable to board concerns that the union will take advantage of potentially harmful provisions in the contract. The union may point out that the provisions in question have been in the contract for several years without leading to any of the abuses that the board fears. The board's response should resemble the argument posed above: Union negotiators and union leaders come and go; hence, the board should not rely upon the good will of union officials who will not hold their positions forever. Unfortunately, boards do not emphasize this point as often as the unions do.

II. The Organization of This Handbook

The organization of this handbook posed several difficult trade-offs, but the plan adopted was deemed most useful to a wide range of readers. Contractual issues are grouped into nine broad categories, with a chapter devoted to each category (Chapters 2 through 10). Within each chapter, the main issues are discussed briefly and are usually followed by examples that highlight the important points to be made. Each example is usually followed by brief comments that summarize the points made by the example. Because actual contract terminology varies widely, readers especially interested in a particular contractual issue should rely on the index as well as the chapter outline to locate the discussion of specific items of interest.

In actual contracts, most of the items referred to in this handbook are categorized in several different ways. For example, sometimes districts give teachers a certain amount of "released time" with pay to conduct union business; contractual provisions involving this practice can be categorized under "union rights," "leaves of absence," "grievance procedure," or "miscellaneous," to cite just four examples. Consequently, it is important to search for items under different headings. Also, discussion of an item under one heading does not necessarily preclude discussion of other facets of it under other headings. Finally, the way contractual items are categorized here frequently differs from the way they are often categorized in their contracts; in fact, some of the chapter headings, such as "Released-Time Subsidies," will not be found in any contract.

III. The Examples of Contract Language

Most of the examples in this handbook, good and bad, are taken from actual contracts, but their identity has been removed. It was not feasible to show every contractual nuance in the examples; instead, I have tried to clarify the most common contractual issues that relate to teacher unions. As will be evident, these issues frequently have a much larger impact upon school districts than the items that explicitly affect teachers.

Generally speaking, the examples of contract language in this handbook are listed in order of their appeal to management; the most highly recommended language is usually that of the last example. Again, it should be emphasized that "management" in this context is a government agency—the board—that is legally responsible for operating public schools in the public interest. In this context, as I evaluate the pros and cons associated with the various examples, I refer to the "management position" or the "board position" as the one that best reflects the public interest.

The discussions frequently refer to examples, which are numbered in parentheses; thus "(2)" refers to example (2). It must also be emphasized that contractual clauses are often modified by contractual provisions located elsewhere in the contract. For example, a contract may include a no-strike clause, but the definition of "strike" that affects the clause's applicability may be located in a separate section of the contract.

IV. Limitations of This Handbook

At the outset, readers should be aware of the limitations of this handbook. First, it does not take account of statutory differences between the states on bargaining issues. This limitation requires a careful approach to evaluating the terms of contracts or board policies on terms and conditions of employment which are not incorporated in contracts. The collective bargaining contract or board policies may not include a specific policy on an issue because such a policy is already incorporated in state law. For example, in New York, nonmembers are required to pay "agency fees" to the union from their first day of employment. ("Agency fees" are fees, usually two-thirds or more of dues, that nonmembers of a union must pay to the unions for union representation.) As a result, many teacher unions in New York do not include the agency fee requirement in the contract. Without knowledge of New York law, one would erroneously conclude from New York contracts that teachers are not required to pay agency fees. In short, the mere absence of a policy in the collective bargaining contract does not necessarily mean that the district is not subject to the policy.

Another caveat relates to the fact that contractual items or board policies often cannot be interpreted correctly in isolation from other items in the contract. For instance, the contract in district X might provide the union with more benefits than the contract in district Y. However, in district X, management might have more discretion to curtail or terminate the benefits. In the absence of the complete picture, one might draw erroneous conclusions about the extent of union benefits in district X.

Even apart from the statutory provisions not included in the contract, the contractual obligations of the school board are not always fully set forth in its collective bargaining contracts. For example, the contract may state that the board will continue various "past practices" relating to terms and conditions of employment. One such past practice may be to provide one class period per day for the union president to conduct union business. In fact, even without an explicit past practice clause in the contract, the board might be obligated to continue the practice until it is changed in negotiations.

Another limitation of this handbook is that it cannot adequately reflect the tremendous variability among teacher union contracts. These contracts vary in the following ways:

- Which items are included or excluded
- How items are headed or categorized—for example, teacher rights to use controversial materials may be included under "academic freedom," "teacher rights," "curriculum," or "miscellaneous," or may be omitted altogether
- The distribution of rights and obligations between the parties
- The extent to which the union is an actor or is designated in the items negotiated

The last point is especially relevant to this handbook. The union negotiates all the items in the contract, which could be two to three hundred pages long and could include hundreds of specific provisions. Nevertheless, the union is not explicitly mentioned in most of the provisions. Consider the following items from a school district contract:

(A) The union shall have the right to post notices on a union bulletin board in the teacher lounge in every school.
(B) Teachers shall be entitled to ten (10) days of sick leave for every year of service.

The union has negotiated both of these provisions, but the union itself is involved in (A) in a way that it is not involved in (B).

Table 1 shows the extent to which the union is explicitly mentioned in a large Midwestern urban school district contract. This contract includes an unusually large number of items that explicitly refer to the union; in effect, the union is a co-manager in this particular district.

V. Unions of Support Personnel

This handbook does not discuss issues pertaining specifically to support personnel, such as bus drivers, custodians, and cafeteria workers. Nevertheless, on most issues relating to unions per se, the teacher union contract is likely to be

Table 1. Union involvement in contract provisions in a large Midwestern school district

Article		Article	
Recognition	✓	Health Examinations	×
Definitions	✓	Payroll Changes	✓
Agency Shop	✓	Teachers-In-Charge	✓
Building Privileges	✓	Administrative Appointments	✓
Grievance Procedure	✓	Academic Freedom	✓
Seniority	✓	Music	✓
Teaching Assignments	✓	Reading Teachers	×
Elementary Schools	✓	Art Teachers	×
Secondary High Schools	✓	Special Education	✓
Team Teaching	×	Audio-Visual Coordinators	×
Transfer Policy	✓	Library/Media Specialists	×
Tutors and Hourly Teachers	×	Visiting Teachers	×
School Closings	×	School Consultation Program	✓
Class Size	✓	Driver Education	×
Recall from Layoff Status	✓	School Nurses	×
Conditions of Teaching	×	Physical Education Specialists	×
School Facilities	✓	Teachers on Special Assignment	×
Building Supplies	✓	Retiring Teachers	×
Property	✓	Insurance	✓
Lunch Period	×	Duration, Renewal, No Strike	✓
Evaluation of Certified Personnel	✓	Integration of Faculties	✓
Substitutes	✓	Special Education Referrals	×
Grading	✓	Assignment Preference Forms	×
School Funds	✓	Guidelines for Student Discipline	×
Student Discipline	✓	Guidelines for New Educational Programs	✓
Student Teachers	✓	Guidelines for Substitute Work	✓
Teachers' Meetings	✓	Insurance Benefits	×
School Intervention Team	✓	Equipment for Vocational Teachers	×
School Calendar	✓	Controversial Materials	×
Arrival, Dismissal Time	✓	Jury Duty Procedures	×
Staff Development	✓		
Department Chairpersons	✓		
Leaves	✓		
Summer School	✓		
Night School	✓		
Personnel Files	✓		
Discharge, Review, Discipline	✓		
Salary Schedule	✓		
Vocational Teachers	×		
Extracurricular Stipends	×		
Special Services Salaries	×		

✓: Union is an actor in the contractual provision.
×: Union is not an actor in the contractual provision.

similar, if not identical, to contracts with these other unions. One reason for this is that it would be difficult for school boards to accept union proposals in one union contract while not accepting them in another union contract in the same district. If an objectionable item is found in a teacher contract, it will probably be found in other district contracts as well. The same point applies to school district policies outside the contract. Whatever rights and privileges are accorded to teacher unions are likely to be accorded to other unions as well. Furthermore, in many states and school districts, support personnel are represented by the teacher unions, and the practice is likely to increase in the future. For these reasons, it can be essential to review nonteacher as well as teacher union contracts when planning an action strategy. If an offending provision is included in nonteacher as well as teacher contracts, unions of support personnel will also be opposed to removing or amending the provision.

VI. Legislative Dimensions

For the most part, collective bargaining in public education is authorized and regulated by state law, not federal law. State laws often differ on several issues discussed in this handbook. The major differences include:

- Whether collective bargaining is authorized, allowed, or prohibited
- Union rights to payroll deduction of dues
- The legality of agency fees, that is, fees that must be paid to the union as a term or condition of employment
- The rights of teacher union employees to become or remain active members of the state teacher retirement system
- The scope of collective bargaining in public education
- The legality of teacher strikes

The critical point is that certain issues may be resolved at either the local level or the state level. In some situations, it may be easier to reach a statewide solution than a local one. For instance, it may be impossible to prohibit agency fee payments in some districts, while a statewide prohibition of agency fees is politically possible. By the same token, reforms that are not feasible on a statewide basis may nevertheless be feasible in certain school districts in the state. This handbook emphasizes local solutions, but whether they are more feasible than statewide solutions must be resolved on a case-by-case basis.

In some school districts, local solutions are highly unlikely because of the acrimonious relationship between a particular board and the union. In other districts, relationships may be relatively calm and cooperative and more might be accomplished. In the former situation, proposing a change opposed by the union might exacerbate tensions, or might induce the union to be less cooperative because its prerogatives are threatened.

VII. Understanding the Union Role

A thorough understanding of unions and the bargaining process is a prerequisite to successful negotiations and school board/union relations. Yet, in the midst of assembling comparative data, developing board proposals, and analyzing the impact of union proposals, few board negotiating teams assess the union as an organization. Understanding the union, its role, and its needs is necessary, however, for the board to set realistic bargaining expectations, plan effective bargaining strategies, and develop a productive ongoing school board/union relationship. This section will provide some discussion of union dynamics that will be helpful to those who wish to understand union goals and operations.

Most interactions between school boards and school district unions occur in an environment marked by conflict as well as cooperation. For example, arbitration involves an appeal of school board decisions, and unions try to limit the administration's flexibility and increase the board's allocation of district resources to employees represented by the unions.

The dual nature of board/union relationships results from the differing responsibilities and perspectives of the two parties. The union is the advocate of employee interests; the board represents the entire district. Consequently, the board must balance employee interests with the needs of students, the district educational program, taxpayers, and parents in order to meet its responsibilities. At the same time, despite the inherently adversarial aspects of the relationship, board/union interdependence is also a fact. Generally speaking, a board cannot legally change terms and conditions of employment without obtaining agreement from the union, nor can the union achieve its goals without the board's agreement. The exceptions are cases in which the parties have bargained to an impasse without reaching agreement; in these situations, the board is usually free to act unilaterally. To avoid situations in which board/union relations deteriorate badly, the ability to cooperate and to reach agreement is essential. Unfortunately, the conflicting perspectives of the board and the union frequently lead to hostile attitudes which weaken the parties' ability to cooperate. One should not make the mistake of assuming that better understanding necessarily leads to a more benign attitude toward the union. Sometimes a "better understanding" justifies the most determined opposition to union proposals and union bargaining strategies.

The Union as a Bargaining Agent

The teacher union is the exclusive bargaining agent of the teacher bargaining unit. As such, the union's objective in bargaining is to improve the terms and conditions of teacher employment. The interests of others become union considerations only in later stages of bargaining, when the union must assess the realities of reaching a settlement. During most of the bargaining process, the teacher union will focus on additional benefits for teachers and oppose any efforts to reduce existing benefits.

Employee welfare is regarded everywhere as the union's primary objective, but this is really not the case. The union's primary objective is the continued existence of the union as an effective organization. To be sure, this objective is also justified in terms of teacher welfare, but conflicts between teacher welfare and union welfare are usually resolved in favor of union welfare. For example, if a full-time union negotiator must choose between another half-percent salary increase for teachers and an agency fee clause for the union, the choice will virtually always be the agency fee clause.

Understandably, board members are often offended, angered, and frustrated by the union's positions and tactics. Board members may tend to react negatively to what they perceive to be (or what are!) selfish, narrow-minded negotiating positions that ignore the needs of the district. Despite their rhetoric about standing up for good education, the unions' role is to promote both teacher and union welfare; the board's responsibility is to represent and to protect the needs of the district. The unions assert that their proposals are in the public interest, even when this is obviously not the case. Much as they might wish these problems did not arise, board members must be prepared to deal with them.

The Union and the Teachers

Board members sometimes characterize a union's bargaining proposals as "the union talking—our teachers would never support that position." Although this assessment may be accurate occasionally, it is usually not accurate, especially in the later stages of negotiations. Indeed, on some occasions, tentative agreements have been rejected by a union's membership and the teachers have sent the union back to the table for a better deal. Generally, however, teachers support their union's bargaining positions. After all, most people, including most board members, find it easy to exaggerate how much their self-interest is also in the public interest.

Sometimes, union leadership may keep the membership uninformed about the progress of negotiations, or may deliberately misrepresent board positions. In such instances, board members are naturally motivated to tell the teachers the truth. Although justified from this perspective, direct communications from the board to the staff about the progress of negotiations can backfire unless such communications are drafted carefully. The board's communications to teachers may be perceived as a self-serving attempt to bypass and discredit the union; in response, teachers may rally behind union leadership and more vigorously support union positions.

Although not every teacher fully endorses every union position or is in complete agreement with union priorities, teachers assume that the union, not the board, represents them at the table. Teachers trust the union because they believe that the union exists to protect their interests. After all, the teachers have chosen it to represent them in negotiations. Repudiation of the union is far more likely to result from the perception that the union is too friendly with the board and is not sufficiently aggressive in protecting teachers' interests than from a sense that the union is disliked by the board because it is too demanding. Furthermore, teachers know that a show of unity during negotiations may be necessary to achieve their bargaining goals. Thus, a lack of trust in the union and its leadership will generally be reflected in future elections for union office, not by repudiation of the union's efforts during negotiations. The bottom line is that in most negotiating situations, teachers support and defend their union. However, efforts to discredit union leadership are sometimes essential, though boards must have a solid case and be prepared for a protracted battle over the issue.

The Union as an Organization

Local teacher unions are virtually always affiliated with a statewide and a national union. Most are affiliated with the National Education Association (NEA) or the American Federation of Teachers (AFT). The state and national unions provide locals with a wealth of information concerning legislation, negotiations, and economic trends; in addition, most NEA locals utilize the services of a professional negotiator (also called a "UniServ director") provided by the state association. Legally, however, the local association, not the state organization, is the teachers' bargaining agent.

Regardless of its affiliation or its degree of cohesiveness with its parent organizations, the local association has goals: it collects dues for itself as well as for the county, state, and national branches; it is governed by a constitution and by-laws; it holds periodic elections in which the leadership is accountable to the membership. As such, the local association is subject to the same pressures, problems, and needs of any other membership organization. These internal problems will affect the union's behavior at the table; therefore, awareness of them is helpful in the bargaining process.

Goal Attainment

The union's primary goals are union and teacher welfare. The most common ways to promote teacher welfare are by achieving safeguards against abuse of administrative discretion, providing appeal procedures to administrative actions, limiting teachers' workload, and increasing teacher compensation. Special goals also emerge when court decisions or new legislation indicate a need to address a particular issue affecting the local membership.

Teachers judge their local leadership primarily by its ability to promote teacher welfare. Leadership which is perceived to be unsuccessful in meeting local needs, or which is perceived to be lagging behind other associations in delivering benefits, may be replaced in the next election by other individuals perceived to be more aggressive in promoting teacher welfare. Membership dissatisfaction seldom leads to decertification of the incumbent union, mainly because viable alternatives to the NEA or the AFT have not been available in the states with collective bargaining laws.

Comparability is extremely important, both to school boards and to teachers. If the majority of the associations in the area have negotiated dental plans, achieving dental insurance will become a high priority for local affiliates who do not have it. Unions who have dental insurance will perceive proposals to "cap" board expenditures for it as attempts to erode existing employee benefits. Also, a union which has always been in the forefront of obtaining benefits will guard its position as the pacesetter. Thus, a union's goals are virtually always affected by its level of benefits compared to other unions in the same geographical area. In any event, the board should respond realistically to union proposals; this requires board review of how its benefits compare with the benefits in nearby districts. This does not imply that a board must avoid providing the smallest benefit in the region on a particular issue; however, if the board does provide the smallest benefit, it can expect a union proposal and emphasis on that issue in negotiations. The board should avoid focusing negotiations on benefits with respect to which the union is trying to play "catch-up"; an effective way to counter these sorts of demands is to compare the board's total compensation package with the total compensation package in nearby districts.

Maintaining Unity

Union goals are an expression of membership priorities. However, bargaining units include individuals whose priorities frequently differ. A teacher unit can include librarians and nurses whose working conditions differ significantly from those of classroom teachers. The needs of elementary school teachers can be considerably different from those of high school teachers, whose assignments often create unique problems which are not shared by other teachers. Even teachers in bargaining units composed of only one job classification often have conflicting bargaining objectives. Senior teachers may want increases in longevity pay and retirement benefits; younger staff may seek tuition reimbursement to foster professional development and a compressed salary guide to accelerate their movement toward higher salaries. Teachers who are the primary wage-earners in their families want health insurance coverage for dependents, while single teachers or secondary wage-earners may be much more interested in higher salaries.

The union leadership and its bargaining team must try to resolve these internal differences and to create unity amid the diversity. To that end, the union leadership may base its bargaining priorities upon the number of unit members who are strongly committed to proposed changes. The tentative settlement presented to the teachers for ratification must be approved by a majority of the membership; the greater the improvements and the greater the number of diverse needs addressed in the settlement, the better the chances of acceptance and membership unity.

The union's bargaining team often initiates the process of achieving unity before it enters into negotiations. Unions frequently poll the membership to determine what changes in terms and conditions of employment teachers desire, and their negotiators include the most frequent responses in their proposals. The board team should assess the number of unit members who will be affected by a proposal and their influence within the bargaining unit. An understanding of the diversity of union needs can also assist the board in arriving at a settlement that would gain union acceptance.

During the negotiating process, the union team reports on the progress of bargaining to the union's executive committee and/or to the membership. Areas of board opposition are discussed, and the membership is usually prepared for union defeat on some matters and compromise on others. A skillful union team, just like its board counterpart, is aware that negotiations are marked by slow, incremental movement, shaped by compromise, timing, and political reality. By letting its membership know what is achievable and what is impossible, the union is demonstrating its efforts for the membership as well as working toward realistic membership expectations, ratification, and unity. If a union's bargaining team is unsuccessful in persuading the membership that the tentative agreement represents the best achievable agreement, the settlement will not be ratified, or its approval by a narrow majority will threaten the unity of the union. Understandably, the union bargaining team seeks compelling explanations to present to its membership.

In preparing to support their bargaining positions, board negotiators must develop rationales which will be persuasive to the union's bargaining team. Board positions that reflect considerations of the impact of proposals on the union and teachers, as well as on the district, will be more convincing than generalized emotional responses. The union negotiators should be able to utilize the board's arguments to explain to their membership why the union's proposals are unattainable at this time.

The intensity with which union leadership will seek to deliver additional benefits is affected by many factors, including the leadership's sense of its own security. A bargaining team representing a bargaining unit that is torn by dissension, that includes a small majority of union members, or that faces a challenge by either a rival union or a rival slate of officers, may feel intense pressure to demonstrate its success in achieving teacher benefits. A threatened leadership may be dominated by its own internal needs, and members of such a leadership may become intransigent advocates of a position that is outside the realistic range of settlement. In contrast, secure leadership is less likely to lose sight of the interdependence of union and district needs that is necessary for a settlement.

Although boards of education should avoid becoming involved in a union's internal affairs, the relationship between the board and the union inevitably affects the dynamics of bargaining. Union leadership that is bypassed or ignored by the board will be perceived as lacking in effectiveness and credibility; leadership whose role and status are recognized by the board is much more likely to receive membership respect and support. By responding to the union with acceptance of its bargaining role, a school board can enhance the union's willingness to accept an agreement that enables the board to fulfill its own responsibilities.

VIII. Unfair Labor Practices

In some states, the teacher-bargaining statute applies only to teachers or to school district personnel; in other states, teacher unions are authorized to bargain collectively pursuant to statutes that cover state and/or local public employees generally. Both types of statutes are referred to as "teacher-bargaining statutes" in this handbook. In the states which have enacted teacher-bargaining statutes, school board negotiators must avoid unfair labor practices. These are practices which constitute violations of the bargaining statutes or the regulations established by the state labor boards responsible for administering the statutes.

Generally speaking, the state labor boards follow the guidelines established by the National Labor Relations Board (NLRB) in evaluating charges of unfair labor practices. The NLRB guidelines utilize two tests to assess the lawfulness of bargaining conduct, that is, to determine whether a party has committed an unfair labor practice. For "per se" violations, the issue is whether the conduct in question undermines the purpose of the law regardless of the intent of the acting party. For instance, if one of the parties refused to meet with the other party, there would be no need to ascertain the intent of the party refusing to meet; its conduct would "per se" violate the duty to meet and negotiate in good faith.

The most common "per se" violations of the duty to negotiate in good faith are the following:

- Bargaining with individual employees or any third party without permission of the union
- Changing a term or condition of employment without making any effort to bargain on it
- Refusing to meet at reasonable times and places to negotiate
- Refusing to negotiate on a mandatory subject of bargaining
- Negotiating to an impasse on a nonmandatory subject of bargaining

Although only an employer would commit the first two "per se" violations, either party could commit any of the others. Again, it should be emphasized that if one of the parties has committed one of the actions listed above, it will normally be regarded as having committed an unfair labor practice. The penalties can be severe, although this will depend on several factors, including the conduct of the other party in negotiations.

In addition to "per se" violations, some unfair labor practices are based upon a judgment that the offending party's conduct was characterized by "bad faith," that is, a subjective intent to refuse to bargain with a sincere desire to reach agreement. Bad faith that rises to the level of an unfair labor practice can be inferred from the following conduct:

- Refusing to provide relevant information when asked to do so
- Refusing to reduce matters agreed to in negotiations to writing
- Refusing to agree to a reasonable bargaining schedule and/or repeated failure to observe an agreed-upon schedule
- Designating bargaining representatives who lack authority to bargain
- Repudiating tentative agreements without a valid reason for doing so
- Insisting upon concessions as a precondition of bargaining
- Introducing new proposals certain to be rejected when agreement appears to be within reach
- Making proposals that are consistently more difficult for the other party to accept
- Adopting a rigid, inflexible position toward proposals by the other party
- Surface bargaining, that is, giving the appearance of bargaining while adhering to a course of conduct that clearly evinces intent to avoid reaching agreement
- Insisting on bargaining items only in the order desired

- Proposing a contract that is of unreasonably brief or unreasonably long duration
- Engaging in delaying tactics in efforts to reach an impasse without bargaining
- Refusing to consider union security proposals, such as those involving the payroll deduction of dues, agency fees, and "maintenance of membership"
- Repudiating tentative agreements without a valid reason for doing so

Usually, a party who commits an unfair labor practice on the basis of the party's "totality of conduct" has engaged in more than one pattern of conduct that evinces bad faith. The above indicators of bad faith often appear to be highly subjective to inexperienced observers, but experienced practitioners usually agree on whether the facts of a case do or do not rise to the level of an unfair labor practice. The issues have been litigated thousands of times, and the result is widespread agreement on what constitutes an unfair labor practice.

In what follows, it is especially important to recognize the distinction between "hard bargaining," which is legal, and a failure to bargain in good faith, which is not. In hard bargaining, there may be intent to derive the maximum benefit from the weakness of the other party, but there is a sincere desire to reach agreement on terms that are not outrageous; some of the contract clauses and recommendations in this handbook can be considered examples of hard bargaining by either the school board or the union. Nevertheless, readers should never lose sight of the distinction between hard bargaining and a refusal to bargain in good faith.

IX. Summary: The Board's Response

In spite of their appreciation of union needs, boards should not agree to terms and conditions which will interfere with the effective administration of the district's educational program. A refusal to agree, however, should be based on the long-range and short-range implications of agreement. It should not be based upon the board's dislike of the union negotiator, its resentment of the bargaining process, or its desire to "win big" and to bring the union to its knees. Appropriate board responses are based upon careful consideration of the needs of both the union and the board.

Well-reasoned board responses do not change the adversarial relationship between the board and the union, but they may reduce the antagonism that interferes with the parties' ability to reach agreement. Reasonable board responses do not necessarily lead to acceptance in the short run, because union leadership may have raised unrealistic expectations among the membership. Sometimes previous boards have made unrealistic and unwise concessions that should be changed, even deleted. Boards that must play "cleanup" are likely to be attacked by the unions no matter how reasonable the boards' positions may be. Although reaching agreement is important, it should never receive a higher priority than a board's ability to administer its district effectively.

2

School Board/Union Relations

Although all the items in a contract between a school board and a teacher union have the potential to affect school board/union relations, it may be helpful to begin by discussing bargaining issues that affect—or can affect—all of the other items in the contract. One example of such an issue is a contract's no-strike clause, which establishes a condition—a prohibition on strikes—that typically applies to all other items in the contract. This chapter discusses several issues of this sort: the preamble, union recognition, union exclusivity, management rights, no-strike clauses, consultation rights, joint committees, statutory benefits, contract printing/distribution, and contractual definitions.

I. Preamble

A collective bargaining contract is a legal document that spells out the legal rights and obligations of the negotiating parties. Language that is not essential for this purpose should not be included in the contract. There is no good reason, from the perspective of the board, to negotiate language that does not spell out legal rights or obligations.

The primary purposes of a labor contract are to (1) state the terms and conditions of employment of employees, (2) place limitations on the ability of the employer to change those terms and conditions, and (3) specify certain kinds of duties or requirements of employees. Except for definitions and clarifications of terms in a contract, there is little need for language in the contract that does not fulfill one or more of these three purposes. Consequently, there is seldom any need for a preamble that goes beyond identifying the parties and the date of the agreement.

Referring to clauses in the preamble, the General Counsel of the NEA has said that they are not strictly necessary as a legal matter. However, he notes, arbitrators and courts, when trying to interpret ambiguous provisions in the contract, may examine these clauses to consider the intentions of the negotiating parties. Thus, the General Counsel warns, the language of these clauses must be carefully drafted.

"Feel-good" preambles are usually included at the union's request. The school board should refuse from the outset to bargain over items that are outside the scope of negotiations, and preambles are typically such items unless they are confined to identifying the parties and the date of the contract. A less desirable alternative for the board would be to insist upon a quid pro quo: for example, if the union insists upon language in the preamble to the effect that the purpose of the contract is to "improve instruction," the board should insist upon language to the effect that an additional purpose of the contract is to separate teachers who are not fulfilling their professional responsibilities. It is best not to get into this sort of exchange, but occasionally it may be appropriate. Remember that preambles are sometimes cited during arbitration or legal proceedings to ascertain the intent of the parties at the time of negotiations, so preambles can affect legal rights or obligations. The goal of the board is to avoid preamble language that can be interpreted in a manner that is disadvantageous to the board.

Discussion of examples

Examples (1) and (2) below include language that school boards should not accept in a preamble:

(1) WHEREAS, the Board and the Association recognize and declare that providing a quality education for the students of the _____ School District is their primary aim and that the character of such education depends predominantly upon the quality of teaching, the availability of materials, the functional utility of facilities, the release of imagination in planning, the application of democratic processes in administration, and the maintenance of high morale among the teaching faculty, and

   WHEREAS, the members of the teaching profession are particularly qualified to advise the formulation of policies and programs designed to improve educational standards, and

WHEREAS, the Board has an obligation to negotiate with the Association with respect to the terms and conditions of employment, and

WHEREAS, the parties have reached certain understandings which they desire to confirm in this Agreement, be it

RESOLVED, in consideration of the following mutual covenants, it is hereby agreed as follows . . .

(2) This Agreement is made and entered into by and between the _____ School District and the _____ Classroom Teachers Association this 1st day of September, 1998.

WHEREAS, the _____ Board of Education and the _____ Teachers Association, the parties to this Agreement, agree that providing the highest standards of education for the children of the District is their mutual aim and that the character of such education depends predominantly upon the quality and morale of the teaching staff, and

WHEREAS, the Board of Education is the duly elected governing body of the District, and

WHEREAS, the members of the teaching profession are particularly qualified to assist in the improvement of educational standards, and

WHEREAS, a free and open exchange of views is desirable and necessary by and between the parties hereto in their efforts to negotiate in good faith and with respect to wages, hours, and conditions of employment, and

WHEREAS, members of the teaching staff in the District have the right to join, or not join, any organization for their professional or economic improvements:

NOW THEREFORE IT IS AGREED . . .

Any interpretation of the contract that follows (1) will be tilted toward union positions. In a salary dispute, for example, the union will point to the clause stressing "the quality of teaching" to justify to a factfinder its demand for higher salaries. Similarly, if sound administration requires some actions that teachers do not like, as is usually the case, the union will cite the clause that stresses "the maintenance of high morale among the teaching faculty" to support its arguments that a district action violates the contract, or to argue that a factfinder should uphold the union's position during an impasse in negotiations. Example (2) has similar problems. In both examples, the school board should have added the clause, "consistent with the limited resources available to the district," to those clauses stating that quality education is the objective of the contract.

However, it is preferable not to waste time at the bargaining table on such peripheral matters.

Examples (3) and (4) below are businesslike preambles that avoid the rhetorical dangers discussed above:

(3) This Agreement made and entered into July 1, 1998, by and between the _____ Board of Education, whose address is _____ _____, hereinafter referred to as the "District," and the _____ Teachers Association, whose address is _____, hereinafter referred to as the "Association," constitutes a bilateral and binding agreement pursuant to Chapter _____ of the Government Code.

(4) This Agreement is entered into this 1st day of July, 1998, by and between the _____ Board of Education, hereinafter called the "Board," and the _____ Association, hereinafter called the "Association."

II. Recognition of the Union

The union represents teachers who fill certain positions. These positions are set forth in a "unit determination." If a position is not included in the unit determination, the union is not legally authorized to bargain over the terms and conditions of employment for teachers who fill the excluded positions. For example, if substitute positions are not included in the unit determination, the school board is not required to bargain over the terms and conditions of employment for substitute teachers unless the latter are included in a different bargaining unit. If included in a different bargaining unit, the substitutes may or may not be represented by the union that represents teachers. The unit determinations may be agreed upon by the board and the union or, especially in case of disagreement, be resolved by the state labor board.

The recognition clause should state clearly and unambiguously the positions whose occupants are represented by the union as well as the positions whose occupants are excluded from representation. The exclusions can be summarized by stating that "positions not specifically included in the bargaining unit are excluded from it." This issue should be resolved prior to bargaining so that the parties mutually understand which employees are represented by the union and are covered by the contract. It should not be left in doubt whether the union is legally authorized to bargain for employees holding certain positions.

Discussion of examples

Consider the following example:

(1) The Board hereby recognizes the Association as the sole and exclusive bargaining representative for a collective bargaining unit consisting of, but not limited to:

Classroom teachers
Contract substitute teachers
Attendance teachers
Librarians
Guidance counselors
Speech and hearing teachers
School psychologists
School social workers
Library and media specialists

This recognition shall be applicable for a period not to exceed the expiration date of this Agreement.

A joint committee of the District and the Association shall be established to study all implications, including financial and fiscal impact, seniority and tenure rights, etc., of recognizing school instructors and/or home/hospital teachers as members of the teachers' bargaining unit.

The recognition clause in (1) is undesirable for three reasons. First, the "consisting of, but not limited to" clause implies that the union represents additional positions; if the union does, these additional positions should be spelled out. The list of positions included in the bargaining unit should be accompanied by a list of the excluded positions in order to remove any doubt on the issue. Furthermore, the board should itself determine the status of these positions whose inclusion in the bargaining unit is uncertain; this should not be left to negotiation. If the union disagrees with the board's determination, it has the right to challenge it by filing unfair labor practice charges with the state labor board.

If the positions are likely to be included as a matter of law, the union is not likely to acquiesce to their exclusion. If the legal issue is in doubt, the board should resolve the issue as it deems appropriate. There is no reason why the board should agree to a joint committee to study the inclusion of new positions in the bargaining unit; the language in (1) agreeing to such a committee is a second reason that example (1) is undesirable. The union can say whatever it has to say about the issue without a joint committee.

A final reason that example (1) is undesirable is that the statement about the period in which the recognition is in effect is gratuitous. The union is the exclusive representative of the teachers until it is decertified. No purpose is served by stating the duration of the recognition.

The language in the following example is also problematic:

(2) A. The Board hereby recognizes the Association as the sole and exclusive bargaining agent for all employees defined in the certification instrument ordered by the Public Employees Relations Commission on the ___ day of _____: Entered the ___ day of _____, in _____.

B. The term "teacher" when used hereinafter in this Agreement shall refer to all employees represented by the Association in the negotiating unit as determined by Paragraph A, above.

C. The Board agrees not to negotiate with any teachers' organization other than the Association for the duration of this Agreement on matters concerning terms and conditions of employment.

D. In being granted recognition as the sole and exclusive negotiations representative, the Association shall represent all personnel in the defined unit regardless of membership in the Association, and without discrimination.

E. The Board agrees not to negotiate individually with any teacher on matters covered by this Agreement. The parties agree that this provision shall not apply to grievances.

In (2), clauses C, D, and E simply repeat legal obligations of the parties and should not have been included in the recognition clause. Clause E reflects confusion between negotiating a procedure for dealing with grievances (which is a matter for board/union negotiations) and negotiations with respect to a particular grievance. Most negotiated grievance procedures allow employees involved in grievances to represent themselves or choose another party to represent them; however, even when the grievant does not choose to have union representation in processing a grievance, the employee is not free to negotiate a separate grievance procedure. Therefore, clause E's prohibition on board negotiations with individual teachers is confusing, because some authorities regard processing grievances as an extension of negotiations.

Also, the contract should state the unit determination instead of merely identifying it by reference to another source, as clause A does in (2). If the contract does not state the unit determination, then over time the parties will forget or fail to take the unit determination into account; there is no need to run this risk.

In (3), the board unwisely agrees to a clause that states that the appropriateness of including a "new class or division of employees . . . shall be determined jointly by the Board and the Association":

(3) The Board of Education (hereinafter referred to as the Board) hereby recognizes the Association and agrees that the Association shall be the exclusive bargaining agent for classroom teachers, guidance counselors, pupil personnel (teachers and social workers), curriculum coordinators, team leaders, department heads, vocational teachers, occupational specialists, librarians, teachers of the homebound, teachers of migrants, case workers, diagnosticians, psychologists, and ROTC instructors, hereafter referred to as teachers.

The appropriateness of any new class or division of employees belonging to the bargaining unit shall be determined jointly by the Board and the Association. If agreement is not possible, the matter shall be referred to the Public Employment Relations Board.

It is acceptable to get the views of the union on these issues, but the use of the phrase "determined jointly" in the above example would require the board to negotiate with the union over these matters. The board should make and implement its own determination; as noted above, the union can, if it so desires, challenge the board's decision by filing charges of unfair labor practice with the state's public employment relations board.

Example (4) below is a straightforward recognition clause that simply lists the included and excluded classes. Note that (4) does not require the board to negotiate over the inclusion of new positions; also, it does not convert any statutory obligations into contractual ones:

(4) The District recognizes the Association as the exclusive representative of the following unit:

Included: All certificated teachers, temporary teachers, summer school teachers, regular part-time teachers, credentialed school nurses, speech and language specialists, credentialed librarians, student development specialist teachers, department chairpersons, but excluding:

Excluded: Superintendent, assistant superintendents, principals, assistant principals, adult education principal, hourly employees, adult education teachers, substitutes, area administrators (deans), teaching principal, home teachers, psychologists, counselors, coordinator of instructional materials/staff development, coordinator of vocational preparation/special projects, district nurse, coordinator of bilingual/compensatory education, at risk/special education coordinator, and any other designated managerial, supervisory, or confidential employee.

III. Exclusivity

In legal and bargaining terminology, the union is an "exclusive representative." This means that the union, and only the union, has the right to negotiate on behalf of the employees in the bargaining unit; the union's right to negotiate is not shared with any other organization or individual. The same union can represent employees in more than one bargaining unit, but in that case, it is the exclusive representative for all the employees in each unit.

It does not follow, however, that the other privileges and rights granted to the union in negotiations are necessarily exclusive. Whether they are or not depends on what happens in negotiations. The union ordinarily seeks the exclusive right to:

- Utilize payroll deduction of dues
- File grievances
- Carry grievances to arbitration
- Use the district mail system
- Meet in school buildings
- Use district facilities
- Address faculty meetings
- Have a reserved seat at board meetings

Whether the union is granted these rights, and whether they are "exclusive," depends on the outcome of negotiations between the union and the board. Boards are not legally obligated to grant these rights to anyone, let alone to grant them only to the exclusive representative. Many boards are under the erroneous impression that the union is entitled to these rights exclusively, but this is not the case.

In the context of board/union bargaining, "exclusivity" should apply only to other organizations that seek to represent teachers on terms and conditions of employment. Once this is granted, however, there is no valid reason why boards should deny the rights listed above to organizations that do not and will not seek to represent teachers on employment-related matters. The union's objective in attempting to keep these privileges from other groups is to forestall any challenge to its status as the exclusive representative. If no other organization can utilize payroll deduction to raise funds or utilize district facilities to communicate with teachers, the development of an effective rival union is very unlikely. The question is whether the board should assist the union in the latter's effort to avoid criticism or competition.

From the teachers' point of view, there is no benefit to union demands for exclusivity. Why should the teachers deprive themselves of additional sources of information? In view of the common tendency of organizations to communicate only favorable information about their activities, denying rival teacher organizations the ability to access teachers easily can hardly be in the interests of teachers. The fact that the union has the exclusive right to represent teachers in negotiations does not imply that it should have the exclusive right to communicate with teachers, or to maintain its organizational existence. The reality is that granting the union exclusive rights to communicate with teachers is a benefit to the union but a disservice to the teachers that the union represents; this is an issue that clearly demonstrates the conflict between union interests and teacher interests.

Whether school boards should deny various rights to teacher organizations other than the exclusive representative can be a difficult practical issue. Incumbent unions try to persuade boards that it is in the latter's best interest to do so. Their argument is that the competing unions would try to gain teacher support by promising to extract more benefits from boards. This sort of competition is not in the best interest of the boards, unions argue; hence, boards should make it difficult for rival unions to compete with the exclusive representative. If there is no competition among unions for teacher support, the argument runs, the incumbent unions will be much more willing to accept reasonable board proposals that are unpopular with teachers.

Unfortunately, many boards uncritically agree to exclusivity when its only function is to protect the exclusive representative. These boards buy peace with the union, but the price is paid by the teachers. They lose the opportunity to get information that the union wishes to conceal from the teachers.

To be sure, granting a rival union the privileges and rights listed above ordinarily involves some risk to the school board. With another union in the picture, the board is more likely to be charged by the incumbent union with an unfair labor practice for negotiating with an entity other than the exclusive representative. Given this, relatively few boards want to allow competing unions to function in the district. However, without the payroll deduction of dues, access to bulletin boards and the district mail system, and/or the right to meet in district buildings, it is practically impossible to maintain an organization that is able to challenge the exclusive representative. The evidence to this effect is overwhelming. For example, when NEA and AFT affiliates compete to become the exclusive representative, the losing union usually withers away due to a lack of access to teachers, even if it has lost the representation election by a very narrow margin.

Note that boards are allowed to establish criteria for access to their facilities; for example, boards can insist that rival unions or nonunion organizations are entitled to certain privileges, such as the use of district facilities. However, it is illegal for boards to condition access to district facilities and services upon an organization's point of view. Boards can deny access to district facilities to all organizations, even the incumbent union, but if they allow access to one organization, they must allow it to others under the same conditions. Thus, a board could not legally grant access to district facilities to the Democratic Teachers Club while denying it to the Republican Teachers Club. The exclusive privileges granted the incumbent union are an unfortunate exception to this ruling of the U.S. Supreme Court.

Suppose an incumbent union has negotiated exclusive access to bulletin boards and use of the district mail system. Suppose that subsequently 30 percent of the teachers sign a decertification petition, thus triggering a vote by all teachers on what organization, if any, they wish to represent them. It seems manifestly unfair that the incumbent union should have the exclusive access to bulletin boards and use of the district mail system, but that would be the outcome if the board had agreed to exclusivity of access.

To summarize, school boards should allow exclusivity only with respect to the right of representation; the board should not assist the incumbent union to maintain a monopoly over communications to district teachers. To do so is to undervalue criticism and the rights of teachers to receive nonunion communications. Exclusivity with respect to payroll deduction of dues is defensible only if the incumbent union does not have sole access to district facilities for communications to teachers.

Discussion of examples

Example (1) below is an example of overbroad protection of an incumbent union's exclusive rights:

(1) Only the exclusive bargaining agent, the _____ Federation of Teachers, shall have the right to enforce this Agreement and hold Union meetings or group activities on school grounds for Union purposes. The use of district facilities requires mutual agreement of the Principal/Site Supervisor and the Union Representative.

As drafted, (1) would prohibit two or more teachers from meeting in a school to discuss a decertification petition or an effort to oust incumbent union officers. Because it prohibits even these minimal attempts to challenge the incumbent union, the language of (1) is overbroad. Example (1) also suffers from other flaws. The requirement of mutual agreement between the principal or site supervisor and a union representative does not provide any criteria for the parties to use in discussing union use of district facilities. (The omission of such criteria was more of a mistake by the union than by the board's negotiator.) Note also that part of (1) is redundant; only the union *could* enforce the contract unless the contract itself allowed another party to do so.

Example (2) below simply repeats the board's statutory obligation not to bargain with anyone except the exclusive bargaining agent:

(2) The rights granted by statute to the certified exclusive bargaining agent shall not be granted to any other association, union, or employee organization.

The clause is completely redundant; the board would be committing an unfair labor practice by bargaining on terms and conditions of employment with any other organization. Note, however, that there may be several disagreements over the statutory rights of the union, hence (2) gives the union a contractual opportunity to test its statutory rights.

(3) All rights and privileges granted to the Association under the provisions of this Agreement shall be for the exclusive use of the Association subject to any statutory exceptions.

To the extent that the contract provides the incumbent union with rights in addition to exclusive representation, example (3), like (1) above, grants the union an unwarranted extension of exclusivity. For example, (3) might obligate the district to deny specialized teacher organizations, such as organizations of science teachers, the ability to meet in district schools or to use the district mail system.

The best approach is to omit any reference to exclusivity from the contract. Examples like (1) and (3) above are highly unfair to teachers who want to be represented by a different union; inasmuch as these rival unions lack access to district teachers in the schools, they are severely—if not hopelessly—disadvantaged in any effort to replace the incumbent exclusive representative with a different union. At the very least, boards should insist that exclusive access to teachers should not apply to the window periods for decertifying an incumbent union.

The union will sometimes propose language that states that the contract between the board and the union supersedes contracts between individual teachers and the school district. Example (4) illustrates such a proposal:

(4) Any individual contract between the District and a unit member shall be subject to and consistent with the terms and conditions of this Agreement.

Such proposals are more propagandistic than substantive because the contract between the board and the union takes precedence even in the absence of language stating this to be the case. Actually, in bargaining-law states, it would be an unfair labor practice for the board to negotiate with an individual teacher.

Example (4) is especially undesirable from the board's perspective because it enables the union to utilize the grievance procedure for alleged violations of the union's statutory rights.

Like (4), example (5) contains language that is superfluous from a legal standpoint:

> (5) This Agreement shall constitute School Board policy for its duration, and shall not be amended or changed in any way except by a written agreement between the Union and the School Board.

Even in the absence of language like that in (5), the contract would be board policy for its duration, and any change in it would have to be approved by both parties to the contract. The only possible change in the rights of the parties made by (5) would be to rule out claims that the contract had been amended by an oral agreement of one kind or another.

The recommended option is to avoid the kind of contractual language illustrated by all of the foregoing examples.

IV. Management Rights[1]

Prior to negotiating any labor agreement, management negotiators should have a clear understanding of their objectives in the negotiations. In the private sector, management negotiators have generally relied on the management-rights doctrine as their guiding philosophy. Briefly stated, the management-rights doctrine is that management retains all those rights that it does not negotiate away. The concept underlying this doctrine is that it is management's duty to act and it is the union's duty to challenge the management's action if the union believes that the action violates the contract. In other words, management acts and the union reacts.

When applied in the public sector, the management-rights doctrine does not allow the union to become a "joint manager" of the district because, according to the doctrine's conceptual framework, unions are not functionally managers. Nonetheless, public employee unions, particularly teacher unions, are increasingly asserting the right to codetermine matters of public policy. As in the private sector, proposals that require management (in this case, the school board) to obtain the union's agreement before acting should be avoided. These "mutual agreement" or "veto" clauses give the unions authority without accountability to the electorate. Boards should not allow this to happen; the board is not required to negotiate matters of inherent managerial policy. Always bear in mind that boards are accountable to the public, but the unions are not. The electorate can vote out an incumbent board if the board's policies fail, but it cannot vote out a union that is also responsible for the failed policies.

Since the board's rights come from the duty of the board to carry out its public policies and to operate efficiently, the board should be the "acting" party and the union the "passive" party insofar as the day-to-day relationships of the parties are concerned. Union leaders should never participate in day-to-day decision-making under a labor contract.

If union representatives are not to participate in day-to-day decision-making, then what is their function under a contract? Of course, during the negotiation of a school board/union contract, union representatives must be recognized as having bargaining rights equal to those of the board; however, once the contract is executed, the union representatives should assume an entirely different role. Their new role should be to monitor the contract to determine whether actions taken by the school district are contrary to the contractual commitments previously agreed upon by the board and the union. Thus, the union's function under the contract can best be described as a "watchdog" function—watching the actions of the employer, the "acting" party—to see whether such actions are in compliance with the contract.

In addition to providing a basic framework within which to negotiate a contract, the management-rights doctrine provides a test by which to analyze union proposals. Thus, to preserve the board's right to carry out its designated public functions and to efficiently manage its operations, one fundamental question should be asked about each union proposal: Does the proposal prevent the district from taking those actions that are necessary to implement efficiently the public policy goals entrusted to it by law? If it does, the proposal should be resisted.

If a statement of the board's rights is to be included, it can be a single comprehensive statement granting the board broad power, or a series of statements spelling out the board's retained rights. The latter option is preferable because it will prevent later confusion between the parties, but it is important to avoid the inference that the list is exhaustive. This can be done by adding the phrase "including but not limited to" before spelling out the specific rights that are retained by the board. If this is not done, a short list of the board's rights may be less desirable than no list at all, because if it is taken to be exhaustive, that list could seriously limit the board's powers. Any list of the board's retained rights should include language that asserts that the board's rights are not limited to the enumerated rights. In any event, the shorter the list of board rights, the greater the risk that the board will lose its rights that are not enumerated.

Bear in mind that parties who assert rights during contract negotiations but fail to get them included in the contract are in a weak position to assert that they have the rights under the contract. To propose a contractual right in bargaining but not get it in the contract is often tantamount to losing the right. Thus, whenever a contract does not include a management right that the board has proposed, the board should make sure that the union recognizes that the board's withdrawal of the proposal is without prejudice to a future assertion of the right in an arbitration or legal proceeding.

If the contract does not spell out the board's rights, these rights can often be incorporated in the contract by adding language that clearly implies their existence. For example, suppose the issue is the district's right to change the schedule of days in which school is in session, so long as the change does not increase the total number of regular school days. The contractual language might read as follows: "The number of instructional days may not exceed 180, nor shall the District change the schedule of instructional days prior to notifying the Union and providing an opportunity for it to express its views on the change." Such language clearly implies that the district has the right to change the schedule of instructional days without bargaining over the change; the board need only notify the union and let the union express its views on the change.

To protect the district's rights, the management-rights section of the contract should include a clause that relieves the board from the duty to bargain during the contract. This is usually achieved by using a "zipper clause," a clause by which the parties, especially the union, waive their rights to bargain during the term of the contract. The importance of such a clause cannot be overestimated. For example, the union has the right to bargain over teacher salaries. Even after a contract is signed, however, the union will retain the right to bargain over salaries (and other mandatory subjects of bargaining) unless the union explicitly waives the right. Such waivers will not be inferred from ambiguous language; unless a waiver is phrased in clear, unambiguous language, the union will not be deemed to have waived its right to bargain.

To appreciate the importance of the issue, suppose that in the second or third year of a three-year contract, the district receives more in state aid than was anticipated. In the absence of a zipper clause, the union could reopen negotiations on teacher salaries and/or fringe benefits—something it could not do if the contract included an appropriate zipper clause.

The management-rights philosophy should be incorporated into the labor contract in the form of a management-rights clause. Such a clause usually begins with a provision to this effect:

> It is understood and agreed that the Board retains the right to operate the District and that all management rights are reserved to it, but that such rights must be exercised consistently with the other provisions of this contract. These rights include but are not limited to the following. . . .

After this kind of preamble, the basic rights of the district should be listed. These basic rights include the rights to:

- Hire, assign, or transfer employees
- Determine the mission of the school district
- Determine the methods, means, and number of personnel

- Introduce new or improved instructional methods or facilities
- Change existing instructional methods or facilities
- Establish and require observance of reasonable rules and regulations
- Discipline and discharge employees for just cause
- Contract out for goods or services

Undoubtedly, the union will oppose any attempt to obtain a strong management-rights clause, but this should not deter boards from attempting to negotiate as strong a clause as possible. Any contract that includes a section on union rights or employee rights should include a section on management rights.

State legislation may constitute a kind of statutory management-rights clause by limiting the scope of representation. For example, the California bargaining statute limits the scope of union representation to "wages, hours of employment, and other terms and conditions of employment." The statute goes on to define "terms and conditions of employment" as meaning:

> health and welfare benefits, . . . leave and transfer policies, safety conditions of employment, class size, procedures to be used for the evaluation of employees, organizational security, . . . and procedures for processing grievances. . . .

The statute further provides that "all matters not specifically enumerated are reserved to the public school employer and may not be a subject of meeting and negotiating." In effect, this language relieves the board of the obligation to negotiate over matters that are not specifically listed in the statute.[2] Despite this statutory recognition of the right to manage in certain areas, public school employers should still try to secure a management-rights clause in their labor contracts for the following reasons:

1. Although the union has the statutory right to negotiate over certain subjects, it has the legal power to waive these rights during the term of the labor contract. A management-rights clause covering these subjects will protect the district from having to bargain over these subjects during the term of the agreement. Thus, the board has a duty to bargain over class size when negotiating a contract, but it should seek a provision stating that the district has the right to change class size during the term of the contract.
2. A management-rights clause constitutes contractual recognition by the union of the school district's statutory and contractual rights.
3. A management-rights clause notifies the union and its members that the district expects to exercise its statutory rights.
4. A management-rights clause reinforces the position that union activity that interferes with the district's rights is prohibited.

5. A management-rights clause protects the district in the event that the present statutory guarantees are modified or eliminated. If the union is adamant about the inclusion of a statutory benefit, the board should insist upon the inclusion of the district's statutory rights in the contract.

Remember that specific clauses of the contract can limit the exercise of district rights, no matter what the language of the management-rights clause states. Accordingly, the draftsman of an agreement must recognize that a management-rights clause, standing alone, is only a general charter of reserved rights. The district's management rights often will be limited, in whole or in part, by the general language or specific terms of the remaining provisions of the contract. Any explicit restrictions supersede a general management-rights provision.

The outcome of any negotiations, however, depends upon many factors that necessarily vary from district to district. The chances of negotiating sound collective bargaining agreements are substantially increased, however, if the district's negotiators and the board vigorously defend the right of the district to carry out its designated functions in an efficient and orderly manner.

Discussion of examples

Compare the language of (1) and (2) below:

(1) It is understood and agreed that the Board of Education possesses the sole right to operate the City School District, and that all management rights repose in it, but that such rights shall be exercised consistently with the other provisions of this Agreement.

(2) Nothing contained herein shall be considered to deny or restrict the Board's legal rights, authority, or responsibility as defined and vested in the Board by the laws and Constitution of the United States and of the State of _____, and the rules and regulations of the Public Employment Relations Board. Except as specifically and clearly stated in this Agreement, all the rights, powers, and authority the Board had prior to this Agreement are retained exclusively by the Board.

Example (1) is a minimal statement of management rights that does nothing to strengthen or even uphold them. Example (2) is preferable to (1), since (2) states that any limitations on board "rights, powers, and authority" must be "specifically and clearly stated in this Agreement." By adopting the language of (2), a board retains all those rights that it does not bargain away; the language of (2) thus reflects the fundamental tenet of the management-rights doctrine noted above. However, as noted above, the optimal management-rights clause (from the board's point of view) will include a detailed, though not exhaustive, list of the district's rights. For an example of such a listing, see (3) below:

(3) It is expressly agreed that all rights which vest in and are exercised exclusively by the Board, except those which are clearly and expressly relinquished herein by the Board, shall continue to vest exclusively in and be exercised exclusively by the Board without prior negotiations with the Association either as to the taking of action under such rights or with respect to the consequence of such action during the term of this Agreement. Such rights shall include the right to:

A. Exercise according to law the executive management and administrative control of the School System and all of its properties, facilities, and equipment, and the activities of the employees during working hours.

B. Adopt rules and regulations not inconsistent with this Agreement.

C. Manage and control all fiscal affairs of the Schools.

D. Determine the number and location or relocation of its facilities, including the establishment or relocations of new schools, buildings, or departments, and the relocation or closing of schools, offices, departments, buildings, or other facilities.

E. Determine the type and quantity of supportive services, including all supplies and equipment necessary to operate the district system and to establish the procedures necessary to manage and control this operation.

F. Determine employee qualifications, establish hiring procedures, hire all employees, and determine employee assignments and the condition of their continued employment, dismissal, promotion, or transfer.

G. Determine job content.

H. Determine the size of the management organization, its function, and its authority.

I. Approve in-service training activities for employees.

J. Establish and conduct an evaluation program to determine the effectiveness and competence of teachers, administrators, and all other employees.

K. Determine staffing allocations for all schools, departments, and district operations.

L. Determine curriculum, courses, and methods of instruction.

M. Determine the appropriateness of textbooks, instructional materials and supplies, and teaching aids.

The listing of specific management rights in this Agreement is not intended to be, nor shall it be, restrictive of or a waiver of any rights of management not listed and specifically surrendered herein, whether or not such rights have been exercised by the Board in the past.

Obviously, (3) is a much more effective statement of management rights than (1) or (2). If the union refuses to agree to the kind of listing in (3), the board should inquire into the reason for such refusal. If the union claims that it does not wish to concede that the district has the specified rights, the board should ascertain the basis for the union's position. If this basis is a union belief that the district does not have the listed rights, the board should make sure that nothing in the contract supports the union's position.

The unions prefer a general statement of management rights because it is always possible to argue that specific management rights are not included in or covered by a general statement of these rights. Of course, this is the reason why specific listings of management rights are preferable from the board's perspective.

V. No-Strike Clause

In the private sector, management agreement to a binding arbitration procedure for handling employee grievances is the quid pro quo for union agreement to a no-strike clause that bans strikes for the duration of the contract. In public education, however, teacher strikes are already illegal in most states. For this reason, the conventional quid pro quo in the private sector is a very good deal for the teacher unions—so good that school boards should not agree to it. The unions are giving up a right they do not have in exchange for a right they should not have.

In the context of public education, a strike is the shutdown of a public service until one special interest group, the teacher union, gets the public policies that satisfy it—at least, satisfy it enough to return to work. No other citizens or interest groups have the power to shut down a public service until it gets public policies deemed acceptable to it.

Nevertheless, even in states in which teacher strikes are illegal, a properly drafted no-strike clause is very helpful. In states where teacher strikes are illegal as a result of judicial decision rather than by legislation, the only way to stop a teacher strike is to get a restraining order or injunction prohibiting it. This is not always easy to do; the board must seek out judges who will issue such an order or injunction, and then the board must wait for the order or injunction to be served on union leaders and teachers. These actions require at least a few days, and most teacher strikes do not last for more than a few days. In states in which judges are elected or appointed with teacher union support, the prospects for judicial relief are especially bleak.

To be effective, a no-strike clause should include penalties against the union. For example, the board should insist upon its right to refrain from deducting union dues from employee paychecks if there is a violation of a no-strike clause. This will cause state and national affiliates of the union to pressure the local union to avoid a strike. Some states have laws that penalize teachers for striking, but penalizing the union financially is much more effective. When teachers are penalized, school districts tend to waive penalties against striking teachers. The unions usually insist on a no-reprisal clause when settling a strike, which would prevent the district from taking disciplinary action against union officials and teachers who performed illegal actions. In their eagerness to end strikes, boards usually agree to such a clause, even though the long-range consequences of this encourage strikes. Furthermore, in medium- or large-sized school districts, efforts to penalize all striking teachers are likely to make a settlement virtually impossible. A no-strike clause that authorizes the district to discontinue payroll deduction of dues and other union privileges would usually be a more effective deterrent to strikes.

Contract language that merely states that the teachers will not strike, or specifies that they do not have the right to strike, is inadequate even though it may legitimize disciplinary action against strikers. Contract language should make it clear that the district can apply disciplinary action against strikers on an individual basis. In larger districts, it is not feasible to penalize all teachers who strike, but it may be essential to take disciplinary action against leaders of the strike. If language allowing selective disciplinary action is not included in the contract, the district runs the risk of not being able to discipline anyone unless all the striking employees receive the same penalty. If the disciplinary action sought in this case is termination, the district will not be able to take disciplinary action against all teachers, except in districts with only a few employees.

It is also important that "strike" be defined broadly, to cover more than a single absence from work or from some other type of job-related action. The language in example (4) below illustrates this point. Any concerted effort to refuse full good-faith performance should be considered a strike; for example, teachers may show up for work and "work to rule," that is, insist upon compliance with all district regulations, even when doing so is obviously unnecessary and counterproductive. The result can be extremely disruptive. Or suppose all the teachers refuse to accept any extracurricular assignments for pay. In some states, teachers have a statutory right to refuse such assignments, but if all teachers do so, the resulting pressure on the district may be as intense as the pressure that would emerge from a refusal by teachers to perform their regular duties. Unless the no-strike clause is drafted properly, teachers may be able to wield all the bargaining power of a strike without running any of the risks involved in a refusal to perform their regular duties.

Discussion of examples

If the language of a no-strike clause is not carefully drafted, the results can be disastrous for the board. This can be the case even when it appears that a no-strike clause will prevent strikes during the processing of grievances. Consider (1) below:

(1) The Association agrees that during the processing of a grievance under this Section's procedures and time limits, it shall take all steps necessary and appropriate to assure that all job responsibilities shall be fully and faithfully discharged and the status quo shall be maintained by teachers until the grievance is resolved.

Example (1) is badly flawed. Because the language of (1) expressly denies the right to strike only during the processing of a grievance, (1) implies that when there is no grievance being processed, the teachers have the right not to fulfill their responsibilities "fully and faithfully." In fact, contrary to how it may initially appear, (1) *legitimizes* strikes by prohibiting them only when a grievance is being processed.

It was noted above that a variety of actions other than a strike can give the teacher union significant leverage over the district. Consider how this affects the ability of (2), shown below, to protect the district:

(2) It is hereby agreed by the Association that there will be no strikes, stoppages of work, or slowdown of the operations of the School District during the term of this Agreement. It is hereby agreed by the School District that there will be no lockout of employees during the term of this Agreement.

On the surface, (2) appears to be a reasonable quid pro quo—the union agrees not to strike or engage in a slowdown, and the district agrees not to lock out employees during the terms of the agreement. As previously noted, a no-strike clause in the public sector is not as valuable to school boards as it is to employers in the private sector, but it is still desirable. However, note that the agreement does not prohibit all the actions that the union can take to disrupt district operations without violating the no-strike clause.

Suppose that the union does decide to collectively stop working in order to achieve its objectives. If a large number of teachers call in sick—but do not officially "go on strike"—and the district cannot employ enough substitute teachers to operate efficiently, it may be necessary to shut down all the schools; however, under the no-lockout provision in (2), the district has waived the right to refuse to pay any teacher who does show up for work. The district would be in a position similar to that of a professional baseball team that was required to pay three players who showed up for work on days when the rest of the team was absent. Not only would the union be able to effectively shut down the schools, but it would do so in a manner that could expose the district to significant costs.

Examples (3) and (4) below cover the loopholes that are found in (2):

(3) The Association, in consideration of the terms and conditions of this Agreement, will not engage in, instigate, or condone any strike, work stoppage, or any concerted refusal to perform normal work duties on the part of any member of the bargaining unit covered by this Agreement, and will undertake to discourage any such acts by any such bargaining-unit member.

(4) The Association hereby agrees that neither it nor its members or agents, or representatives, or the employees, or persons acting in concert with any of them, shall incite, encourage, or participate in any strike, walk-out, slowdown, or other work stoppage of any nature whatsoever during the life of this Agreement. In the event of any strike, walkout, slow-down, work stoppage, or threat thereof, the Association and its officers will make a good-faith effort to end or avert the same. Any employee authorizing, engaging in, encouraging, sanctioning, recognizing, or as-sisting any strike, slowdown, work stoppage, or other concerted inter-ference in violation of this Article, shall be subject to discipline which may include termination as provided for in the Education Code.

When comparing these two examples, note that (4) is superior to (3) because (4) states clearly that teachers who engage in a strike may be terminated. How-ever, (4) would be much more effective if it specified that in the event of a strike or similar work stoppage, the district was authorized to decertify a union and revoke that union's payroll deduction of union dues.

To reiterate, the no-strike clause should plug any loopholes in the statutory or judicial prohibition of strikes. It should also require the union to do whatever is necessary to end a strike or strike threat, and the penalties for not doing so should include decertification and loss of union rights, such as the dues check-off.

A consideration of no-reprisal clauses will complement this discussion of no-strike clauses. Although unions sometimes propose a no-reprisal clause in their initial proposals at a bargaining session, such a clause is typically proposed as part of the settlement of an especially acrimonious dispute, such as a strike. The following examples illustrate several points about no-reprisal clauses.

(5) The Association and the District, having resolved the current dispute, agree to return the District to normalcy. To promote this end, neither party, nor its agents, shall take any punitive action or reprisal against each other, or against any individual, including pupils, parents, or orga-nizations, on account of participation, involvement, support, sympathy, or lack thereof as related to any activities involved in the current dispute.

(6) The School Board and the Union agree that the continuation of the dispute leading to this Agreement in the schools is contrary to their interests and the educational interests of pupils. Consequently, each party agrees that it will not engage in activities that tend to exacerbate the disagreements between the parties, and that it will also discourage efforts to carry on the controversy in and away from the schools.

The union will try to use a no-reprisal clause to avoid disciplinary action for illegal activity during a confrontation between the union and the school board. For instance, union officials or teachers may have engaged in vandalism, threatened parents who sent their children to school during a strike, or disrupted district services, to cite just three activities of this kind. The district should not waive its rights to pursue charges for illegal actions of this kind.

Furthermore, it should be noted that it would be illegal for the district to take any "reprisals" per se. It can discipline its employees only for actions that justify disciplinary action; expressions of sympathy for the union would not justify disciplinary action by the district. The proposed no-reprisal clause of (5) would be used to shield union activists for activities that merit disciplinary action or even criminal prosecution. This is why the union proposals will usually be labeled "Return to Normalcy" or by some other feel-good language that makes it easier to gain board acceptance of the proposal.

Bear in mind that a no-reprisal clause is usually intended to protect union activists; after all, the union is not in a position to take disciplinary action against school administrators. Nonetheless, a no-reprisal clause may be useful to the district when the union's membership has been bitterly divided; for example, some teachers may have continued to work during a strike, and they may fear disciplinary action by the union as a result. An agreement may also be desirable in order to minimize continuing controversy and acrimony in the schools. In this situation, a no-reprisal clause may help protect teachers who opposed union positions during a confrontation between the union and the district. In this type of situation, the language in example (6) may be appropriate.

VI. Consultation Rights

The union typically proposes that it have consultation rights. One kind is a consultation meeting, usually taking place once a month, in which the parties can bring up any concerns in an informal way. The union will also propose language requiring mandatory consultation with the union before the district can act on certain issues. For example, the union may propose that it must be consulted before the district can change the schedule, or transfer teachers, or drop a program. The differences between the two types of consultation rights are important and require discussion.

First, the board should make every effort to avoid negotiations during the term of the contract (see the earlier discussion of the zipper clause). In principle, there is no objection to a monthly consultation meeting, but such meetings sometimes become de facto bargaining sessions, an outcome to be avoided. If the union representative in these monthly consultation meetings is aggressive and the district representative is not a strong individual, consultation quickly turns into de facto bargaining. The best solution to this problem is a strong zipper clause and an agreement to consult once a month; however, attention should be paid to the mechanics of the consultation meetings. Will they take place during the regular school day? Will they require released time, that is, require teachers to forgo their normal duties in order to participate? How many union officers or staff will be present? Consultation meetings are most productive when they are one-on-one meetings between parties who can make decisions.

Union proposals that would require the district to consult the union before the district could take specific actions are a different matter. The union does not want to be surprised; surprise embarrasses the union leadership. However, avoiding surprise does not necessarily require consultation. Avoiding surprises in this way comes at a price; under contracts with consultation provisions, many controversies emerge over whether the district really "consulted" the union, since the concept of "consultation" is not very precise. Furthermore, the district may have to act very quickly in some circumstances; having to wait until the union can be consulted can be a significant problem. One feasible solution is to add "except in emergencies" to the clause requiring the district to consult the union before acting on specific matters.

The board should resist the temptation to grant the union a right to be consulted before the board can act on specific issues. In some cases, the union only uses such prior consultation to generate opposition to a district action, or to provide the union with time to launch such a campaign. For this reason, the board should avoid granting a union the right to be consulted before the district can act; at the same time, the district should consult with the union whenever it can reasonably do so. Most importantly, a refusal to agree to a consultation clause in the contract does not mean that the board cannot or will not consult with the union before taking action that affects the union or the teacher(s) in important ways.

Discussion of examples

Examples (1) and (2) below are examples of contractual language that sometimes emerges when the board decides to give the union a right to be consulted on matters of district policy. Both leave the district vulnerable to the exercise of union power.

(1) A. The District agrees to consult with the Association on the following District-wide matters: policies, procedures, objectives, goals, and programs relating to textbook selection, curriculum, course content, educational equipment and supplies, grade-level advancement, guidance, grading policies, pupil testing, records, forms, health and safety, student conduct, student discipline, extracurricular and cocurricular activities of students, and the substantive and procedural rights of students. The requirements to consult shall be met with the appointment of an Association representative to all District-wide committees set up to assess those enumerated items.

B. Each party agrees to notify the other of its intent to consult on matters described in Paragraph A, above, at least seven (7) working days prior to consideration of those matters.

C. Upon conclusion of the consultation on matters enumerated in Paragraph A, above, the District agrees to provide the Association with any recommendation to be made to the Board five (5) working days prior to its inclusion in the Board agenda.

D. It is agreed that failure to meet the procedural requirements outlined above shall be subject to the grievance and arbitration provisions of Article IV, "Grievance and Arbitration." However, the substance of the District's decision on consultation subjects is not grievable.

Example (1) is a most unwise consultation clause from the board's perspective. For most practical purposes, it cripples the district's ability to act promptly on a wide range of important issues. Although the district is technically free to act on matters subject to consultation, the procedural requirements are stifling, and overcoming them will take large amounts of district time.

(2) In the event the Board of Education is considering a change in policy which would come within the scope of this Agreement, or is considering any change in District-wide educational policy which has an impact on the terms and conditions of work, the Board of Education or the Superintendent of Schools shall so notify the President of the Association. The Association shall, within ten (10) days, notify the President of the Board of Education if the Association will exercise its right to negotiate these matters. The Board and the Association shall also negotiate on any appropriation of unanticipated additional sources of public revenue which are not specifically earmarked.

The Association shall also have the opportunity to present its views to the Superintendent, his/her designee, and/or the Board on other revisions of educational policy which the Association may deem desirable at a mutually convenient time.

Instead of negotiating a zipper clause that would free the board from having to negotiate during the term of the agreement, (2) requires the board to negotiate on virtually all changes in policy. Example (2) is even more undesirable than (1) because (2) explicitly obligates the board to negotiate on any change in policy that the union asserts would have "an impact on the terms and conditions of work."

As noted above, however, a right of prior consultation is not the only type of consultation requested by unions. Consider (3) below, in which the board agrees to more informal consultation meetings:

(3) Upon request, the parties agree to consult once a month on matters of mutual concern.

It should be apparent that (3) is far more desirable, from the board's point of view, than the other examples. Its inclusion in the contract does not mean that the district should adopt a cavalier attitude toward the union, but it does not require union consultation without consideration of the need or feasibility of such consultation. Furthermore, if the union does not initiate discussions on certain matters during the monthly consultation meetings, it is in a weak position to contend that union members are deeply concerned about them. In any case, districts must not allow consultation to become de facto bargaining or become tied down by bureaucratic consultation procedures.

VII. Joint Committees

The "joint study committee" typically emerges from one of the most common scenarios at the negotiating table: The union negotiators want something very badly, or at least they say they do. For various reasons, board negotiators reject the demand. Finally, as time is running out and the board negotiators are eager to wrap things up, the union negotiators request that the board establish a joint committee to look into the problem at hand. This committee, union negotiators will argue, shows the union's members that the union tried to achieve something, while not committing the board to any position on the problem.

This appeal can sound very attractive to a board's negotiating team, especially in the final stages of negotiations. Granted, a proposal for a joint committee sometimes does make sense for both sides. On the other hand, many boards eventually discover that they have opened up a Pandora's box by agreeing to a joint committee.

When do joint committees make sense, and when are they a bad idea? As a general rule, it is unwise for a board to agree to establish a joint committee when the board knows that nothing can be done about the substantive problem involved. The sense of relief that boards feel when an issue is temporarily resolved through the creation of a joint committee will eventually be replaced by dismay over teacher feelings of outrage ("The administration agreed to a joint committee as a subterfuge!"). At that point, it will not help for the board to point out that it had told the union negotiators that nothing could be done. The union representatives may have sincerely regarded the joint committee as just a device to reach an agreement by bypassing a sticky issue. However, the union negotiators are not likely to put the matter this way to the teachers, because to do so would destroy the value of the joint committee from their point of view. Even if union negotiators privately believe that the administration will do absolutely nothing about a problem, they are not going to say that to the teachers, at least before the teachers ratify the agreement under consideration. Instead, they will hold out the possibility of using the joint committee as a way to achieve something when the committee reports. In other words, regardless of the private thoughts of the union negotiators, joint committees can raise false hopes in union membership.

Sometimes the parties in negotiations do not fully realize that refusing to make concessions on a proposal can be as legitimate as accepting the proposal or agreeing to consider it. It is the union's refusal to take "no" for an answer that leads to a joint committee. Instead of getting closure on negotiations, the board and the union may find themselves negotiating endlessly in joint committees. Furthermore, once a joint committee is appointed, the union representatives on the committee will want released time for committee work and meetings. This can be a drain in a smaller school system.

Joint committees should not negotiate. Sometimes, while negotiating an agreement, it is helpful to refer particular issues to subcommittees of the negotiating teams. Remember, however, that the binding agreements are made between the board and the union, not between their representatives on the subcommittees. In any case, referring a problem to a subcommittee *during* negotiations is different from having a problem referred to a joint committee *after* an agreement is reached. Committees of the latter sort must have clearly defined tasks, or else the board may discover that it is embroiled in continuous negotiations after an agreement on the contract has been reached.

Many problems that are referred to joint committees will be the subject of negotiations in the next contract. The union will use the report of a joint committee as a point of departure if there is anything in the report favorable to the union's position. If there has been a report by a joint committee, especially on a matter subject to negotiations, members of the board's negotiating team should know what the report says about the issue. If the board were to display ignorance of the committee report, such ignorance would encourage the belief of teachers that the administration was not negotiating in good faith.

Board negotiators should avoid having joint committees do work that should have been done by the union prior to negotiations. If the facts were available but the union did not collect and present them, the board negotiator should insist that the union negotiators be better prepared at the next set of contract talks if they want progress on the item. If the board permits the creation of a joint committee to study something that the union has itself failed to research, then the board is simply encouraging poor preparation by the union in the future.

On the other hand, there may be new issues, proposals, or questions from either side that legitimately require data—the "facts" of the matter—that are not available during negotiations. If the union proposes the formation of a joint committee to find this data, the burden should be put on the union to make its case; it is the union's proposal, and if the union cannot support it adequately, boards should not bail them out by agreeing to study the issues or proposals. If, however, there is uncertainty or honest disagreement between the board and the union over the facts of a particular issue, it may make sense to have a joint committee mutually ascertain the facts and report back to both parties.

Having joint committees explore a problem *before* negotiations begin can eliminate a great deal of unproductive controversy by facilitating the development of a set of facts that both groups accept. However, it is a mistake to believe that agreement on these facts means that the parties will reach agreement on the issues involved. As Richard H. Tawney, the famous English historian, once pointed out, the conflicts that really matter in life are not those which result from misunderstanding the other fellow, but those that result from understanding him too well.

Discussion of examples

Though joint committees pose problems for school districts by diverting resources into unproductive use, one should also note that contractual provisions involving committee membership can also create problems. Consider example (1):

(1) A joint committee of the Administration and the Association shall be established to review all existing and proposed outside funded projects and to recommend future projects and study the impact of such projects on the regular instructional program. Such committee shall be composed of ten (10) persons. Five (5) persons will be appointed by the Association, one of whom may be a parent. Five (5) persons will be appointed by the Superintendent, one of whom will be a parent selected by the PTA. All project proposals shall be submitted to the joint com-

mittee prior to Board approval and/or submissions to the appropriate government agency.

A. The working conditions of teachers working on outside funded projects shall conform to the terms of this Agreement.

B. All positions under such programs will be posted in accordance with existing procedures.

C. The committee shall meet as the need arises, and shall make its report available to both the Association and the Board on or before February 1 and May 1 of the school year.

Example (1) obviously places severe restrictions on school management. By creating a joint committee, (1) adds another layer of bureaucracy that the district must negotiate before it can act on proposals for external funding; in addition, it requires both the district and the union to devote some resources to the joint committee.

Note also, however, the specifications of the committee's membership. By ensuring that up to two parents will be on the committee—one that the district superintendent must appoint, and one that the union may appoint—example (1) essentially gives the union two of the ten slots of the joint committee. If the union appoints a parent, that parent will be one who can be depended upon to support union interests. The same will be true for the parent appointed by the superintendent, since that parent is actually selected by the Parent-Teacher Association (PTA), an organization that rarely opposes union positions.[3] The parents would not necessarily represent other parents. Also, there is no reason why there should be a parent on every committee to review externally funded projects. For example, why should it be necessary to have parents on joint committees that review district budget procedures? If it is desirable that parents understand the issues involved in such procedures, the designation of individual parents to serve on a joint committee is a poor way to achieve this objective.

Example (1) is also marred by other flaws. The requirement that working conditions in externally funded projects conform to the contract is indefensible; the clause renders it impossible to experiment, even on a trial basis, with conditions of employment that differ from the contractual conditions.

Furthermore, the language of (1) provides no clues as to why such a joint committee is necessary. The members of the committee appointed by the administration should include administrators knowledgeable about the issues under study. However, these administrators can typically report directly to the district; there is no need for them to report separately to the board as committee members. Also note that the scope of this committee should be limited; potentially at least, many externally funded projects have no impact on the "regular instructional program."

Example (2) is not about joint committees per se, but it illustrates a different approach to union participation on district committees:

(2) If the Board shall determine to appoint a District-wide committee that includes teacher representatives, the Union shall be invited to submit to the Superintendent the name of at least one (1) teacher who shall be named to the committee. Such Union-selected teacher shall meet the District requirements for committee participation prior to such appointment as the Union representative.

Although different, this approach is also unsatisfactory. If a joint committee is studying matters that are subject to bargaining, the union will have ample opportunity to present its point of view during the bargaining process. If the subject matter to be studied is not subject to bargaining, there is no automatic reason why the union should appoint any members of the committee. If the union's point of view is relevant, the board can get it without giving the union the right to name a member of the committee.

Even when joint committees have clear goals, they can still be extremely disadvantageous to the district. Example (3) illustrates one such case:

(3) A. Membership. No later than October 1, 1998, the Board and the Association agree to establish an Evaluation Committee consisting of seven members, three appointed by the Board, and four members appointed by the Association.

B. Responsibility. This Committee shall develop specific criteria for the evaluation of teachers.

C. Report Date. The recommendations shall be submitted for adoption to the Board and the Association no later than February 1, 1999.

Example (3) sets forth a specific task and completion date, but developing specific criteria for teacher evaluation is not an appropriate task for a joint committee. If the criteria are negotiable, the joint committee's discussions will probably be repeated in negotiations; if the criteria are not negotiable, it is probably a mistake to refer them to a joint committee. In effect, (3) allows the union to determine the criteria for teacher evaluation; the union designates a majority of committee members, and the committee's recommendations "shall be submitted for adoption to the Board and the Association." This is an invitation to a management disaster. If the board refused to accept the proposals, it would pay a heavy price for the time that district representatives spent working for the joint committee.

Finally, consider the language of example (4):

(4) A committee of five (5) teachers and four (4) administrators will work

on the details of the peer review program during the 1997–98 school year; the program will begin during the 1998–99 school year.

In (4) the joint committee's task is very poorly drafted. First, the language of (4) lacks a specific deadline by which the committee's work is to be completed. Furthermore, to state that the peer review program will begin during the following year is a categorical commitment that is unwise in the absence of an agreed-upon plan. Nothing would have been lost by merely stating that the parties "hope" or "plan" to begin the program during the 1998–99 school year.

To summarize, the best outcome from the board's point of view is to include no joint committees in the contract. If and when joint committees are included, the contract should specify their task and date of completion.

VIII. Contract Printing and Distribution

The union typically proposes that the school district print the contract and give the union copies to distribute to teachers and others. These proposals are often accepted after being modified; for example, the board and the union may agree to share the costs of printing, or the board may grant the union the right to be consulted on the format of the printed contract.

Although consultation with the union should not ordinarily be a problem, some union proposals on the subject can have serious negative consequences for the board. The collective bargaining contract is board policy for the duration of the contract. Therefore, boards should be extremely careful not to allow anyone else to have a veto power over how the board presents its policies to teachers and others. Because the union is one of the contracting parties, it is acceptable for it to share the printing costs. However, if as a quid pro quo for splitting these costs, the union demands a right to codetermine the contract's format or a right to include commentary about the contract, then the board should not accept the union's help. If the union insists upon including extraneous material when presenting the contract, it should print and distribute the contract at its own expense.

For example, suppose the board has agreed to a maintenance of membership clause. Such a clause requires teachers to remain members of the union except during a short "window" period, usually in effect for a few weeks before the expiration of the contract. The board may wish to alert teachers to the window period during which resignation from the union is permissible. Of course, the union will oppose having any attention drawn to this feature of the contract.

Bear in mind that the union has the right to publish the contract and say whatever it wishes about it. The union wants to emphasize teacher rights; the board may wish to emphasize teacher responsibilities. Normally, contracts are printed without interpretive material, but boards may have legitimate reasons to include such material (an addendum or preface, for instance) in some way that does not change the wording of the contract.

The board should not accept any restriction on who will print the contract and how the copies are disseminated. For example, some districts operate print shops, which can print the contracts at a considerable savings over commercial printing. An agreement to consult the union with respect to the printing of the contract before publication is about as far as a board should go on this issue. If the union has more power over the printing process, the results can be problematic. For example, sometimes the union will use its designer or printer to try to convert the contract into a publicity piece for the union or union leadership. The names of union officers and the union's negotiating team will be prominently displayed, along with those of board members and the board's negotiating team.

Every teacher should receive a copy of the contract and any amendments to it, but a requirement that everyone considered for employment receive a copy is not desirable and is probably outside the scope of negotiations. As noted above, the union represents teachers in an appropriate bargaining unit; teachers being "considered for employment" are not in this bargaining unit and thus the board is under no obligation to bargain over what publications they receive from the board. That said, giving prospective employees a copy of the contract can be a desirable way of informing them about the terms and conditions of their employment. There is nothing objectionable in providing this information to prospective employees before they are offered a position in the district, but the board should not obligate itself contractually to do this. However, boards can agree to provide the union with a specified number of copies at no charge.

Discussion of examples

Example (1) contains language that creates many of the problems cited above:

(1) Copies of this Agreement shall be reproduced by a union print shop which shall be selected by mutual agreement. The cost of such reproduction shall be shared by the Association and the Board with the Association paying a maximum of $1,500. Copies of the Agreement shall be distributed by the Association to all unit members employed at the time the printed Agreement is available. Unit members subsequently employed by the Board of Education shall be provided copies of the Agreement at the time of hire. The format of the contract copy shall be jointly developed by the Association and the Board.

Several objections apply to example (1). First, the identity of the contract's printer is not a term or condition of teacher employment. For this reason, proposals on the issue are outside the scope of bargaining and thus should not be negotiated. Also, as noted above, allowing the union to be jointly responsible for determining the format in which the contract is published is an undesirable policy. The board might, however, allow the union to help develop the format of items that supplement the contract. In that case, if the union insisted upon a format objectionable to the board, the latter would be free (as it would be in any case) to publish the contract as it sees fit.

Example (1) is also problematic because it forces the board to use a union print shop. The board might wish to have the agreement printed in the least expensive way that is consistent with good quality. Ideally, the board should have printers compete to provide the printing. In some districts, a high school printing class prints the contract, at a considerable savings to the district. At the very minimum, school boards should retain these options, which may result in district savings that would exceed the union's contributions to the cost of printing.

Sometimes instead of giving the union a right to consult with the board over questions of printing, contractual language may imply such a right. For example:

> (2) A copy of this Agreement shall be provided for each member of the bargaining unit. The Board's representative agrees to meet with the Federation after the signing of this Agreement for the purpose of arranging for printing of this Agreement. The Board and the Federation will share the cost of providing such copies on an equal basis.

Example (2) implies that the union has the right to negotiate the arrangements for printing the contract, but the board should reject any such implication or language giving rise to it. The contract is board policy for its duration, and the board should not agree to negotiate how its policies will be printed. If there is disagreement between the union and the board on a printing issue, the union's willingness to share the costs of printing is not worth the time and trouble of negotiating over the issue.

Given these problems, one may wonder what sort of clause involving contract production and distribution could be acceptable to school boards. The two examples below are acceptable models:

> (3) Copies of the Agreement shall be printed at the expense of the Board within sixty (60) days after the Agreement is signed. The printed Agreement shall be distributed to all employees now employed or employed during the duration of the Agreement. Twenty-five (25) additional copies shall be provided to the Association.

(4) Within thirty (30) days after the execution of this contract, the District shall provide without charge a copy of this contract to every unit member. Employees who become unit members after the execution of this Agreement shall be provided with a copy of this Agreement by the District without charge at the time of employment. The District shall notify unit members of contractual changes.

Examples (3) and (4) are satisfactory and are good examples of how far the board should go in accommodating the union with respect to the printing and distribution of the contract. Of course, there is no objection to consulting with the union on this matter, even if this is not required by the contract.

IX. Statutory Benefits

Collective bargaining in public education establishes a dual system of employee benefits: contractual benefits and legislative benefits. Unfortunately, in most states, the state legislatures ignored this duality when they enacted public employee bargaining laws.

Every state has some legislation dealing with teacher welfare. State retirement systems are probably the most important example, but payroll deduction of dues, agency shop fees, minimum salaries, tenure, sick leave, and duty-free lunch periods are also common subjects of state legislation. A few states have even enacted statutory grievance procedures. Legislators, school board members, and interested parties should carefully consider the relationships between statutory benefits and union contracts.

For example, suppose state law mandates that teachers receive at least one thirty-minute duty-free lunch period each day. During negotiations, the teachers may ask for a sixty-minute duty-free lunch period. If the school board cannot provide a duty-free lunch that is longer than thirty minutes, the union may ask the board to include the statutory benefit in the contract. The union will argue that this is only a case of the board giving the teachers something that the teachers already have by law. The union will also urge the board to include statutory benefits in the contract to make it more attractive to teachers, and to do so, apparently, without any concession by the board. What should be the board's reaction to such apparently harmless requests?

First, incorporating a statutory benefit into a collective bargaining agreement is not a harmless concession. On the contrary, such incorporation constitutes an important concession to the union. To see why, we must compare the benefits of a contractual right to those of a statutory right.

Suppose a controversy arises as to whether a teacher's right to a duty-free lunch period was violated. If the right is only statutory, the teacher and the union would have to bring a lawsuit against the district to achieve redress. Most teachers would be unwilling to initiate such a lawsuit. Furthermore, the statutes involved in such lawsuits seldom prescribe or even authorize any remedy for the teacher; even if the statutes did, the remedies involved would rarely compensate for the time and expense of a lawsuit. Of course, the board might redress the grievance in the absence of a lawsuit, but it might not. In contrast, teachers who have a duty-free lunch period pursuant to a union contract typically have recourse to a grievance procedure terminating in binding arbitration by an impartial third party, to remedy any alleged violation of their contractual rights.

Contractual grievance procedures that culminate in arbitration are far less costly and less time-consuming than lawsuits, for both the board and the union. Nevertheless, the board may prefer to avoid binding arbitration of grievances because this cheaper method of resolving contractual disputes would allow frivolous grievances. Furthermore, the union can often pursue a grievance in ways that it could not pursue a lawsuit. For instance, the union cannot sue the school board in order to handle the complaint of one of its members; the member would ordinarily be required to file such a lawsuit himself. While the union could provide the member with the necessary funds for either arbitration or litigation, the union, like individual teachers, is much more likely to initiate a grievance rather than a lawsuit to remedy alleged grievances. In short, unions initiate and pursue arbitration for many grievances that would be ignored if the union's only recourse were a lawsuit. Ironically, although the teacher unions are opposed to privatization when it could affect school district employees adversely, they aggressively support the private resolution—through arbitration—of their claims that the board has violated its contract with the union.

Suppose the union agrees that inclusion of the statutory benefit in the contract is a significant concession, but tries to negotiate for inclusion of the benefit on its merits. If the board sincerely believes that grievances should be resolved quickly, the union may argue, why would the board force a teacher to file a lawsuit if the teacher sincerely believes the board violated the teacher's right to some statutory benefit?

This argument has some merit, but overlooks the possibility that the introduction of arbitration as a method of dispute resolution could lead to abuse. As noted above, the more expensive it is for a teacher to resolve a dispute, the less likely it is that the teacher union will be able to use grievance arbitration to harass the administration. If the district reduces the cost of resolving disputes by allowing them to be resolved through arbitration rather than by lawsuit, the district will increase the likelihood that teachers will initiate both valid and invalid claims. By including statutory benefits in the contract, the board renders dispute resolution less expensive, thereby increasing the possibility of abuse.

It is sometimes appropriate to include statutory obligations in a contract. Suppose, for example, that a statute prescribes certain penalties for teachers who break their contracts. It can be to the board's advantage to have this sort of statutory obligation included in the contract. Incorporation of the statutory obligation into the contract would be a valuable means of publicizing the obligation among teachers. Also, if the contract incorporates the teachers' statutory obligation to renew their employment for the coming year in a timely fashion, the teachers cannot escape this obligation by arguing that the terms of the contract take precedence over those of the statute. Furthermore, if a statute that is advantageous to the board is repealed or weakened, the contractual provision will help the board avoid the problems that arise when teachers break their contracts.

There is merit in the view that negotiations between the board and the union should govern the relationships between the parties. If this argument is valid, however, the union should be required to accept the consequences of it. Among other things, this would require that teachers give up their statutory remedies for the infringement of contractual rights. Public policy should require statutory remedies for statutory rights, and contractual remedies for contractual rights; providing both statutory and contractual remedies for the same school district action enables unions and teachers to "shop" for the forum most likely to support their position. One important way for the board to avoid "forum shopping" is to refuse to include statutory benefits in the contract.

Needless to say, unions oppose any effort to delete statutory benefits from union contracts. Ideally, the problem should be avoided by state legislation; state legislation should prohibit bargaining over statutory benefits. For instance, if state law provides a certain amount of sick leave, the law should prohibit unions from bargaining for a larger entitlement. This is justified because statutory benefits are disadvantageous to school boards during bargaining. When a legislature enacts a benefit, the unions do not have to make any bargaining concession to get the benefit, whereas unions would have to make concessions if the benefit were negotiated at the local level. The most important objection against including statutory benefits in a union contract is that the dual system is inconsistent with the rationales for statutory benefits and for collective bargaining. The statutory benefits were provided because teachers allegedly did not have recourse to adequate procedures for resolving their terms and conditions of employment, while the rationale for collective bargaining is that the terms and conditions of teacher employment are best resolved through negotiations at the local level.

A less abrupt way to remedy the problems that arise when there are two systems of benefits would be for the states to incorporate the statutory benefits into teacher contracts for two or three years while state legislators simultaneously repeal the corresponding statutes. This would obviate the argument that it would be unfair to deprive teachers of legislative benefits that they have struggled for years to achieve.

As a practical matter, the only action that can be taken in some states is to ensure that the problem is not exacerbated. Every time state legislators propose a new statutory benefit for teachers, the proposal should carry a provision stating that the benefit is no longer a subject of school board/union bargaining. Better yet, legislators and school boards should refuse to extend the dual system of benefits; no statutory benefit that is a subject of bargaining should even be considered by state legislative bodies. This would not undo the damage caused by the dual system, but at least it would prevent more of the same.

Discussion of examples

The clause in example (1) renders alleged violations of any statutory "rights, benefits, and privileges pertaining to [teacher] conditions of employment" subject to the grievance procedure:

(1) Except as modified herein, teachers shall retain all rights, benefits, and privileges pertaining to their conditions of employment contained in the School Code at the time of the execution of this Agreement.

Note how completely the language of (1) entrenches teachers' rights; even if the legislature repealed or weakened any of these conditions of employment, the teachers would continue to have them. A clause of this kind is usually found only in extremely pro-union contracts in districts where the board negotiators are subject to strong union pressures.

Example (2) incorporates the federal antidiscrimination statutes in the contract, and then adds several state statutory rights and benefits to the provision:

(2) The District shall comply with Titles VI and VII of the Civil Rights Act of 1964, Title IX of the Education Amendments of 1972, the Rehabilitation Act of 1973, the Age Discrimination in Employment Act of 1967, and shall prohibit discrimination because of race, color, national origin, religion, sex, sexual preference, age, handicap, disability, marital status, economic status, political affiliation, domicile, membership in an employee organization, participation in the activities of an employee organization, union affiliation, or exercise of the rights contained in this Agreement.

Though this may seem quite expansive, it is actually less sweeping than (1), which incorporates all "rights, benefits, and privileges" in the "School Code." Example (2) thus gives readers some idea of the enormous scope of (1); needless to say, (2) is also highly objectionable.

No matter how innocent the incorporation of a statutory benefit may seem to be, it should be rejected; once a board makes an exception to this rule, it will come under pressure in the future to include other statutory benefits in the contract. The board should only include statutory benefits in a contract as a trade-off for language that the board believes to be very important, or in exchange for a union waiver of some other statutory right or benefit. Note that in some states, however, the bargaining statute itself precludes any such trade-off by providing that bargaining shall not diminish any statutory rights or benefits.

X. Definitions

Theoretically, the definitions section of a contract is intended only to point out the meaning that the parties should give to words and phrases in the contract. Boards should not be opposed to a definitions section, but they should be alert to avoid making inadvertent concessions by choosing definitions that are disadvantageous. Every use of a defined term should be reviewed carefully to ensure that it does not require concessions that the board is unwilling to make.

Discussion of examples

Examples (1) and (2) illustrate union efforts to achieve concessions by defining terms in ways that favor their efforts:

(1) "Paid Leave of Absence" means that a unit member shall be entitled to receive wages and all fringe benefits, including, but not limited to, insurance and retirement benefits; to return to the same or similar assignment which he/she enjoyed immediately preceding the commencement of the leave; and to receive credit for annual salary increments provided during his/her leave.

(2) "Unpaid Leave of Absence" means that a unit member shall be entitled to the same benefits accorded unit members who are on paid leave, excluding wages.

Before we examine how these definitions achieve concessions for the union, note that it would be possible to define "paid leave of absence" and "unpaid leave of absence" at the time the parties negotiate over leave benefits. This would make more sense than to negotiate over leave benefits in the definitions section and then again under the section on leave benefits.

Example (1) favors union interests by incorporating an expansive set of privileges into the definition of paid leave. A requirement mandating the return of teachers who are on paid leave "to the same or similar assignment which he/she enjoyed immediately preceding the commencement of the leave" might be objectionable to the board; it might prefer not to grant leaves of absence if required to honor this requirement. Similarly, the requirement that teachers on paid leave of absence should receive "all fringe benefits" that they receive when working might be a reason to deny paid leaves of absence. It would be preferable to spell out the fringe benefits that accompany leaves of absence, whether paid or unpaid.

Similarly, (2) is an effort to negotiate benefits under the guise of defining terms. Suppose a teacher wants a leave of absence to study for an advanced degree, ostensibly in order to find another job. The district may have legitimate objections to subsidizing this teacher, who is unlikely to return after the expiration of the unpaid leave. Or a teacher may want unpaid leave to serve as a full-time union officer for an extended period of time; in such cases, there is no obvious reason why the district should pay for the teacher's health insurance or guarantee the teacher's ability to return to the "same or similar" position.

The best alternative for the board is to avoid including any definitions of contractual terms that implicitly provide concessions to the union. For example, the definition of paid leave could include a provision like that in the following.

(3) Teachers on leave of absence shall not be entitled to salary and benefits unless explicitly provided in this Agreement.

Example (3) is included to emphasize a different approach to leave benefits. Instead of asserting that teachers on leave receive all or virtually all benefits, (3) asserts that they shall receive only the benefits explicitly provided in the contract. The district should adhere to this position until the union clearly recognizes that the district will not grant all benefits to all kinds of leaves.

3

Organizational Security

In this handbook, "organizational security" refers to contractual provisions that protect the union's status as the exclusive representative of teachers in an appropriate bargaining unit. The most important of these provisions are those dealing with union revenues: membership fees, dues, and/or agency fee payments. As defined in Chapter 2, agency fees, which are sometimes referred to as fair-share fees, are the fees that nonunion teachers must pay to the union as a condition of employment. Note that other items relevant to organizational security may be found in other sections of this handbook. For example, the union's rights to meet on district property or to use the district's mail system are sometimes included under organizational security, but in this handbook they are discussed in Chapter 4, "Union Rights."

Contrary to popular opinion, unions and school boards cannot contractually require teachers to be dues-paying members of the union. In four states, however, nonunion teachers are required to pay agency fees to the union upon employment; in twenty-five other states, the teacher unions can negotiate the requirement. The remaining twenty-one states are right-to-work states in which it is illegal to require union membership or payment of any fee to a union as a condition of employment, or they are states that prohibit collective bargaining in public education.

I. Payroll Deduction of Dues

From the union's point of view, provisions involving the payroll deduction of dues, political action committee (PAC) contributions, and agency fees are among the most important items in the contract. School boards often agree to these provisions without thinking about their implications for the district or its teachers. This section considers payroll deduction of dues, and the following sections discuss PAC contributions and agency fees. In several states, these issues are resolved by statute, but the discussion here considers the issues only from a contractual perspective.

Although contracts typically provide that the district shall deduct and transmit union dues to the union, most contracts do not include a copy of the authorization form that must be signed by the teachers to allow for the deduction. However, when the unions prepare the form, it frequently authorizes and directs the district to implement payroll deduction for other matters, such as PAC contributions, as well. The ramifications of any clause involving payroll deduction of dues cannot be fully understood without understanding the authorization form and who is authorized to prepare it. This is evident from Figure 1 below, which is part of a dues deduction form prepared by a teacher union. Obviously, forms prepared by the school district might be very different; for example, forms prepared by the school district would be less likely to provide for payroll deduction of PAC contributions.

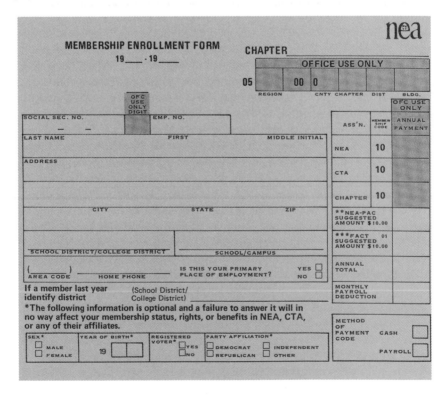

Figure 1. Dues deduction form prepared by a teacher union

The union is an organization providing representational services. Teachers are the customers. What other business has the benefit of a third party collecting the revenues from its customers at no cost to the business? It is difficult to think of any. Yet by having the school district deduct union dues from teachers' paychecks, teacher unions receive this rare benefit.

The amount of money that unions raise through dues is quite large; altogether, the NEA's and the AFT's revenues at the local, state, and national levels exceed $1.3 billion annually. This amount does not include their PAC funds, foundations, special-purpose organizations, and member-benefit corporations; there is very little public awareness of the fact that the NEA and the AFT are huge financial conglomerates.[1] Although boards have not charged the unions for collecting union dues in the past, they should at least consider language that would terminate the concession in case of egregious union conduct.

The unions pay close attention to every aspect of payroll deduction of dues, and districts should do likewise. The dues deduction article should include the following safeguards for the school board:

- Union certification of the amounts to be deducted from teacher salary checks
- Adequate time for the district to make payroll changes from month to month and transmit funds to the union
- Cancellation of payroll deduction of union revenues if the union engages in a job action
- An adequate hold harmless clause (see section V of this chapter)
- No district liability for any errors in the payroll deduction process
- No district involvement in collecting unpaid dues or agency fees from delinquent teachers
- No district obligation to deduct the balance of annual dues from teachers who leave district employment during the school year
- No district obligation to accept whatever dues deduction form is prescribed by the union
- Adequate provision for district needs and legal obligations that may be ignored in union-sponsored authorizations for payroll deduction
- Avoidance of a provision that would require union approval for any other deductions
- A satisfactory time schedule for paying teachers
- No district obligation to collect contributions to union PACs—this is not an appropriate function of a government agency
- If there is an agency fee, a religious exemption that allows the employee with religious objections to union membership to select a charitable organization to receive an amount equivalent to the agency fees

Although none of the examples below includes all of these safeguards, (3) includes most of them; for example, it is the only one to explicitly avoid payroll deduction of contributions to union PAC funds.

Discussion of examples

Sometimes unions demand contractual language that will ensure that the district will help the union collect dues from workers who receive no union benefits. Consider the following:

(1) A. Dues of the Association or fees paid to the Association shall be deducted from the employee's salary in sixteen (16) equal installments beginning with the first salary check in October of each year. Employees desiring to have the Association dues or fees deducted shall sign a request for payroll deduction on a form provided by the Association. Requests shall continue from year to year until the employee leaves the District.

B. Teachers joining the Association at a date later than September 30, or new employees who choose to be fee payers, will have the dues or fees deducted in equal installments from their remaining salary checks for the balance of the school year.

C. The District shall deduct outstanding dues or fees from the final paycheck of a teacher terminating his/her employment early.

D. The Association agrees to indemnify and hold the Board harmless against any liability arising from any action taken by the Board to comply with the provisions of this Article, including reimbursement of any legal fees, back pay, or expenses incurred. This indemnification shall not apply to any claim, demand, suit, or other form of liability which may arise as a result of negligence or willful misconduct by the Board.

Example (1) requires the district to deduct the balance of full dues from an employee's pay regardless of when the employee was hired or resigned. It is indefensible for a school board to force its employees to pay for services that the employees cannot possibly use or benefit from. Even if the employees have agreed to pay in this situation, the district should not participate in efforts to force the employees to pay.

The contractual language in the second paragraph of (2), below, illustrates how a district may involve itself—unnecessarily—in the collection of dues:

(2) A. Payroll Deduction

The District agrees to promptly remit membership dues and agency fees to the Association with an alphabetical list of unit members for whom such deductions have been made, categorizing them as to membership or nonmembership in the Association and indicating any changes from the list previously furnished. There shall be no charge to the Association for such deductions and employee lists. Unit members choosing to pay membership dues or service fees directly to the Association who do not make timely payments shall have a membership dues or service fee deduction initiated by the District.

B. Delinquent Employees

1. The Association may take appropriate legal action against the delinquent employee if, after the next pay period, dues are not paid. Such legal action shall be limited to recovery of the Association dues to the extent provided by law.

2. The District will not undertake dismissal or other disciplinary action against an employee who refuses to pay dues to the Association.

3. In the event the dues are not timely paid, the District, upon receiving a signed statement from the Association indicating that an employee has failed to comply with this provision, shall notify said employee that he/she is delinquent.

C. Other Payroll Deductions

1. Upon appropriate written authorization from the employee, the District shall deduct from the salary of any employee and make appropriate remittance for District-approved annuities, credit unions, charitable donations, or other plans or programs jointly approved by the Association and the District.

2. Employees on authorized leaves of absence from the District are not required to pay dues or agency fees to the Association.

In example (2), the district has agreed to warn employees who are delinquent in their payments to the union; there is no good reason why the school district should perform this task for the union.

Example (3) below also illustrates how school districts promote union agendas at the expense of district employees. Clause C refers to fees that are "equivalent" to dues, but no agency fee should be "equivalent to dues"; such fees should always be much less than dues if the spirit and letter of the state bargaining laws and U.S. Supreme Court decisions governing agency fees are followed.

(3) A. Any employee who is a member of the Association, or who applies for membership, may sign and deliver to the District an assignment

authorizing deduction of unified membership dues, initiation fees, and general assessments in the Association. Such authorization shall continue in effect from year to year unless revoked in writing. Pursuant to such authorization, the District shall deduct one-tenth of such dues from the regular salary check of the employee each month, as long as teachers are paid in ten (10) monthly installments. Deductions for employees who sign such authorization after the commencement of the school year shall be appropriately prorated to complete payments by the end of the school year. The District shall not be required to provide payroll deductions for political purposes or for any other purpose not specifically required by law.

B. Any employee who is a member of the Association as of the date this Agreement becomes effective (following approval by the District and the Association) shall remain a member in good standing until thirty (30) days prior to the expiration of this Agreement. Any employee who is not a member of the Association as of the effective date of this Agreement shall either become a member or pay to the Association a fee equal to unified membership dues, initiation fees, and general assessments unless the District is notified by the employee within fifteen (15) working days of the effective date of this Agreement that he/she elects not to do so. New employees shall have fifteen (15) working days after the first duty date of employment to make such election. The District agrees to provide the Association with a list of unit members electing not to become a member and/or pay fees equal to membership dues, initiation fees, and general assessments within seven (7) working days after the deadlines provided for in this Article.

C. With respect to all sums deducted by the District pursuant to authorization of the employee, whether for membership dues or equivalent fees, the District agrees to remit such monies to the Association promptly, accompanied by an alphabetical list of employees for whom such deductions have been made, and indicating any changes in personnel from the list previously furnished.

D. Employees who do not become members of the Association but who do pay equivalent dues, fees, and assessments may authorize payroll deductions in the same manner as provided in Paragraph A of this Article.

E. The Association and the employee(s) shall indemnify and hold the District harmless of any and all claims, demands, suits, or any other action arising from the organizational security provisions of this Agreement.

Example (4) provides that district obligations to collect union dues are terminated thirty days after teachers revoke the authorization form. Practically speaking, example (4) takes the school district out of the business of enforcing the collection of dues from union members.

(4) A member of the bargaining unit, and only such a member, may present written authorization to the Board to deduct Union dues from his/her salary. Each authorization shall be effective until the earlier of the following two occurrences:

A. Loss of certification by the Union as the bargaining agent for the teachers covered by this contract.

B. Thirty (30) days after written notice of revocation of said authorization by the teacher to the Board and the Union.

The Union shall pay to the Board a fee of two hundred fifty dollars ($250.00) per year for payroll deduction for Union members. The Board shall transmit to the Union any and all deductions within fifteen (15) days, except in the case of reasonable delays.

The Board's obligations with respect to said funds are the collection and transmittal of the funds within fifteen (15) days whenever possible. The Union, its officers, agents, and members will hold the Board and its agents harmless for the cost and results of any action which may be brought by any of its members, groups of members, or agencies of law with respect to the use or disposition of said funds after they have been transmitted to the Union.

The Board is prohibited from any involvement in the collection of fines, penalties, or special assessments levied or attempted to be levied upon its teachers by the Union, its officers, agents, or members.

Example (4) is also interesting for its imposition of a service fee that the union pays the district for the collection and transmittal of dues. The union is much less likely to engage in a job action if it fears that the school board will charge the union a substantial amount for the payroll services that are vital to union viability. The $250 fee in this district is minimal, but it establishes the important principle that a board can charge a union for the services it provides the union.

II. Agency Fees

As previously noted, "agency fees" refer to amounts that nonunion employees must pay to the union as a condition of employment. In public education, such fees are illegal in twenty-one states that either have not enacted a teacher bargaining statute or have enacted right-to-work laws. In twenty-five others, the teacher unions have the right to negotiate for an agency fee. In Hawaii, Minnesota, Rhode Island, and New York, nonunion teachers are required by statute to pay agency fees from the beginning of their employment; the unions in these states do not have to negotiate for the fees or include an agency fee clause in the contract because school districts must by law deduct the fees from teacher salaries and transmit them to the union.

The U.S. Supreme Court has held that nonunion teachers are required to pay agency fees to their state and national unions as well as to their local affiliates.[2] The amount of these fees varies from year to year and from union to union; supposedly, the amount is based on the nonmember's pro rata share of union expenditures for collective bargaining, grievance processing, and contract administration in the previous year. Nonunion teachers cannot be charged for any other expenditures. In most cases, the charges to nonunion teachers are 65 to 90 percent of dues, but only because the teacher unions have substantially exaggerated the amounts that nonunion teachers are required to pay.[3]

The rationale for agency fees is that every teacher in the bargaining unit benefits from union representation, hence every such teacher should pay his or her "fair share" of union dues. The reality is that many teachers do not benefit from union representation; some are even clearly disadvantaged by it. For example, some teachers who lose their jobs when there is a reduction in force (RIF) would be retained if not for a union contract that requires the district to make layoffs in reverse order of seniority. These teachers hardly "benefit" from union representation. Mathematics and science teachers also frequently suffer from union representation because the unions negotiate single salary schedules that require all teachers to be paid solely on the basis of their academic credit and years of teaching experience. Mathematics and science teachers would frequently be paid more than other teachers if it were not for such single salary schedules, because the talent required to be a good mathematics or science teacher can usually command salaries higher than those that are paid to most other teachers.

Unions give single salary schedules high priority in order to avoid internal divisions over which groups of teachers should be paid more and which groups should be paid less. Unfortunately, single salary schedules function to the detriment of school districts that can hire teachers in fields where qualified candidates are scarce only by paying higher salaries to all teachers. Furthermore, even if every teacher benefits from union representation, they do not benefit equally. Finally, requiring the payment of agency fees deprives rank-and-file teachers of the leverage provided by resignation, their most effective way to influence the union. Threats to resign from the union are not an effective way to influence the union if the resigning teachers must nevertheless pay agency fees to the union.

Despite these and other valid objections to agency fees, school boards often accept the imposition of the fees. Agency fees are extremely important to the unions; next to payroll deduction of dues, agency fees are the most important source of union revenues. Consequently, the unions frequently offer important concessions for an agency fee, and since the fees are paid out of teachers' pockets rather than from school district revenues, many boards succumb to the temptation to agree to the fee. In subsequent contracts, the unions usually achieve the objectives that were allegedly sacrificed to get the agency fee clause.

Discussion of examples

The examples below illustrate the language found in strongly pro-union agency fee clauses. They are "pro-union" in the sense that they require the school district as well as nonunion teachers to act promptly to ensure maximum union revenues. Note that in both cases the optional procedure for religious objectors is just as costly to the employee as are union dues, but unlike the authorization of dues, the optional procedures are replete with obstacles that would discourage all but the most committed of those who would object on religious grounds.

(1) Organizational Security and Payroll Deductions
   A. Any employee who is a member of the Association who signs and delivers to the District an assignment authorizing deduction of unified membership dues, initiation fees and general assessments of the Association, or a service fee (representation fee), shall have such authorization continue in effect from year to year unless revoked in writing between June 1 and September 1 of a given year. Any such revocation should be effective for the next school year. Pursuant to such authorization, the District shall deduct such dues, fees, or assessments (or a service fee) from the regular salary check, in ten (10) equal installments each year, for the duration of this Agreement.
   B. The District will provide bargaining-unit employees new to the District with a copy of the Collective Bargaining Agreement and the employee will sign a form, a copy of which will be forwarded to the Association within ten (10) days of the employee reporting to work.
   C. Any employee who is a member of the unit, who is not a member of the Association in good standing, or who does not make application for membership within thirty (30) days from the first day of active employment (except as provided hereafter in the Optional Procedure), shall pay a service fee to the Association: an amount equivalent to the unified membership dues, initiation fee, and general assessments uniformly required to be paid by members of the Association.
   D. In the event an employee fails to comply with this Article, at the request of the Association, the Superintendent or his designee shall notify the employee within ten (10) days that he/she is not complying

with his/her contractual obligation to the Association and the District. A copy of such notice shall be sent to the Association.

E. The District shall deduct service fees from the salary or wage order of the employee who is not a member of the Association, or has not complied with the Optional Procedure.

Any employee may pay service fees directly to the Association in lieu of having such service fees deducted from the salary or wage order.

In the event that a unit member shall not pay such fee directly to the Association or authorize payment through payroll deduction as provided in Paragraph A, the Association shall so inform the District and the District shall immediately begin automatic payroll deduction in the same manner as set forth in Paragraph A of this Article.

Any payment to a charity must be made on an annual basis.

F. The parties further agree that the obligation of this Article shall be grounded in the individual contract for employees, which shall state — "this contract is subject to a collective bargaining agreement heretofore or hereafter negotiated by the District and the exclusive bargaining representative of employees employed by the District. The terms of such collective bargaining agreement are incorporated herein, and by accepting this contract, you agree to be bound by all such terms, including the Organizational Security and Payroll Deductions provisions thereof."

G. The District agrees promptly to remit monies collected through payroll deduction to the Association accompanied by an alphabetical list of employees for whom such deductions have been made.

H. The Association agrees to furnish any information needed by the District to fulfill the provisions of this Article.

I. Upon appropriate written authorization from the employee, the District shall deduct from the salary of any employee and make appropriate remittance for annuities, credit unions, and savings bonds. Deductions for any other plans or programs shall be jointly approved by the Association and the District.

J. Dues check-off authorization in effect on the date of the signing of this Agreement shall remain in effect but shall be subject to the conditions set forth in this Article.

K. The Association agrees to indemnify and hold the District harmless from any and all claims arising from a bargaining-unit member represented by the Association concerning the implementation of this Article, provided such implementation is done by the District in good faith and in a non-negligent manner. In such case, the Association shall have the exclusive right to defend such suits and to determine which matters shall be compromised, resisted, tried, or appealed.

L. The District agrees to deduct dues or service fees pursuant to the schedule submitted by the Association for employees who execute a form currently in use or any mutually agreed-upon form. The Association is to submit the schedule each year by September 7. The schedule may be amended once each school year with thirty (30) days notice.

Optional Procedure

M. Any employee of this unit who has bona fide religious beliefs which prohibit him/her from joining or financially supporting employee organizations shall not be required to join or financially support the Association or its affiliates. However, that employee shall utilize the following Optional Procedure:

1. Submit a notarized statement to the Association with a copy to the employer by the end of the first month (September) of each school year. The statement shall state that the person does not desire to join or contribute to the Association because of religious beliefs that prevent him/her from joining or contributing.

2. Make payment equal to unified membership dues to a nonreligious, nonlabor organization exempted under Section 501(c)(3) of Title 26 of the Internal Revenue Code. The list of designated charitable organizations is: Heart Fund, Cancer Fund, Cystic Fibrosis Foundation, or others approved by the Association.

3. Proof of such payment (i.e., payment to one of the charities on the list of designated charities) shall be submitted to the Association with a copy to the District by the end of the first month of each school year (September).

This procedure is applicable only to employees who have elected not to join in financial support of the Association and/or its affiliates based on personal beliefs and who annually continue to exercise that option.

In example (1), the agency fee equals the cost of union dues and assessments. The unions often continue to negotiate agency fees that equal regular dues and assessments even though they are aware that the fees should be substantially lower; at the bargaining table, the unions take the position that the amount of the agency fee is an internal union matter. The unions often succeed in enforcing these agency fees because many teachers are not aware of their legal rights or are not aware that they can receive legal help without charge from the National Right to Work Legal Defense Foundation (NRTWLDF). Unions are also aided by the fact that many school boards elected with union support do not care very much about the rights of individual teachers.

The optional procedure in (1) illustrates the minimal concern for individual rights that is frequently reflected in teacher union contracts. The optional procedure applies only to teachers who refuse for religious reasons to pay dues or agency fees; the group of teachers that has such religious objections to paying dues or agency fees to the union is relatively small. Even such bona fide objections do not release the teachers from an obligation to pay; they serve only to release the teacher from an obligation to pay the union. So the teacher has to pay, but to whom? The optional procedure allows these teachers to donate to charity in lieu of their union dues. However, the designated list of charities in the contract is extremely narrow and cannot be expanded without union approval (according to the second subsection of section M). In some contracts, the designated list of charities includes only union foundations or scholarship funds; in those cases, the nonunion employee who does not wish to contribute indirectly to the union can look forward to an endless stream of litigation by union lawyers.

Finally, to safeguard against the possibility that teachers might drop their religious objections but continue to avoid payment, section M.1 requires that teachers who wish to use the optional procedure to avoid paying the union must formally opt for it each year. Parenthetically, one reason the unions are so adamant about restricting the religious objections to agency fees is that the union receives no income from religious objectors. Unlike teachers who object to union fees on religious grounds, those who object on other grounds must still pay the agency fee to the union.

The union's contractual focus on dues and service fees is further illustrated by section G, which ensures that the union will not lose any interest due to district tardiness in transmitting funds to the union, and that the union will be able to identify immediately those teachers who do not pay. By requiring joint approval between the union and the board before payroll deduction can be used for any plan or program, section I ensures that there will be no payroll deduction for any plans or programs opposed by the union. The language of (1) suggests that the school district is completely subservient to the union; this is illustrated by the fact that the district cannot suspend the collection of dues while the teachers are on strike, a development that has occurred occasionally in the district in question. Not surprisingly, the union in this district was very influential in school board elections, and thus clearly exercised considerable influence over agency fee issues.

Example (2) below shows how the unions try to prevent teachers from faking religious convictions to avoid paying service fees. Section A requires teachers to pay "sums equal to the service fee" to one of the listed charitable organizations. Since this amount equals the amount that a teacher would pay the union if he or she was a member, this provision removes teachers' financial incentive to claiming a religious objection.

(2) Religious Objection
- A. Any employee who is a member of a religious body whose traditional tenets or teachings include objections to joining or financially supporting employee organizations shall not be required to join, maintain membership in, or financially support the Association as a condition of employment; however, such employee shall be required to pay sums equal to the service fee to one of the following charitable funds exempt from taxation under Section 501(c)(3) of Title 26 of the Internal Revenue Code:
  1. American Cancer Society
  2. American Heart Association
  3. Children's Memorial Hospital
  4. School District Educational Foundation
- B. Any employee claiming the religious exemption shall, as a condition of continued exemption, provide the Association with copies of receipts from the charity selected as proof that such payment has been made, or shall authorize payroll deduction of such payments.

III. PAC Contributions

Payroll deduction of PAC contributions is one of the most neglected issues in teacher bargaining. One reason for the neglect is that the unions rarely, if ever, explicitly propose payroll deduction of PAC contributions. Instead, they propose—and school boards invariably accept—payroll deduction of union dues. The contract explicitly states that such deduction will be implemented pursuant to an authorization form—sometimes one prepared by the union, sometimes one mutually agreed upon by the parties, and sometimes a district form. In all of these scenarios, the union is virtually always successful in including spaces on the form whereby the teacher can authorize payroll deduction of PAC contributions for local, state, and national union PACs.

Most board members never look at the authorization forms, and even when they do, most do not pay any attention to the spaces authorizing payroll deduction of PAC contributions. The common attitude among board members is that inasmuch as the teacher is authorizing deductions from his or her own salary checks, there is no reason for the board to be concerned about the practice. This attitude is typical even though the incumbent unions can and do prohibit payroll deduction of PAC contributions to any PACs other than that of the union. Thus, in districts in which the NEA and AFT affiliates are the exclusive representative, individual teachers are not allowed payroll deduction of contributions to Republican PACs.

The importance of this issue should not be underestimated. Teacher unions typically generate five to fifty times more revenue from payroll deduction of PAC contributions than from cash contributions by teachers; this source of revenue is one of the most important factors undergirding the teacher unions' tremendous political clout.

If we think of the practice in political terms rather than labor terms, the routine acceptance of the practice by school boards is difficult to defend. Essentially, the practice amounts to the collection and dissemination of political contributions by a government agency; not only is this done without any charge to the interest group that is the beneficiary of the practice, but that beneficiary is also given the power to veto the payroll deduction of PAC contributions for all other PACs. Analyzed in these terms, as it should be, the practice is clearly indefensible.

Discussion of example

Example (1) below specifies that the district shall prepare the payroll deduction form:

(1) Upon appropriate authorization by any teacher, the Board will provide direct deposit to the Union credit union of a part or all of the teacher's salary. Such deductions and remittance by the Board shall be made in accordance with regulations established by the Superintendent.

The Board shall deduct from the pay of each employee all current membership dues and uniform assessments of the Union provided that at the time of each such deduction there is in the possession of the Board a valid signed authorization for each such deduction, executed by the employee, in the form and according to the terms of the authorization. Such authorization shall continue year after year unless revoked by the employee. Authorization cards in a form approved in advance by the Superintendent and provided by the Board shall be distributed by the Union.

The impact of this provision with respect to payroll deduction of PAC contributions is potentially enormous. If the district does not wish to collect PAC funds for the union, it can omit this option from the form. In contrast, if the union prepares the form, the PAC option will be included. The strongly recommended position is that school boards should not participate in the collection and distribution of PAC contributions for any individual or special interest group. To ensure that the district is not involved in such activities, school boards should demand the right to prepare the form.

IV. Mailing Lists

More and more unions are proposing that school districts provide them with an up-to-date mailing list each month that shows who has contributed dues or agency fees during the last payroll period. These proposals often have a political rationale, because up-to-date mailing lists are extremely valuable in electoral politics. Congressional and state legislative districts often include a large number of school districts. The ability to target mailings to teachers accurately can be very helpful to the union as it attempts to influence elections.

In recent years, union involvement in political campaigns has revealed that the union mailing lists were not up-to-date. As a result, the unions were wasting a great deal of money sending campaign literature to teachers who had moved, died, or retired; furthermore, the campaign literature often did not reach newly employed teachers. Consequently, local unions frequently request a monthly updated address list of teachers who have recently contributed to union revenue, or even of all teachers in some cases.

Most school board members, even most school board negotiators, do not appreciate the value of this concession to the union; they are not aware of the implications of address lists for union political activities. Typically, the board focuses on how much the concession will cost the board. Since providing updated mailing lists is inexpensive, boards rarely insist upon union concessions in exchange for the board's agreement to provide the lists.

The critical point is not necessarily that boards should refuse to provide the lists. Some boards may agree readily, while others may not; each may be acting appropriately. What is important is that school boards be aware of the implications of the concessions. Strictly from a tactical point of view, they should know the importance of updated mailing lists to the union; such knowledge could allow the board to secure a union concession that might otherwise not be obtained.

V. Hold Harmless Clause

Recall example (1) from this chapter's previous section on agency fees; section K of this example is a hold harmless clause. Such clauses are included in school board/union contracts because agency fee clauses are frequently challenged by teachers for various reasons, and school boards as well as unions must frequently defend their actions relating to agency fees. Inasmuch as requiring and collecting agency fees are services that boards provide for unions, boards often insist, as they should, upon contractual protection against legal challenges to school board actions on this issue.

Discussion of examples

Example (1) below sets forth a typical hold harmless clause; inasmuch as the district is providing a benefit to the union, the union should protect the district from any liability in this matter:

(1) A. In any case in which the provisions of this Article are contested, and it is necessary for the District to defend a position, engage legal counsel, and incur expenses in so doing, the Association agrees either to provide the defense and costs for the District, and/or pay for such legal and defense costs at the election of the Association.

B. The Association shall indemnify and hold the District harmless from any and all claims, demands, suits, or any other actions arising from the organizational security provisions contained herein.

C. The Association shall have the exclusive right to decide and determine whether any such action shall be compromised, resisted, defended, tried, or appealed.

The following proposal reflects widespread union thinking on the essentials of a good hold harmless clause:

(2) The Association agrees to pay to the District all reasonable legal fees and costs incurred in defending against any legal and/or administrative action challenging the legality of the agency fee provisions of this Agreement or their implementation. The Association shall have the exclusive right to decide whether any such action referred to above shall or shall not be compromised, resisted, defended, tried, or appealed.

There are several objections to this language from the board's perspective. First, there can be honest differences of opinion over what fees and costs are "reasonable" in this context. Second, the board and the union may have conflicting interests in a legal challenge to the agency fee; it is quite possible that the union would agree to a resolution that was good for the union but bad for the board. The critical point is that the agency fees are a high union priority, whereas the board can function very well without them. Consequently, there is no policy reason why a board should accept a union's weak hold harmless proposal (like the one above).

The following language gives the school board control over the defense of any action against it, while the union is nevertheless required to hold the board harmless for its actions in all matters pertaining to organizational security:

(3) The Union and the employee(s) shall indemnify and hold the District harmless of any and all claims, demands, or lawsuits, or any other action arising from the organizational security provisions of this Agreement.

Note that the above language protects the board from actions against it relating to dues as well as agency fees.

VI. Maintenance of Membership

Under a maintenance of membership clause, teachers must maintain their union membership, usually until a date close to the expiration date of the contract. For example, a three-year contract might include a maintenance of membership clause that allows members to resign only during the fifteen days preceding the expiration date. Sometimes the window period for resignations comes at the beginning of the contract rather than at its end, but placing it at the end is the more common practice.

Reasons for resigning from the union may or may not be union-related: possible reasons include a desire to be with a spouse who is being transferred, a desire to live elsewhere, employment opportunities outside of education, and dissatisfaction with the union. Whatever the reason, resignations result in a loss of union revenues. For this reason, the unions try to prohibit or limit resignations as much as possible.

At the present time, the critical issues of the right to resign have not been definitively resolved by the courts. Meanwhile, the teacher unions continue to negotiate maintenance of membership in their contracts; the unions realize that most teachers are not sure of their rights to resign, and will rarely spend personal funds to contest the unions on these issues. It may be several years before the U.S. Supreme Court rules on the issue. Unions argue that when teachers become members, they are aware—or should be aware—of the limits on resignation; therefore, the school district should not interfere with the contractual agreement between the union and its members. As a practical matter, however, most teachers are not aware of the restrictions on resignations until they wish to resign—at which time it is too late to do anything about the restrictions.

A maintenance of membership clause requires the school district to enforce the teachers' obligation to remain members of the union in good standing. In the absence of any enforcement power, unions could not insist that, as a condition of employment, teachers must remain members in good standing until the beginning of an applicable window period for resignations. Without the school board's agreement to require union membership as a condition of employment, the unions would have a very difficult time enforcing restrictions on resignations from the union. Essentially, the unions would have to sue teachers for the unpaid dues, which are relatively small amounts of money. The cost and adverse publicity generated by such lawsuits would render it practically impossible for the unions to enforce maintenance of membership without school district help in enforcing the requirement. Given this, why should school boards be responsible for enforcing teacher obligations to the teacher unions? The candid answer is that the unions are frequently able to coerce the school boards into the enforcement mode.

Note the difference between a maintenance of membership clause and a restriction on resignation clause. A maintenance of membership clause provides that if the teacher joins the union, the teacher cannot resign from the union until the expiration of the contract or the beginning of the window period preceding expiration. A resignation clause may contain a provision that requires teachers who resign to pay the balance of dues for the school year. By itself, a maintenance of membership clause would not require teachers leaving district employment to pay the balance of the annual dues. The union usually tries to negotiate both a maintenance of membership clause (under which you must be a union member as long as you are employed by the district, except during the window periods) and a clause that requires teachers who resign from the union to pay the balance of their annual dues.

Especially in multiyear contracts, maintenance of membership virtually eliminates the rights of teachers to resign. No matter how objectionable the union is to the teacher, the teacher must remain a union member for virtually the duration of the contract. In states that allow contracts to be in effect for three to five years, maintenance of membership is especially onerous.

Although many contracts include maintenance of membership provisions, union members probably would not be prevented from resigning at any time during the duration of a contract if they were determined to do so. Many teachers are not aware of this and would not pay membership dues and fees if they knew that the provision probably would not be enforced in the courts.

Discussion of examples

The examples cited below illustrate the objections to maintenance of membership clauses. Consider the following:

(1) Any employee who is a member of the Association on September 1, 1998, or who joins the Association during the term of this Agreement, will retain membership status for the duration of this Agreement. The Association agrees to furnish information required by the District to fulfill the provisions of this Article.

Example (1) provides no window period whatsoever for those who wish to resign from the union, and undoubtedly could not be enforced against any employee who wanted to resign. Here again, the teacher unions rely upon the fact that most teachers are not aware of their rights and that teachers do not realize how hard it is for unions to challenge those teachers who wish to resign.

Examples (2) and (3) below, both negotiated in Pennsylvania, demonstrate two different problems. As we shall see, (2) is too vague, while both (2) and (3) show how a maintenance of membership clause can provide a backdrop for problems noted in the previous chapter, namely, those problems that emerge when teacher unions are able to pursue rights both through contract and by statute:

(2) The Board agrees that all employees of the Association shall be subject to the Maintenance of Membership provision as defined in the Public Employee Relations Act (PERA) of 1985.

(3) All members of the bargaining unit who are dues-paying members of the Association shall be subject to the Public Employee Relations Act (PERA) of 1985 which provides:

. . . [A]ll employees who have joined an employee organization or who join the employee organization in the future must remain members for the duration of a collective bargaining agreement so providing with the proviso that any such employee or employees may resign from such employee organization during a period of fifteen (15) days prior to the expiration of any such agreement.

Example (2) leaves teachers uncertain what their obligations are, and they are taking a big risk by relying on union officials to tell them. Since both examples are from Pennsylvania school districts, teachers under the language of both examples must follow the provisions of the PERA listed in (3). Unlike (3), example (2) provides no specification of these obligations. This is misguided; teachers should not have to rely on union staff to find out that they have a window period in which they can resign from the union.

Examples (2) and (3) also illustrate why legislatures should not pass legislation covering issues that are dealt with by school board/union contracts. The teacher unions in these cases justified collective bargaining on the grounds that the terms and conditions of teacher employment should be negotiated by boards of education and teacher unions. After the enactment of the bargaining laws, however, the unions then lobbied for a statutory resolution (the Public Employee Relations Act). This statute clearly affected one of the terms and conditions of employment by establishing a legal obligation to maintain union membership. This was an extremely pro-union resolution for which the school boards received no concession in return.

In any event, school boards interested in protecting teacher rights should avoid maintenance of membership even though unions are willing to make important concessions to get it. Maintenance of membership is highly coercive and deprives teachers of the right to resign from the union, which is often the only way—or the most effective way—for teachers to express their dissatisfaction with the union or influence union policy. The only benefit that the school boards get from such a clause is whatever concessions the union is willing to make for this deprivation of teacher rights.

VII. Right to Resign

Although the right to resign is an important aspect of the maintenance of union membership, it also raises several independent issues. Note the distinction between the two concepts. Resignations from the union reduce union revenues; for this reason, unions try to make sure that teachers who leave the union will still be forced to pay their union dues. Maintenance of membership forces district employees who leave their union—or who attempt to stay out of the union altogether—to pay their dues. Yet maintenance of membership is only one provision that unions use to achieve their goals. Even with such a clause, for instance, an employee who resigns from district employment could still resign from the union. Quite often, contracts provide that if a teacher resigns from district employment during the year, the balance of that teacher's annual dues must be deducted from the teacher's final paycheck. Thus, a teacher who had to resign because of a spouse's transfer would nevertheless have to pay annual dues in full. Restricting a teacher's right to resign is, therefore, another way that unions can prevent the loss of revenue that comes from resignations from union membership.

Unions argue that this is acceptable because the issue has been resolved by the teachers and the union; since the teacher agreed to pay the union the full amount upon joining the district, the school board should not interfere. Unions will also point out that the school board does not pay anything for its agreement with a union proposal that restricts the right of teachers to resign; the balance of the dues comes out of teachers' money, not school district funds.

The fact is that many teachers are not aware of their obligation to pay full dues until it is too late for them to avoid the obligation. Consider a teacher being interviewed for employment by a district. The union contract may or may not be included in the letter of appointment, but in either case most teachers are not aware of their obligations to the union. When they accept a position, most teachers do not focus on what happens if they must leave the district for one reason or another. The common perception among job applicants is that raising the issue during a job interview would send the wrong message to the district.

The school board might insist that teachers be made aware of the problem. For example, the board could demand that the union require each teacher to sign a statement that demonstrates that teacher's awareness of his or her obligations to the union upon resignation. This solution involves the school district in union affairs and would evoke strong opposition from the union. Furthermore, an understanding of these obligations to the union may also discourage teachers from accepting employment in the district. However, if the district is going to require teachers to meet these obligations, the principle of fairness toward one's employees justifies the district's insistence that employees be made aware of these obligations upon employment. Better yet, the board should refuse to agree to any proposal that would require district employees to pay full union dues or fees upon termination of employment with the district.

Some contracts include maintenance of membership and also require teachers who resign during the year to pay full annual dues—this is a sad commentary on school district determination to protect the rights of individual teachers. It is unconscionable for the union to collect a full year's dues from teachers who must quit district employment during the year for all sorts of reasons, many of them unanticipated. The union may assert that it does not insist upon the dues when the teacher must quit for unanticipated reasons; if this is the case, the union should not insist upon a contractual right to collect the full amount of annual dues from all teachers who resign during the school year.

Currently, the extent to which employers and unions can legally limit resignations from unions is an issue that has not yet been resolved by the U.S. Supreme Court. Logically, if a teacher is not legally obligated to join the union, then the teacher should be allowed to resign at any time. It must be emphasized, however, that in twenty-one states, unions and school boards cannot require teachers to pay service fees to unions as a condition of employment, and a federal right-to-work law is pending in Congress at the time of this writing.

Discussion of examples

Teacher union contracts virtually never include "Resignations" or "Teacher Resignations" as a heading in the contract; obviously the unions do not wish to publicize a process that diminishes union revenues. Nevertheless, because discouraging resignations requires school district participation, the subject of resignations cannot be completely excluded from the contract; the issue is usually resolved in a section on dues deduction or some related section.

Example (1) makes clear one way in which the unions try to utilize district involvement to delay or frustrate teacher resignations:

(1) No later than October 15 of each year, the Association will provide the District with a list of those employees who have voluntarily authorized the District to deduct dues for the Association. Copies of the executive dues authorization for all employees shall be submitted to the District. The Association will notify the District monthly of any changes in said

list. Any employee desiring to have the District discontinue deductions previously authorized must notify the Association in writing between July 1 and July 15 of each year for the next school year's dues, and the Association will notify the District in writing to discontinue the employee's deduction. The Association shall enjoy the exclusive right to dues deduction.

Example (1) is a good illustration of how the unions minimize teacher resignations via indefensible procedural requirements. There is only a fifteen-day window period, from July 1 to July 15, in which teachers can resign and discontinue previously authorized payroll deductions. Obviously, most teachers will not be in the schools during this period; many will be in other states or foreign countries.

Interestingly enough, although the issue has not yet reached the U.S. Supreme Court, teachers may have the right to resign from the union at any time. Nevertheless, this possibility has not had much impact on the treatment of resignations in teacher union contracts. Most school boards are not sensitive to the issue, and the unions' attitude is that nothing is lost by insisting upon brief window periods for resignations. If teachers successfully challenge restrictions on resignation, the worst that can happen is that unions will be forced to pay back dues that they should never have received in the first place.

Under (1), teachers resigning from the union must send their resignations to the union first, thereby providing opportunities for the union to pressure the teachers not to resign. Note that the article does not require the union to send resignations to the board within a specified time. The union has strong incentives to delay the submission of resignations to the board:

- Delay gives the union more time to pressure teachers to withdraw their resignations.
- The union receives the amount of full dues as long as the teacher is a member.
- The union has the right to discipline members but not nonmembers for good cause.

Example (1) is indefensible for another reason. There is no reason to deny payroll deduction of dues to a teacher organization that does not seek to represent teachers on terms and conditions of employment. The exclusivity clause here enables the union to dominate every teacher organization, union or not, whose viability depends on payroll deduction of dues.

The language of (2), like that in (1), involves the district in union efforts to frustrate teacher resignations.

(2) Upon termination of employment with the District of any employee, the remaining amount of dues for the Association will be deducted from the employee's final check.

In agreeing to deduct dues, the District is performing an administrative function on behalf of the Association for its convenience and is not a party to any agreement between the Association and its members regarding the deduction of dues. The Association, therefore, agrees to hold the District harmless and to reimburse the District for any and all costs, including legal fees it may incur in relation to any deductions made at the direction of the Association and contrary to the instructions received from the individual teacher. If there are not sufficient funds due to garnishment, the District is not liable for failure to collect such dues so long as the funds are not available.

Example (2) reflects the district's intention to implement the union's directives relating to payroll deduction of dues while making sure that no liability accrues to the district for doing so. It is regrettable that even school boards that are scrupulous in protecting themselves in these matters are so indifferent to the rights of the teachers whom they employ. This comment is applicable to most of the issues discussed in this chapter.

From the board's perspective, the best alternative is to refrain from including any contractual limitations on a teacher's right to resign. Note that the union can spell out any limitations on the right to resign in the union form used to enroll members. If a teacher signs such a form limiting his or her right to resign, the district could legitimately honor the agreement between the individual teacher and the union; however, it is indefensible to have teachers agree to become union members, only to discover that the school board has limited their right to resign from the union.

Example (3) combines elements that enforce maintenance of union membership with clauses that restrict teachers' rights to resign:

(3) Any employee who is a member of the Association as of the date this Agreement becomes effective (following approval by the District and the Association) shall remain a member in good standing until a thirty (30) day period commencing May 15 of the year of the expiration of this Agreement. Any employee who is not a member of the Association as of the effective date of this Agreement shall either become a member or pay to the Association a fee equal to unified membership dues, initiation fees, and general assessments unless the District is notified by the employee within fifteen (15) working days of the effective date of this Agreement that he/she elects not to do so. New employees shall have fifteen (15) working days after the first duty date of employment to make

such election. The District agrees to provide the Association a list of unit members electing not to become a member and/or pay fees equal to membership dues, initiation fees, and general assessments within seven (7) working days after the deadlines provided for in this Article.

Under the language of (3), new teachers have fifteen working days after the first day of employment to decide whether or not to join the union. All teachers who are members when the contract becomes effective must remain members until the thirty-day period preceding the expiration of the contract. Employees who are not members on the effective date must notify the district within fifteen days after the effective date of the contract that they wish to remain nonmembers.

Example (3) can be criticized on the grounds that it requires new teachers and nonunion teachers already on the staff to notify the district in a timely fashion that they wish to remain nonunion teachers; union membership should result from an affirmative act, not from a failure to express a preference for nonunion status.

4

Union Rights

Chapter 4 focuses on union rights that are not discussed elsewhere in this handbook. Again, it must be emphasized that union rights are discussed under several different headings in contracts as well as in this handbook. For example, the union's rights to payroll deduction of union dues are usually set forth in sections entitled "Organizational Security" or "Dues Deduction"; the details of leave with pay to conduct union business are often included in the section on leaves of absence. These are just two examples of this general trend in contracts.

The union rights discussed in this chapter relate mainly to the union's rights to use district facilities and services for union purposes. The importance of these rights is often overlooked because they do not appear to require any district expenditures or changes in educational policy; nevertheless, their cumulative importance to the union should not be underestimated. For example, union access to school bulletin boards might seem to be a trivial matter to many school board members, but if such access were denied, the unions would have to spend a great deal of their own resources communicating with teachers in some other way.

I. Union Access to and Use of District Buildings

The union will invariably request a contractual right to access and use district buildings for union meetings. These requests raise the following issues:

- Is advance approval by the administration required in order to use a building? If advance approval is not required, how much advance notice is the union required to give to the principal?
- Can the district charge the union for any expenses that result from the use of the building?
- Does the contractual permission ensure that union use of the building will not interfere with or disrupt any educational activity?
- Can the district rescind the union's right to meet on school property if the union abuses the right (for example, by damaging property, interfering with educational programs, conducting unruly meetings, or by using the right to help organize a strike)?

Discussion of examples

Example (1) below does not provide even minimal protection for the district:

(1) The Association and its representatives shall have the right to use school buildings at all reasonable hours for meetings. The principal of the building in question shall be notified in advance of the time and place of all such meetings. No approval shall be required.

Under the contractual language above, the union's obligation to notify the principal "in advance" is virtually useless—notification only a few seconds "in advance" of a meeting would still be in compliance with the contract. An even more egregious flaw in the contractual language is its failure to require the union to seek prior approval from the district before using district facilities for meetings. It might have been wiser, from the union's perspective, to delete the last sentence, since no approval would be required if the contract did not specify it; however, the importance of being explicit about the issue might depend on other articles in the contract.

Example (2) below authorizes the union to interfere with extracurricular activities, counseling, study halls, library work—anything that is not "classroom instruction." School boards should not accept union interference on such a broad scale.

(2) The Association representative shall have the right of access to areas in which employees work, the right to use designated bulletin boards and mailboxes, and the right to use the facility for the purpose of meetings. Use of all of the above mentioned is with the understanding that such activities or use do not interfere with classroom instruction.

From the board's perspective, the following example is unwise contractual language because it is very vague:

(3) The Bargaining Agent and its representatives shall have the right to use school buildings for meetings after normal working hours. A time and date must be cleared and approved through the normal procedures of the Employer.

The "normal procedures of the Employer" should be set forth or incorporated into the contract by a specified reference to the specific board policy. Also, suppose the board changes its specified "normal procedures" for reasons that have nothing to do with the union, but the procedural changes nevertheless disadvantage the union. Would the union have a sustainable grievance? One would have to review the rest of the contract to decide the issue.

Example (4) below ensures that the district is adequately protected with respect to the union's use of district buildings. An especially valuable safeguard in the language is the district's ability to revoke the union's right to use district buildings if the union abuses that privilege.

(4) From the effective date of this Agreement to its termination, the Association shall be allowed the use of school buildings and premises for Association meetings and activities on regular school days as long as arrangements have been made with the principal of the building. Such activities shall not conflict with any regular or special educational activities and such use shall not involve additional or extra custodial services and/or other unusual expenses to the School District. Use of buildings on other than school days requires the approval of the Superintendent in addition to the school principal. Any added expense resulting from the Association use shall be paid by the Association. If the privilege extended herein is misused by the Association or any of its designated representatives, it may be immediately revoked by the Superintendent. Individual teachers will not be prohibited from the responsible use of the school facilities. Disputes arising from the revocation of privileges granted under this Article shall be resolved in an expedited manner.

II. Union Use of the District Mail System

In any school district with multiple schools, especially schools that are several miles apart, use of the district mail system is important to the union, just as it is to the school district. In many instances, the time saved by using the system is even more important than the money saved by not having to use the U.S. postal system. Nevertheless, the school board should make sure that the district mail system is not used simply to avoid paying U.S. postage; such use of the system is illegal.

The board should also insist that prior administrative approval be given to all union materials that are disseminated through the district mail system. Otherwise, the district administration will be required to allow the union to use the union to use the mail system to disseminate strike notices or defamatory material of one kind or another. The purpose of prior approval is to protect the district, not to censor union publications that disagree with board policies; also, for the sake of effective administration, principals should know what is being disseminated in their schools. The examples cited below differ primarily in the extent to which they require the union to obtain prior approval of the documents that they disseminate, and the extent to which unions are required to observe certain safeguards in their use of the mail system.

Discussion of examples

Example (1) below provides the union with complete freedom to use the district mail system in any way that it sees fit. Even an inexperienced school board should have had the sense to reject such an unwise provision.

(1) The Association shall have the right to use the interschool mail facilities and school mailboxes as it deems necessary and without the approval of building principals or other members of the Administration.

School boards should also be wary of the language used to grant individual employees the right to use the district mail system. Consider the following:

(2) The Association shall have the exclusive right to use school mailboxes and the interschool mail service and faculty bulletin boards for organizational material, provided that all such material is signed by an Association officer or is clearly identified as Association material and the Association accepts the responsibility for such material. Copies of all such material shall be given to the building principal. Individual employees will not be prohibited from judicious use of the school mail service and faculty bulletin boards.

Example (2) would require that union material be signed by a union officer; in this respect, this example is more restrictive toward union rights than (1). However, the language of (2) would provide individual employees with the right to use the district's mail system, a rather risky provision despite the qualification that their use be "judicious." The larger the district, the more likely it is that some employees will adopt a highly idiosyncratic interpretation of "judicious" or ignore the qualification altogether. Districts should grant individual employees the right to use the district mail system, but districts should also retain the right to terminate or regulate the practice if necessary. Note also that even though the union "accepts responsibility" for items placed in the district mail system, this does not necessarily relieve the district of responsibility for any defamatory material sent through the system.

Even a provision that may seem fairly restrictive can actually be quite vague. Consider (3) below:

(3) Within the guidelines of the U.S. Postal Service and related quasi-judicial rulings, the Union shall have the right to use the interschool mail facilities and school mailboxes, so long as such use does not include boxes, books, or other bulky material.

The restrictions in example (3) are vague, since only a few teachers and administrators at most will know the guidelines of the U.S. Postal Service or understand the content of the "quasi-judicial rulings" cited in the provision; the prohibition against "bulky material" is also vague. Furthermore, the clause above provides the district with no protection against potential legal problems involving defamatory or obscene material.

Example (4), which is the best of the examples from the board's perspective, provides ample protection for the district without getting into detailed arrangements on use of the mail system:

(4) Subject to reasonable regulation, the Union shall have the right to use without charge District bulletin boards, mailboxes, and the District mail system. The District reserves the right to terminate contractual rights to such use for violation of District regulations governing same.

III. Electronic-Mail Service

In recent years, the teacher unions have proposed contractual language that would give unions unlimited and unregulated access to district interschool and intraschool electronic-mail service (e-mail). Because there are so many unresolved issues pertaining to e-mail, it is recommended that districts adopt a cautious attitude toward granting the union unfettered access to district e-mail systems.

Discussion of examples

A critical point in contractual discussions involving e-mail is the amount of scrutiny that the district can give to union communications. Consider the following:

> (1) The Union shall have the right to use the District electronic-mail service and unit member electronic mailboxes for communications to unit members without interference, censorship, or examination of such communications by the District.

The school district will not wish to be a censor of union publications, but the district is responsible for the communications that are sent through its e-mail system. The contractual provision above would allow the union to send strike instructions, defamatory material, or libelous statements via district e-mail; the board should not tolerate this.

The language of (2) below is as permissive as a district should allow with respect to e-mail issues:

> (2) Subject to reasonable regulation which includes but is not limited to prior review of Union communications sent via the District's e-mail system, the Union shall have access to the system. The Union agrees to hold the District harmless from any and all costs arising out of Union use of the system. The District reserves the right to revoke Union access to the District e-mail system if such access is abused in any way or in case of any violations of District regulations pertaining to access to and use of the District e-mail system.

Given that most districts lack experience with allowing unions access to their e-mail systems, districts should allow such access only if they can also secure the rights to revoke union access and to change the regulations governing such access.

IV. Bulletin Boards

Unions want to post notices on bulletin boards where members will read them. There is no reason for the board to oppose this, but the union proposals on these matters usually involve several issues that are often overlooked. For this reason, the following caveats concerning union notices and bulletin boards should be considered carefully.

Suppose the union posts obscene or defamatory material. Does the district have any contractual protection against such an action? What if there is a disagreement over the issue, as is likely, between the union and the district? Unless the district maintains the right to remove such material, the district will be criticized—and possibly subject to legal action by injured parties—for allowing its facilities to be used this way.

On the other hand, censorship of union communications also raises problems. Suppose the union asserts or implies that the district's superintendent is having an affair with a board member at district expense, for example, by claiming that while attending conventions together, the two shared rooms paid for with school board funds. This sort of allegation can emerge when the union is trying to pressure the board and administration to make concessions during bargaining. In the past, the union negotiators may have sincerely disclaimed any thought of using such tactics, but negotiators and circumstances come and go.

As with use of the mail and e-mail systems, the board should grant the union reasonable access to bulletin boards, but the district should insist upon protection against abuse. It is reasonable for the board to require that all material to be posted must be approved by the principal or site administrator prior to posting; this does not imply censorship, but does provide time for remedial action if necessary. A further justification for the requirement of prior approval is that principals and site administrators should know what is being posted, especially if it includes editorial comment about school matters. The district's objective in establishing a policy of prior approval is not to prohibit criticism of district policies or personnel, but rather to ensure that such criticism is consistent with professional standards. Potential abuse of bulletin board access justifies a requirement of prior approval. It may also justify placing limits on the subject matter that may be posted on bulletin boards; for example, the board may feel that the union should only be allowed to use bulletin boards to post notices of union meetings.

It is preferable to have a separate union bulletin board in order to avoid controversies over the posting or removal of district notices. It is desirable for the board to have the right to terminate use of bulletin boards in schools in case the union abuses its right, but it is not essential if the union needs prior approval from a district administrator before it can post anything on its bulletin boards.

Note that in some contracts, various issues, such as approving notices for bulletin boards, are resolved at the school level. In these situations, aggressive union representatives may intimidate those principals who are afraid of confrontations. If the criteria for appropriate notices are not spelled out in the contract, the district should make sure that everyone who must approve bulletin board material knows what the criteria are. It is better to negotiate common rules at the district level, and leave open the possibilities for exceptions.

Discussion of examples

The examples range from those that give the district neither a right to prior approval nor a right to regulate the content of bulletin board postings to those that provide ample protection for the district. If the school board can do nothing about union abuse of bulletin board space until the contract expires, it should insist on appropriate restrictions in the next contract.

Example (1) provides no protection whatsoever for the district. Insofar as the contract is concerned, the union can post defamatory materials, strike notices, or other disruptive documents without any district right to prohibit or restrict such posting.

(1) The Association shall have, in each school building, the exclusive use of a bulletin board in each faculty lounge and teachers' dining room. The Association shall also be assigned adequate space on the bulletin board in the central office for Association notices. The location of the Association bulletin boards in each room shall be designated by the Association. Copies of all materials to be posted on such bulletin boards shall be given to the building principal, but no approval shall be required.

Example (2) also fails to provide any protection for the district:

(2) The Association shall have the right to maintain a bulletin board in each faculty lounge.

Unlike (1) and (2), example (3) limits the kind of material that can be posted. The language of (3) also provides some indirect protection for the district; if the principal does not initial a document, the union cannot post it.

(3) The Association shall have, in each school building, the use of a bulletin board for the posting of official Association notices concerning meetings and other Association programs. Any item to be posted shall be initialed by the building principal.

Example (4) does not limit the content of union postings in any way, but it does provide a few safeguards for the board with respect to posting procedures:

(4) The Union shall have the right to post notices of activities and matters of Union concern on commonly used bulletin boards, at least one of which shall be provided in each school. The school principal shall either provide space on the commonly used bulletin board or make provisions for space for the Union on a centrally located bulletin board. Posting notices on bulletin boards and putting items in teacher mailboxes shall be the exclusive responsibility of the Union and shall take place at times other than duty time of the individual performing such activities, and all

information shall be presented to the school principal, or his or her designee, for review before distribution.

Note that this example refers to the use of "commonly used" bulletin boards. Generally speaking, it is preferable to provide the union with its own bulletin board in order to avoid conflict over removed or damaged notices, allowable space, and other issues that could arise.

Finally, consider the following two examples:

(5) Items that may be placed upon Union bulletin boards shall be restricted to: A) meeting notices, B) notice of social and/or recreational events, C) elections and appointments, D) Association services, E) progress reports on commissions and committees, F) Association legislative programs, G) news clippings, H) messages from officers and/or boards, I) social messages, e.g., Christmas greetings, J) directories, i.e., names and numbers to call for services, K) names of building representatives and Uni-Serv representatives, L) information on Association organizational structure, M) affiliate and/or cooperating organizational notices, N) community service notices.

The District Superintendent shall have removed from mailboxes (except U.S. mail) and bulletin boards any material that is abusive or libelous, or any material in violation of Board policies or regulations in effect on the execution date of this Agreement.

(6) Subject to reasonable regulation, the Union shall have the right to use without charge District bulletin boards, mailboxes, and the District mail system. The District reserves the right to terminate contractual rights to such use for violation of District regulations governing same.

Example (6) provides adequate district protection, especially because the contractual language allows the district to terminate union use of bulletin boards if the union abuses its privileges. Example (5) also gives the district some protection, but it does not allow the board to rescind the union's bulletin board privileges, as (6) allows. Suppose the union posts notice of a meeting to discuss its strike plans. Could the district prohibit such a notice on union bulletin boards when it has agreed to allow the union to post "meeting notices"?

V. Union Rights at Faculty Meetings

The union usually tries to minimize the number of faculty meetings and limit their duration; the union will also try to ensure that it has the opportunity to address the faculty at those meetings. These objectives apply to meetings of teachers from the same school or district, or who teach the same grade or subject. Although the number of times that each of these groups meets may vary, the union objectives regarding faculty meetings are the same in each case, and are treated similarly here.

Unions argue for limits on the number and duration of meetings by claiming that administrators (usually principals) do or may require teachers to attend numerous long, unproductive meetings. Allegedly, if the number and duration of meetings are limited, administrators will get down to business promptly during those meetings that do take place; hence, unions argue that limiting the number and duration of meetings would still give the district adequate time to conduct district business. Sometimes the union will make this argument while refusing to identify the administrators who allegedly require teachers to attend these long, unproductive meetings.

Of course, the district should not have the right to call a limitless number of meetings held after the regular school day is complete. However, the union's proposals, if implemented, would usually create serious inefficiencies. This is because it is impossible to anticipate the number and duration of meetings needed to deal with district concerns. A fire, an accident, the defeat of a school bond issue—these are only a few of the events that might justify a number of meetings within a brief period of time, or meetings longer than some predetermined duration. One solution to this problem that would be consistent with the union's objectives would be to negotiate a maximum number of meetings that the district could call in a given timespan, with district discretion as to when the meetings are held. If no meetings are necessary, then the district retains its "meeting bank"; it would also retain some of the flexibility that is essential for the scheduling of meetings that are necessary.

Union proposals to limit the duration of faculty meetings typically attempt to limit the length of meetings to one hour. This is indefensible. An alternative is to give the district an allotment of longer meetings that it can hold at its discretion; if the need for the meetings does not arise, they need not be held.

Although unions often denigrate faculty meetings as a waste of time, the real underlying reason that the unions attempt to limit the number and duration of meetings is often that the unions are responding to the needs of "moonlighting" teachers or teachers who want the time to meet their private responsibilities. However, it should be possible for the district to respond adequately to these needs without being required to conduct essential business within an arbitrary, inadequate time frame. Sometimes unions argue that teachers deserve additional compensation for the time they spend working outside the classroom. School boards should not accept this argument, because an adequate job description for teachers would make it clear that some of their regular duties, such as meeting with parents, must be performed outside of the regular school day.

Nevertheless, there should be limits on the amount of time that teachers are required to work outside of the regular school day.

Ironically, unions and teachers who complain about the lack of opportunity for teachers to participate in school district policymaking are often the most adamant opponents of teacher obligations outside the regular school day. Typically, these teachers have no objections to faculty meetings that occur during the regular school day; thus, the real issue is not so much whether teachers can participate in policymaking, but rather whether their participation can take place during the regular school day or outside of it. The regular school day, however, should be time where teachers focus on pupil needs and interests, and the teachers' lack of involvement in policymaking should not be regarded as a limitation on the teacher workday.

Boards must consider complaints that faculty meetings are a waste of time, but they must also consider the possibility that those complaints are substitutes for objections to faculty meetings that unions do not lay on the table. Furthermore, even if some meetings are not essential or productive, restricting the district's rights to require attendance at faculty meetings is not necessarily the best remedy for this problem; after all, when classroom instruction is not productive, no one advocates eliminating classroom instructional time. Instead, the best solution may be to retrain or replace the administrators responsible for the unproductive meetings.

Unions typically request a contractual right to preempt a certain amount of time during faculty meetings. Quite often, these requests are part of a series of proposals that would also limit the number and duration of faculty meetings. Boards should scrutinize all such proposals very carefully; while reserving time for unions at faculty meetings may not have had deleterious consequences in the past, this is no guarantee that problems will not emerge in the future.

One reason that boards should be wary of reserving time for unions at faculty meetings is that faculty meetings are called to conduct district business, not union business. The union would object, and rightly so, if school management insisted upon reserving a certain amount of time at union meetings. Also, while allowing the union to make announcements seems to be harmless, it raises several issues that are potentially problematic: What is an "announcement"? If a building's union representative announces union objections to a district policy, is that an "announcement"? Is this the best way to approach district/union differences? Typically, the union has access to district mail facilities and thus it need not preempt any district time during faculty meetings in order to communicate with its members.

If the board/union relationship is harmonious, then the district could allow the union to make announcements at faculty meetings without any contractual provision. Any contractual provision that does provide the union with time during faculty meetings should be hedged with safeguards to protect the district.

Bear in mind also that granting the union time at faculty meetings is, in effect, a taxpayer subsidy to the union; the district is paying teachers to listen to union concerns.

Discussion of examples

The following examples illustrate several problems that can emerge from contractual language that reserves time for union representatives during faculty meetings:

(1) The Association building representative shall be given an opportunity at building faculty meetings to present brief reports and announcements not to exceed fifteen (15) minutes at the end of and prior to the conclusion of the meeting.

The language of (1) mandates that the union's building representative is to have fifteen minutes prior to the conclusion of each faculty meeting. This requirement is problematic because it will force the district to interrupt important discussions in order to comply with the provision. Also, fifteen minutes is a long time for the union's faculty representatives to preempt the time of teachers who are paid by taxpayers.

Example (2) below does not guarantee that the union representatives will receive fifteen minutes, but the language sets no cap on the time allowed:

(2) The Senior Representative or a designee shall be allowed to present the views of the Organization at any faculty meeting as a last agenda item. The Administration shall make every effort to forward to the Senior Representative any and all agenda items relative to said faculty meeting. Unless an emergency exists no faculty meeting shall be held without forty-eight (48) hours notice.

In the following example, the union representatives are entitled to fifteen minutes after the conclusion of faculty meetings:

(3) The Association shall be granted no less than fifteen (15) minutes immediately after the conclusion of a faculty meeting to present such items as determined by the Association faculty representative. This time may or may not be within the bargaining-unit members' workday.

In addition, the Association faculty representative or bargaining-unit members may request that items concerning educational issues be placed on the agenda of faculty meetings. The school administrator or supervisor shall consider such requests as time allows. He/she will attempt to schedule in the faculty meetings those items which he/she feels are relevant and appropriate.

Presumably, the additional meeting is a union meeting; if the district faculty meeting is over, the union presumably can meet for as long as it wishes to do so. Example (4) avoids the problems discussed above:

(4) With the approval of the building principal, the Association shall have an opportunity at the conclusion of faculty meetings to present reports and announcements to those professional employees who choose to remain.

According to the above language, union requests to address the faculty after faculty meetings must be approved by the principal, and the provision explicitly states that teacher attendance at these union meetings is voluntary. Although these are useful safeguards, school districts should avoid this sort of involvement in union meetings; the unions can, if they wish, schedule union meetings after faculty meetings without the district's contractual involvement.

VI. Union Rights at School Board Meetings

Unions frequently propose that they be accorded special rights at school board meetings. The proposals may include provisions for special seating at school board meetings and the right to address the board before the board acts on certain matters. The union may also request that, before each board meeting, the board deliver to union officials copies of the agendas, minutes, and collateral material going to each board member.

Prompt delivery to the union of board agendas, minutes, and collateral materials should be acceptable. All of these things are public documents, and other parties in addition to the union may be on the mailing list to receive them. However, the other union requests mentioned above are more problematic. After all, teachers are in constant contact with school administrators, as are union representatives in the schools. The union also seeks the right to address faculty meetings at both the school and district levels. The upshot is that no organization or interest group has as much opportunity as the union does to convey its views to the administration. Adding to this access by giving the union special privileges at board meetings seems highly questionable, especially since the union has so many opportunities to convey its views during contract negotiations and consultation meetings. Inasmuch as most citizens are unable to meet with school authorities during the day, allowing the union to preempt time during school board meetings in the evening may deprive others of their own relatively scarce opportunities to address the board.

Justified or not, however, many—perhaps most—boards grant the union some type of special rights involving board meetings. Boards that agree to special rights for the union should ensure that these rights do not deprive others of opportunities to address the board during board meetings. After all, even if the union lacked any special rights, union members would still have the same opportunity as others to attend board meetings and speak about matters that concern them.

Note also that school boards typically must deal with more than one union. If the board grants the teacher union special rights at board meetings, the same argument that justifies granting the teacher union such rights will apply to other unions of school district employees, and to administrator organizations as well. Except for the fact that the teacher union is usually the most powerful interest group to attend board meetings, there does not appear to be any reason to grant any special rights to the union at these meetings. If any rights are granted, they should be made conditional upon the requirement that they cannot be exercised in a way that deprives others of an opportunity to address the board. The board should also consider carefully how granting any special rights to teacher unions will affect other unions of school district employees.

Discussion of examples

Another right that teacher unions sometimes seek is the right to influence the agenda of school board meetings. Consider the following example:

(1) The Board shall, whenever appropriate, place as the first item on the agenda of each regular Board meeting, any matters submitted by the Union so long as those matters are made known to the Superintendent's office eight (8) calendar days prior to said meeting. Teachers appearing before the Board during consideration of any item shall be released from duty only for consideration of that item.

Example (1) sets forth a vague criterion with which to decide when union-sponsored agenda items must be the first item on the agenda of a regular board meeting: the item must be "appropriate." If there is a conflict over whether or not a union-sponsored item is "appropriate," the union should win, since there are endless ways to argue that a particular item is "appropriate."

Example (2) below illustrates a provision under which the union has the right to speak on any issue facing the board:

(2) The Association may request that items be placed on regular Board of Education meeting agenda in accordance with rules governing the conduct of the meeting. A designated representative of the Association may speak on any issue before the Board of Education before the Board acts on the issue.

The language of (2) could be troublesome, since not only does it guarantee that the union can speak on any issue before the board, but it may give the union the opportunity to have the last word on every issue. This is because the union representatives need not volunteer to address the board until all other parties have done so, and the board would then be obligated to allow the representatives to speak. Presumably, the normal board regulations involving the duration of speeches—if the board has developed such regulations—would apply to the representative's speech.

In the following example, the board is providing the union—which is, as noted above, the interest group with the most opportunities to express its views in the schools—with preferential seating at board meetings:

(3) A copy of the official Board agenda and folder material shall be provided to the Association prior to each regular Board meeting. Copies of the official minutes of each regular Board meeting will be provided to the Association upon approval of the minutes of the Board. Table space, where available, will be provided at all Board meetings for two (2) Association representatives.

This preferential seating gives the union enormous tactical advantages in dealing with the board, because it gives the union an excellent position from which to monitor informal communications of board members, and it provides the union with an aura of authority at board meetings. From the board's perspective, it is best to give the teacher union no preferential treatment at board meetings.

In summary, the recommended policy is for the board to include no provisions in the contract that would grant the union special rights at board meetings. The board's negotiator at the bargaining table should point out that the district will fulfill its statutory obligations regarding the distribution of information to the union, and that it expects the union to observe its own obligations to the board involving these matters.

VII. Union Identification

Should teachers be allowed to wear items on school premises that identify the wearer as a union member? Although the issue seems trivial, it may not be in certain circumstances. For example, if the union has been involved in a job action, such as a strike, a slowdown, or a period of work-to-rule, the wearing of union insignia may further divide teachers into groups that did or did not support the union. It is difficult to bring everyone together when the union is trying to emphasize the divisions among teachers.

There is also the possibility that the insignia could intimidate teachers who do not wish to become members of the union. From the board's perspective, the best solution to this problem is probably to allow teachers to wear union insignia, but to avoid granting the teachers a contractual right to do so. By proceeding in this way, the district has more freedom to act if circumstances arise that render union insignia a divisive or intimidating factor.

When the issue of union insignia emerges during contract negotiations, the union will probably propose the following clause or something similar to it:

> No teacher shall be prevented from wearing an insignia, pin, or other identification of membership in the Association on school premises.

Any effort that the district makes to restrict the First Amendment right of teachers to wear union identification would probably have to be pursuant to a broad policy restricting all parties in district facilities from wearing dress or insignia that is likely to be disruptive; even then, the district should be certain that there are legal and practical justifications for its position.

VIII. Teacher Orientation

During negotiations with the board, the union frequently requests an opportunity to discuss the role and benefits of the union at orientation sessions for new teachers. The outcome of negotiations over this issue may depend on school board/union relations at the time of negotiations. If the union is conducting an anti-administration campaign, or appears likely to do so, there is no reason why the school board should facilitate union efforts along this line. The union should not be allowed to utilize the orientation sessions for new teachers to promote its positions on bargaining disputes.

Discussion of examples

From the board's perspective, the following example is a highly undesirable provision:

(1) The Union and Board will jointly coordinate new employee orientation at mutually agreed times.

It is difficult to explain why a school district should allow the union to co-manage the orientation of new teachers, as the language of (1) would allow. In addition, it is not clear whether "mutually agreed times" refers to meetings between the board and the union to coordinate the orientation program, or if this requirement applies to the program itself.

Example (2) below specifies the day and the amount of time that the union gets to present its case to new teachers. Note that the principals would be required under this language to provide the thirty minutes on the teachers' first day.

(2) Principals shall provide the Association representatives from their buildings with the opportunity for a thirty (30) minute meeting with new teachers during the opening day of school for teachers.

Example (3) provides the district with more flexibility than does example (2), since it does not force the district to allow these orientation sessions on the teachers' first day. However, note that it is not clear from the language below whether the district or the union is expected to gather the teachers for these orientation sessions.

(3) To inform new teachers of the provisions of this contractual Agreement, and to explain the services available through the Association, the Association shall, during the first month of school, have time for orientation of new teachers for a thirty (30) minute period conducted by the Association at the building level if such time is needed.

Example (4) does not require the district to provide time for the union during the district's orientation program. Note also that there is no limit on the duration of the union presentation because, according to the language of the provision, the union presentation is made after the district's orientation program is completed.

(4) In any orientation program for new teachers, the Employer shall announce and inform new teachers that the Association is the exclusive representative of all members in the bargaining unit and that the Association will explain the services available to the teachers after the conclusion of the orientation program.

Like examples (2) and (3), example (5) below grants the union a specific allotment of time with which to communicate with teachers. The language of (5) would be much more acceptable if it included a district right to terminate the provision if the union abused it.

(5) The Association shall be allowed ten (10) minutes on the agenda of the orientation program for newly hired teachers to explain services avail-

able through the Association. In each building the Association shall also be given ten (10) minutes on the agenda of the first general meeting of all teachers at the opening of school. The Association shall give the Superintendent a two (2) day advance notice of its intention to speak at said meetings.

Most contracts do not provide for union participation in orientation programs for new teachers, and this is the recommended option for school boards.

IX. School Visits by Union Representatives

The union naturally wants access to teachers at the worksite during the school day. The district has an interest in avoiding the interference or disruption of school activities; in addition, school administrators, especially principals, want to know as a general rule who is in the school and why they are there. As the examples below will make clear, there is an extremely broad range of contractual provisions that deal with union access to the worksite.

Discussion of examples

Consider the following example of a contractual provision involving school visits by union representatives:

(1) Whenever possible, the Union representative shall be allowed to conduct Union business throughout the workday other than during instructional time or teacher planning time unless otherwise agreed to by the parties.
    Union representatives shall have access to any worksite for the purpose of enforcing this Agreement.

Example (1) does not require the union to ensure that the visits of its representatives will not interfere with school operations. As long as the visit does not take place during instructional time or teacher planning time, it meets the requirements of the provision. This is an invitation to trouble.

Even contractual language that seems as if it should protect the district's ability to operate may offer less protection than the board desires. Consider example (2) below:

(2) Duly authorized representatives of the Association may transact Association business on school property. This may occur during the regular

workday, except during instructional class time, provided this shall not interfere with or disrupt normal school operations.

Example (2) does not require the union representative to obtain permission from the principal or even announce his or her presence on arrival. Furthermore, the prohibition against interfering with or disrupting "normal school operations" is much too weak. Not only is it likely that the district and the union will disagree about the definition of "normal school operations," but example (2) also implies that it is acceptable for union visits to interfere with or disrupt *abnormal* school operations. The district should have insisted on deleting "normal" from the clause. Finally, the prohibition against conducting union business at times other than "instructional class time" is much too narrow. Suppose, for example, that a teacher has supervisory duties that are not part of his or her instructional time, or that a teacher is working on a report to the principal that is needed immediately. In neither case could such time be said to be "instructional class time."

Example (3) requires that union representatives get the approval of an employee's immediate supervisor before visiting:

(3) Union representatives may be granted access to employees who are members of this bargaining unit during working hours. Such access will be with the concurrence of the employee's immediate supervisor and no substantial interference with job performance will ensue. Such access shall not be unreasonably denied.

While this may seem like an adequate way to protect the district, the force of this requirement is seriously weakened by the proviso that "[s]uch access shall not be unreasonably denied." In view of the lack of other safeguards, the district should not have weakened the supervisor's ability to control the union's access to teachers.

Under the language of the following example, the union representative is required to report his or her presence before visiting a site; otherwise, (4) contains many of the objectionable features of the previous examples. Note that although the union representatives must report their presence, they are not required to secure anyone's approval before they visit.

(4) During the regular workday, Union representatives may visit employees at school provided that the representatives report their presence to the building administrator or his/her designee and they do not interfere with or disrupt normal school operations. No authorized representative shall use this privilege except to conduct Union business.

Even when a contract does require administrative approval, that in itself does not guarantee that the district is protected from potential union abuses. Consider example (5) below:

(5) Field representatives of the Association will be permitted to transact official Association business with individual teachers on school property at reasonable times, provided that permission is secured from the principal/designee.

While the language of example (5) requires administrative approval before visits, this is the district's only safeguard. It would be better to include additional safeguards in the contract to avoid the possibility that weak principals will permit the union to abuse its visitation rights.

As noted above, leaving terms such as "normal school operations" undefined is not a good idea. Boards may attempt to avoid this problem by linking restrictions to the school day. It is important to be as clear as possible in this language; consider the following example:

(6) The Association and its representatives shall have the right to use school buildings to discuss matters pertaining to Association business with professional employees at reasonable times before and after school, scheduling such use in advance with the principal of the school, provided that in any event, such use shall neither interfere with nor interrupt normal school operations or activities, nor be in conflict with a previously scheduled activity.

Example (6) limits school visits to "before and after school," which is somewhat vague but would probably be interpreted by the district to mean before and after the regular school day for teachers. If the union's intention was to allow the visits before and after the regular school day for pupils, that should have been explicitly stated in the contract.

Example (7) below provides the most adequate safeguards for the district:

(7) Subject to reasonable regulation, the Union shall have the right of access to areas in which employees work. Union representatives shall identify themselves and state the purpose of their visit immediately upon arrival at a District facility. Access shall not be used in any way to interrupt or interfere with District operations or the work of an employee. Upon District request, Union representatives shall leave during the employee's work time.

The requirement that union visits be scheduled in advance, together with the union's obligation to accede to administration requests to leave the building, ensures that there will be no on-site controversies involving union visits.

X. Contracting Out

Until the 1990s, the teacher unions did not pay much attention to contracting out. In contrast, school district unions of support-service personnel have always emphasized the importance of restricting district efforts to contract out for support services. School bus drivers, cafeteria workers, groundskeepers, and paraprofessionals were some of the employee groups interested in protection from having their work contracted out.

In the early 1990s, the NEA began to negotiate restrictions on contracting out much more aggressively than it had in the past. The reason was that the state and local associations had begun to organize support personnel on a large scale. The AFT has tried to organize support-service personnel since its inception, but this objective was a major change for the NEA and its affiliates. In fact, before the 1990s, several NEA affiliates did not allow support staff to be members of the state or local associations, and a few affiliates still do not allow it. Today, the NEA's message to support personnel is that the NEA will protect them from "privatization," that is, from having their work contracted out to private companies. Eventually, as a result of the emergence of companies that attempt to provide education services for profit, the teacher unions became concerned that "privatization" would cut into their teacher membership and revenues as well. For this reason, NEA affiliates emphasize restrictions on contracting out much more than they did in the past.

By the late 1990s, the NEA and the AFT had embarked upon a war against privatization that is still ongoing.[1] In doing so, they are simply doing what unions have always tried to do—prevent nonunion personnel from doing the work done by union members. The only difference between the NEA and the AFT and the United Auto Workers (UAW) on this issue is that the teacher unions try harder to cast their opposition to contracting out as an objective that is in the public interest.

Although the unions publicly assert that contracting out by school districts should be evaluated on a case-by-case basis, this is clearly not how they approach the issue. They do not urge citizens to weigh the pros and cons of each school board effort to contract out for services; on the contrary, union publications portray contracting out as an unmitigated evil. School boards should take this into account in thinking about the issues involved in contracting out.

Ironically, the NEA and the AFT are themselves major users of contracting out. For instance, both unions advocate binding arbitration of grievances; as noted previously, this is a procedure whereby privately employed arbitrators decide whether school districts have violated their labor contracts. In the absence of arbitration, claims that a party has violated a contract are resolved in the courts, that is, by government agencies. Thus, it is somewhat misleading to say that the NEA and the AFT are opposed to contracting out per se; they are opposed to contracting out when it threatens losses of union members and revenues.

The position that school boards should take on contracting out is suggested by its importance in our daily lives. When we eat in a restaurant or take soiled clothes to the laundry, we are contracting out services that could be performed in the home. Companies have to decide every day whether to print the annual report themselves, or hire an outside printer to do the job; whether to employ outside legal counsel, or have the work done by in-house counsel; whether to utilize company trucks to transport their products, or hire an outside trucking firm to perform this task. Without the freedom to make these decisions, individuals and companies would not be able to function efficiently, and neither would school boards. Therefore, boards should oppose restrictions on their rights to contract out for services just as vigorously as do private companies. This does not mean or imply that school boards can or should ignore the impact of contracting out on any school district employees who may be adversely affected by the practice. Such consideration, however, should not be an indirect way of preventing contracting out, by requiring school boards to pay exorbitant amounts to such employees.

Discussion of examples

Consider the following two examples:

(1) Work normally performed by bargaining-unit members will not be subcontracted if the contracting out of such work jeopardizes, eliminates, or reduces the work force of the bargaining unit.

(2) The Board shall enter into no contract which will result in instruction being provided, supervised, or otherwise influenced by any person or persons, organization, group, or company other than properly certificated persons directly employed by the Board or by the Association without the express written approval of the Association.

Example (1) could be used by any union of school district employees, whereas (2) applies only to unions of employees that provide instruction. Actually, the language in (2) would prohibit a district from employing paraprofessionals to help teachers in classrooms. Both examples would undercut the district's ability to contract out for services; example (2)'s prohibition against board employment of any "person or persons, organization, group, or company" that might "influence" instruction is obviously overbroad to the point of absurdity.

Ideally at least, the biggest concession that school boards should grant is an opportunity for the union to be consulted before services, instructional or non-instructional, are contracted out. It is also acceptable for the school board to pledge to make a good-faith effort to ease the impact of contracting out on employees who suffer its adverse effects. In making these commitments, however, school boards should insist upon a management-rights clause that explicitly recognizes their right to contract out. In the absence of such a clause, the district should resist any restriction—including those noted above—on their right to contract out.

Union rights present school boards with two dilemmas. The first is that while board refusal to accept at least some union rights will be perceived as mean-spirited or as evidence of an anti-union animus, accepting union proposals on the subject can be very risky.

One solution to this dilemma is to grant defensible union rights as a reasonable concession outside of the contract. In effect, the school board is saying to the union: "We will allow you to exercise certain rights, but we are not going to bind ourselves contractually to provide you with these rights. If we were to do that, it would be necessary to haggle over contractual safeguards against potential abuses, and we see no need to do that. Instead, we will allow you to exercise these specified rights, but we will also retain our right to suspend them for cause, as we interpret it. We do not intend to get involved in arguments over whether the board is justified in suspending the union rights."

The unions will oppose this solution, but it will seem reasonable to many others; after all, everyone is familiar with the idea of terminating or suspending rights that are abused. If the union subsequently alleges that the district unfairly or arbitrarily terminated a union right, the district will be in a better position to see how the union would interpret contractual safeguards if they were incorporated into the contract.

The second dilemma that boards face involving union rights relates to exclusivity. The union seeks exclusivity as a way to stifle opposition or competition. The dilemma arises because it may be to the board's advantage (or seem to be to the board's advantage) to avoid competition between unions over the right to represent the district's employees. As previously noted, however, granting a union exclusivity infringes on the rights of individual teachers. When faced with this dilemma over exclusivity, many—perhaps most—school boards have chosen to protect the unions rather than teachers.

5

Released-Time Subsidies

In many school districts, school boards subsidize union operations in the following ways:

- Granting union members released time and/or leaves of absence with pay (often including fringe benefits) in order to conduct union business
- Performing the payroll deduction of union dues, agency fees, and PAC contributions at no cost to the union
- Giving the union free use of district facilities and services, including the use of space for union meetings, use of the district mail system, and the right to address faculty meetings
- Giving union employees advancement on the teacher salary schedule for time spent working for the union
- Payment by the school district of contributions to the pensions of union officers and staff
- Reimbursing union members for travel expenses for union events

Most school board members are not aware of the magnitude of these subsidies. In school district budgets, the subsidies are never grouped together under the heading "Subsidies to the Union." Instead, the subsidies are included in school district budgets under a variety of headings that may or may not refer to the union: union rights, grievance procedures, leaves of absence, organizational security, salary schedules, and so forth. School districts pay for these subsidies from a variety of line items in the district budget: payments to substitute teachers, teacher salaries, and pension contributions, among others. In most situations, the union subsidy is lumped together with other expenses paid for under the same line item; for example, the costs of hiring substitutes for teachers who are on re-leased time for union business may be included in a budget line for substitutes that also covers substitutes required for other reasons, such as replacing teach-ers on sick leave, personal leave, maternity/paternity leave, and so on. Another reason that board members are unaware of the extent of union subsidization is that the costs involved must be computed from allocations of time or of the use of facilities; for example, if a teacher devotes one period a day to service as a union's building representative, it would be necessary to compute the total cost of that amount of time and count it as a union subsidy. Such allocations may ap-pear to be unnecessary because of the small amounts presumed to be involved; be that as it may, the cumulative amounts of these subsidies can be quite sub-stantial. However, the most important reason why boards misunderstand the ex-tent of their subsidies to the unions is simply that boards never really think about the total cost of these subsidies. If they did, they would undoubtedly be opposed to certain subsidies that boards typically accept without much thought.

Previous chapters have discussed some of the taxpayer subsidies to the teacher unions. This chapter, however, will focus on leaves of absence and re-leased time with pay to conduct union business. These are among the most costly, most unrecognized, and most frequently used taxpayer subsidies that benefit the teacher unions. It is important to think carefully about these re-leased-time issues during negotiations, because when a bargaining crisis erupts, unions frequently scrutinize the contract carefully to find district vulnerabili-ties that were ignored when district/union relations were positive.

School districts vary considerably with respect to how they treat released time for union activities. Obviously, the amount of released time allowed in a contract will depend on several factors: the size of the school district, the way that the contract is drafted, the kind of leadership on each side, the statutory im-passe procedures, the level of sophistication among the district's principals, and the principals' determination to run their schools properly. Also note that, like other contractual provisions, released-time policies can be found in various places in a contract. For example, most contracts treat released time for griev-ances in the provision relating to grievances, but other contracts may have it elsewhere. To ensure adequate district protection from potential union abuses of released time, it is extremely important that the board's negotiating team be aware of how any contractual provision could affect released-time issues.

I. Released Time for Bargaining

One critical subsidy that the board may provide to a union involves the terms of negotiations for the next contract between the union and the board. The union invariably requests that these negotiations be conducted during the regular school day and that members of the union negotiating team be released with pay for this purpose. The union tries to get released time with pay for as many days and team members as it can. School board negotiators sometimes agree to such proposals because they do not want to negotiate in the evening, on weekends, or after the regular school day. Nevertheless, contractual commitments to provide released time for negotiations are generally undesirable for most districts. This does not mean that school boards should never provide it, but they should avoid agreeing to a contractual obligation to do so.

Why do teachers want released time to negotiate with the board? First, some teachers prefer service on the union's negotiating team to teaching. Also, service on the negotiating team presents teachers with opportunities to promote their own agendas; for example, coaches may want to be on the negotiating team in order to ensure substantial raises for coaches. While it is understandable that teachers would wish to pursue their individual agendas, the discontinuities in instruction that result from released-time policies can be a difficult problem for students. No matter how much released time the board allows in the contract, teachers usually utilize it to the hilt and expect that additional released time will be forthcoming; thus, any grant of released time will lead to a corresponding loss of instructional time between students and their primary teachers.

If some concession on released time for negotiations is desirable, the provision should state the maximum amount of released time—not the minimum amount—that will be available for negotiations. Also, be sure that this amount of time covers all "impasse procedures," that is, procedures like mediation or fact-finding, which are used when the two parties cannot reach agreement on a contract. These procedures often require teachers to spend substantial amounts of time as witnesses as well as negotiators.

From the board's perspective, the best policy is not to provide any released time until the parties are close to a final agreement, and then to make it clear that released time will be available only if there is real progress toward a settlement. If a board allows more expansive amounts of released time, the school district will be vulnerable to union stonewalling at the district's expense. The more that a union team that includes classroom teachers must bargain on teachers' time rather than on the district's time, the more likely it is that the union team will adopt a realistic, businesslike attitude toward negotiations.

In addition to setting a limit on the amount of released time, the board should limit the overall duration of negotiations. It is almost always unwise to provide released time months before the existing contract expires; the unions are usually very reluctant to concede very much in the early stages of bargaining, anyway. Their attitude is that there is plenty of time to negotiate: why make concessions before it becomes necessary to do so in order to reach agreement?

Sometimes provisions in a multiyear school board/union contract allow the parties to negotiate over a limited number of items during the term of the contract; these items are called "reopeners." School districts should think carefully before granting teachers released time to negotiate when the negotiations involve these reopeners. If a contract contains such reopeners, then unless the contract provides otherwise, the union would be able to invoke the statutory impasse procedures, even if only one item was holding up agreement on the contract.

Under most statutory impasse procedures, if the parties cannot reach agreement on an issue under negotiation, they are required to enter mediation, followed by fact-finding. These procedures usually require a considerable amount of unproductive time. For example, if the mediator spends a great deal of time with the district's negotiating team, the union's team may spend that time just sitting around. After all, by the time the parties are in mediation, the union team has had ample opportunities to think through its positions and those of the school board; there comes a time when more analysis or discussion of an issue does not result in more insight.

The best way for a school board to avoid protracted contract negotiations is by announcing its opposition to retroactive pay increases and adhering to this position, even if it is the only item holding up agreement on the contract. Under this policy, salary increases included in a new contract would not be effective until there was agreement on the successor contract. Admittedly, it is often difficult for the board to adhere to such a tough stand, but if the union has nothing to lose by dragging out negotiations, it is likely to do just that.

Discussion of examples

Examples (1) and (2) illustrate the kind of commitments that districts should avoid when considering released-time issues. Example (1) is an open-ended commitment on bargaining time, and because the contract in which this clause appears provides released time for bargaining, the clause serves as an open-ended commitment on released time. This is an example of how various clauses can function together in subtle ways that are not always apparent. In contrast, example (2) displays the problem with unlimited released time in explicit form, a problem that is not significantly mitigated by a final sentence that urges that released time "shall not be abused" by the union.

(1) In the event that the Board of Education is considering a change in policy which would come within the scope of this Agreement, or is considering any change in District-wide educational policy which has an impact on the terms and conditions of work, the Board of Education or the Superintendent of Schools shall so notify the President of the Association. The Association shall, within ten (10) days, notify the President of the Board of Education if the Association will exercise its right to negotiate these matters. The Board and the Association shall also negotiate on any appropriation of unanticipated additional sources of public revenue which are not specifically earmarked.

(2) When it is necessary for representatives of the Association to engage in Association activities directly relating to the Association's duties as representative of the teachers which cannot be performed other than during school hours, upon the approval of the Superintendent or his/her designated representative within a reasonable time in advance, they shall be given such time, without loss of pay, as is necessary to perform any such activities. The Association and its officers recognize and agree that this privilege should not be abused.

Providing released time without any caps or other safeguards is folly, and would be even if the union has never taken an excessive amount of leave pursuant to these articles. Circumstances and personnel will be different in the future; in fact, this is one of the main arguments for having collective bargaining contracts. As noted in Chapter 1, even if the district has always acted fairly, unions often point out that administrators and school board members come and go, and that nobody can be sure that future administrators and board members will be as fair as the current ones. Hence, they argue, their rights and privileges need to be established in a contract. By the same logic, school boards should insist on including contractual safeguards against union abuses of those contractual rights and privileges.

Example (3) illustrates language that sets a cap on released time for union business, but provides the district with no other safeguards:

(3) One hundred twenty (120) days of leave with pay shall be made available for Association use each school year. The Association shall reimburse the District for substitute costs when a substitute is employed. When possible, the teacher shall provide twenty-four (24) hours' notice of intent to use Association leave.

Only the Association President or his/her designee may authorize use of Association leave.

This lack of further safeguards may prove costly to a district subject to the contractual language above. Note that the provision gives the union 120 days of leave "each school year." However, if 120 days is enough released time for those years when the union is bargaining on a successor contract, then it is too much released time for the years in which there is no bargaining.

The following language would probably protect the district adequately:

(4) Whenever members of the Association's negotiating unit are scheduled by mutual agreement to participate in negotiations during working hours, the Association agrees to pay the substitutes.

Example (4) would usually be adequate, because the district need not agree to schedule negotiations "during working hours" unless it finds the arrangements satisfactory. However, note that the phrase "the Association agrees to pay the substitutes" is a mistake. It is probably intended to convey the idea that the union will pay the district for the costs of the substitutes, and not the idea that the union will pay the substitutes directly. The district must control the appointment of substitutes, and must be responsible for paying them.

Example (5) below provides more protection for the district than any of the previous examples:

(5) Whenever any representative of the Association or any employee participates during working hours in negotiations, grievance proceedings, conferences, or meetings relating to the administration of this Agreement, he shall suffer no loss in pay when such meetings are mutually so scheduled by the Administration and the Association. The Administration is under no obligation whatsoever to agree to such meetings during working hours. This clause is not applicable if the employee is not scheduled for professional duties, is on any type of leave, or is on strike.

While example (5) provides the district with greater protection than do the other examples, the best outcome would be a contract that does not include any provision granting teachers released time for negotiating. Avoiding these contractual commitments gives the district maximum flexibility. As a practical matter, however, a contract that allows for released time only when the district and the union come to a "mutual agreement" over the terms of the released time may be as satisfactory as a contract including no released-time provisions at all.

However, the advantages of flexibility should not be understated, and thus the board should try to avoid contractual obligations that would provide teachers with released time for negotiating. If school board/union relations are harmonious, the board can provide released time, with or without pay, as it deems appropriate. This way, the board retains the right to discontinue released time immediately if the union or its members abuse it or use it in ways that the board did not intend to allow.

II. Released Time for Grievance Processing

Granting teachers released time for processing grievances leads to the same problems that emerge when teachers are granted released time for bargaining. The more released time with pay that the union receives, the less incentive that the union has to adopt a realistic, businesslike attitude toward the work to be done. If the union's building representatives get one period of released time with pay each day to process grievances, they will tend to encourage or find enough grievances to justify that amount of released time. The more generous the district is with released time, the more it will suffer as a result of its generosity.

Just as it is risky for the board to provide teachers with released time for negotiations, it is also very risky for the board to provide the union with an open-ended amount of released time with pay for grievance processing, since grievants as well as witnesses will also want released time with pay in order to attend grievance hearings. If these hearings take place during the school day, this is likely to have a negative impact on student instruction. Thus, the district should try to include in the contract a provision stating that "insofar as possible, all grievance proceedings will be held after or before the regular school day, or during unassigned time."

Discussion of examples

The following language provides one example of contractual language that could disrupt student instruction:

(1) Designated representatives shall have the right to receive reasonable periods of released time without loss of compensation when participating in the grievance process.

Example (1) discusses released time for grievance processing without making any reference to the workday; this contrasts sharply with example (5) below, which categorically states that grievance meetings will be held "during either unassigned time during the school day or after school hours."

Example (2) places a cap on released time for grievances. This is one way to prevent excessive utilization of released time for processing grievances; in contrast, example (6) below imposes limits for investigating grievances, as distinguished from processing them.

(2) Whenever any representative of the Association or any teacher participates during working hours in scheduled grievance proceedings, the teacher shall be released from duty and shall suffer no loss in pay, nor shall such time be charged to the teacher's limited leave days, nor shall the School District require reimbursement in any form for this time. The time to be so consumed by teachers, including Association representatives, without loss of pay during a school year shall not aggregate more than fifteen (15) teacher days. The School District shall be reimbursed by the Association for time in excess of fifteen (15) teacher days at the substitute daily rate of pay.

When negotiating the procedure under which requests for released time for grievances will be considered, the board should make sure that the procedure can be implemented effectively. Consider example (3) below:

(3) When it is necessary, as approved by the Superintendent, for the Union President and/or his/her designee to engage in Union activities directly relating to the Union's duties as representative of the certified professional personnel which cannot be performed other than during normal school hours, or are the result of an emergency situation, the Union's representative shall be given such time, without loss of pay, as is necessary to perform any such activities.

Example (3) would be appropriate only in small school districts; otherwise, the superintendent might be overworked trying to deal with numerous requests for released time. Example (3) illustrates the reason why contracts should refer to generic entities such as "the district" rather than to specific individuals when specifying who is required to perform certain actions. If a contract does need to refer to the superintendent, the contract should explicitly state that such references also include the superintendent's designees, since the superintendent may not always be available to act in a timely fashion.

Example (4) can be considered adequate from the district's point of view:

(4) Hearings and conferences pursuant to the procedure shall be conducted at a time and place which will afford a fair and reasonable opportunity for all persons, including witnesses entitled to be present, to attend, and will be held, insofar as possible, after regular school hours, or during nonteaching time of personnel involved. When such hearings and conferences are held, at the option of the Administration, during school hours, all employees whose presence is required shall be excused, with pay, for that purpose.

While the following example adequately protects the district from excessive grievance processing during the school day, the language is silent with respect to who is responsible for absorbing the cost of any released time:

(5) All meetings involving grievances shall be held during either unassigned time during the school day or after school hours.

Example (6) provides strong protection for the district against any abuse of released time that the district grants for processing grievances:

(6) The School District agrees that the Association may designate members as representatives authorized to investigate grievances so long as they do

not interfere with instructional time, assignment time, or planning time, or carry on this activity during the representative's instructional time, assignment time, or planning time. Such activity for the purpose of investigating grievances only may be conducted at other appropriate times, if necessary, with the prior approval of the building principal or principals involved. The Association agrees that no Association activities except as provided for in this Agreement shall take place on the School District's property during working hours. It is further agreed that, in the event of an emergency, a bargaining-unit member may receive assistance from a union staff member during the bargaining-unit member's duty-free lunch period only. In the event the union staff member wishes to enter a school building he/she must first present himself/herself to the building principal or his/her designee.

III. Released Time for Union Business

School district budgets often distinguish the costs of released time for union business from the costs of released time for grievance representation. In many situations, however, it is better to show the entire cost of all granted released time in one lump sum. In that case, the district need not bargain separately over grants of released time for several different purposes, such as attending state and national union conventions, attending union conferences, granting union officers leave, and so on. Furthermore, it is much easier to maintain control over costs when the various categories of released time are treated as one whole; otherwise, the union could add a little bit of released time in each of the various categories without drawing the board's attention. Finally, showing the total costs to the district of all released time will provide one large figure that is more likely to shock the board and the district's taxpayers than would an accounting of the various types of released time that is scattered throughout the budget.

Obviously, an important issue concerning released time for union business is who should pay for the time—the union, the teacher(s), or the school district? It seems foolish for the district to pay teachers to attend meetings held for the purpose of training attendees how to squeeze more concessions from the board. Nevertheless, most medium- or large-sized districts probably provide some released time for union business. It is important to ensure that teachers do not take leave on critical work days, days when substitutes are not available, or the days before and after holiday periods. Although a requirement of district approval for such released time is essential, other limitations on the use of such time should also be included in the contract. This will avoid situations in which district administrators have to inform applicants why requests for released time are being denied; it also ensures that teachers requesting released time can be under no illusions if they try to take released time for an impermissible purpose.

Deciding who will incur the costs of released time for union business can be difficult. The more released time for which a district pays, the more such time will be utilized, and the harder the union will bargain for an increase in the amount of released time. If hiring substitutes becomes necessary, the union typically asserts that the district's only cost with respect to the released time is the cost of the substitutes—an interesting argument that ignores any educational loss to students that occurs when the district hires substitute teachers and consequently creates discontinuities in instruction. The board should also protect itself against the use of released time to support union pressure tactics, either in the district or elsewhere.

Discussion of examples

The examples of released-time provisions below range from open-ended provisions without contractual safeguards to more restrictive provisions, and from provisions where the district absorbs all of the costs of released time to provisions where the union absorbs all or most of the costs. There is also a range of provisions relating to advance notice, the number of teachers who can take leave for union business at the same time, and limits on the amount of leave that an individual teacher can take. The latter safeguard is intended to ensure that no particular class is unduly disadvantaged by teacher absences due to leave for union business.

(1)   When it is necessary for representatives of the Union to engage in Union activities directly relating to their Union duties as representatives of the teachers which cannot be performed other than during school hours, upon the approval of the Superintendent or his/her designated representative within a reasonable time in advance, they shall be given such time, without loss of pay, as is necessary to perform any such activities. The Union and its officers recognize and agree that this privilege should not be abused.

Although example (1) appears to require the union to seek approval from the superintendent or a designee before taking released time for union business, the language suggests that such approval is expected automatically. The union is the judge of when released time is "necessary," and the provision sets no criteria by which the district could refuse to grant a request for released time. Furthermore, the statement that "[t]he Union and its officers . . . agree that this privilege should not be abused" suggests that they have considerable opportunity to abuse the privilege should they be so inclined; the statement would not be necessary if this were not the case.

Like example (1), the following provision is very advantageous for the union:

(2) The Board shall provide the Association a base of fifteen (15) days of Association leave, plus one (1) day of Association leave for every ten (10) Association members, or thirty-five (35) days, whichever is greater.

  Leave shall be at full pay, and shall be granted by the Superintendent within twenty-four (24) hours prior to such leave being used.

  An authorization statement from the President of the Association accompanying a letter for such leave will be adequate for justification.

Example (2), like example (1), provides no safeguards for the district, despite the fact that the language of (2) would require the district to pay for the released time and, in the absence of language to the contrary, for the cost of any necessary substitutes as well. The provision gives the superintendent no discretion to refuse to grant a request for released time, and thus the only thing needed to get a request approved is an authorization from the union president.

Example (3) also provides a generous subsidy to the union:

(3) An aggregate of fifty (50) leave days per school year shall be granted to the Association for use at its discretion for Association business. A teacher shall be authorized to utilize such Association business leave only upon submission of written notice to the personnel office by 4:45 p.m. of the day prior to the proposed use, which notice shall bear the approval of the Association President. Teachers utilizing such Association business leave shall suffer no loss of pay as a result thereof.

  If a substitute is provided, only the time for which the substitute has been provided will be charged against the aggregate Association leave days. No teacher, except the Association President, shall use more than twenty (20) Association leave days in any one school year, unless prior written approval is received from the Superintendent or his/her designee.

  In the event that the Association utilizes the entire fifty (50) leave days before the end of the school year, the Association shall have the right to use additional days for Association business upon application as set forth above; the Association shall reimburse the Board for the actual cost of the replacement teachers who are required.

By providing the union with an unlimited right for its members to released time for union business if it pays for the substitutes, the district has made it possible for the union to conduct an effective and legal strike at little cost, especially since the union is only obligated to pay for the actual costs of the substitutes.

Example (4) reflects a district's intent to protect its operations against the simultaneous use of released time by large numbers of teachers:

(4) Each year of this Agreement, representatives of the Union shall be granted up to fifty (50) days of unpaid leave each year to conduct Union business provided the following conditions are met:

    A. No more than two (2) employees may be absent from any faculty on any day.

    B. The employee's supervisor must be given at least forty-eight (48) hours notice of the intent to take leave.

    C. No more than ten (10) employees may be absent on any day.

    D. Except for the President of the Union, no teacher may be absent more than ten (10) days during the school year. The President can be absent no more than twenty-five (25) days.

    E. A minimum of twenty (20) employees will be granted leave to attend the convention of the state Association. A maximum of ten (10) days of temporary duty will be granted by the District for this purpose. Teachers that do not require a substitute will not be charged personal leave for this convention only.

The specific numbers used in the above example will not necessarily be suitable for other districts attempting to protect themselves from union abuses; the limits suitable for other contracts will vary with the size of schools and school districts. Obviously, the most prudent course for the board to follow is to avoid any contractual obligation to provide released time for union business. Without such an obligation, the district can still provide such released time if it wishes to do so, but it maintains the power to discontinue the benefit if it is abused.

IV. Released Time for Union Officers

Released time for union officers is a variant of released time for union business, but it is often a separate item, even in contracts containing sections pertaining to released time for union business. Several questions arise:

- Should the released time be granted at all?
- If the district decides to grant union officers released time, how much time should the district allow the officers to take?
- Should the district pay any part of the officers' salary and benefits while they are on leave?
- What are the teacher's rights with respect to returning to his or her teaching position?

- What happens if the teacher loses the union position before the term of leave expires?
- Should the teacher advance on the salary schedule while on leave?

In small school districts, granting released time for union officers would usually be too disruptive to justify acceptance in any form. The union officers in small districts typically do not have much to do, and their union responsibilities should not require them to conduct a significant amount of travel. If teachers in small school districts become state or national union officers, then the union affiliates, rather than the school district, should defray the costs associated with assuming these positions.

The district may wish to make it possible for teachers to take extended leaves of absence without losing their seniority; conceivably, if it does this for nonunion jobs, it might be considered discrimination against the union if the board does not allow union employees the same opportunity. Another point to consider is that a board might not wish to incur union hostility by denying released time; granting it may help foster good board/union relationships. It must also be recognized that in small school districts, leave for state and/or national union positions is very infrequent.

Arguments about granting released time so teachers can serve as union officers are often arguments about the conditions of the released time. The NEA and the AFT are wealthy unions that can well afford to pay full salary and benefits to individuals that serve as union officers, so the district should refuse to pay for such leave. Also, serving as a union official is a much different job than teaching, hence these individuals should not advance on the salary schedule.

Whether or not a request for released time is granted, it should include adequate assurances that the union will reimburse the district for the district's expenses, that the employee will give timely notice of his or her leave and return, and that the employee understands that there is no "guarantee" of getting the same position upon return. The district should be obligated only to make a good-faith effort to restore the teacher to the same position; however, all rights of return should apply only for a limited time, one year at maximum.

Discussion of examples

In the following example, the school district is clearly subsidizing the union:

(1) The President of the Association shall be provided with full released time from his/her teaching or equivalent duties in order for him/her to carry out Association duties, and shall suffer no loss of pay or employment benefits while performing such duties during his/her term of office. He/she shall have the absolute right of return to his/her former position

when his/her term of office expires. The Association shall pay to the District an amount equal to Step 7 on Schedule A for such release of the President.

By paying the amount specified, the school district in this example is paying for about half of the union president's salary and for all of his or her fringe benefits; the union is paying for less than half the cost of its president's time. In addition, the union officer's absolute right of return in this situation is indefensible.

Example (2) below requires the union to pay its president's "salary and benefits." It would be preferable to spell out these benefits to ensure that there will be no misunderstanding about which benefits the district must pay.

(2) The Association President shall be allowed a leave of absence for his/her term of office with salary and benefits to be paid by the Association for the time that the President is released from teaching duties. In the event the Association requests less than full-time leave, the scheduling of the leave shall be mutually agreed upon prior to starting said leave. Said leave of absence shall count toward retirement and all other purposes of the Master Contract.

Example (3) requires the union to reimburse the district in advance; also, an employee granted released time does not get an "absolute guarantee" of return to his or her former position:

(3) Any professional employee elected to an office in the state or national Association which requires his/her full-time absence from the District will be granted Association leave at his/her request. This leave will normally be for an entire teaching year.

During the period of leave, the employee will receive the salary he/she would normally receive while performing his/her teaching duties, including all rights of tenure, retirement, advancement, and any other rights he/she would normally receive. The School District *must* be reimbursed promptly for the salary and benefits paid to the employee. This section of the Agreement will take effect only upon district receipt of a binding agreement that these funds will be reimbursed by the Association.

Upon completion of the leave, the employee is guaranteed the same or equivalent position to the one he/she left.

The district subsidies to the union are very explicit in the example below; in view of the salary schedule in this particular district, the subsidy to the union was over $30,000 annually:

(4) A tenured teacher who is elected President of the Association shall be granted a leave with pay, fringe benefits, and seniority accrual for a period not to exceed one (1) year. The leave shall be for one (1) complete school year and cannot be taken in conjunction with any other leave. The Association shall pay to the District one-half of the cost of the President's salary and one-half the cost of retirement, health insurance, and life insurance.

A teacher on such leave of absence must give written notice to the Superintendent of Schools by March 1 of the year the leave expires of his/her intention to return on the first day of the following school year or resign. Failure to furnish such notice shall constitute a notice of resignation.

The teacher shall be entitled to return to his/her same position he/she held prior to his/her leave, or apply for a vacancy consistent with the terms of this Agreement.

When a teacher is granted such leave of absence, he/she shall, upon reemployment, retain only the following employment rights held by him/her before such leave was granted:

A. a continuing contract as a tenured teacher.

B. unused sick leave held at the start of the leave of absence.

The language of (5) and (6) below would adequately protect a district's interests:

(5) Teachers who are elected or appointed to full-time union positions with the AFT, or the state federation of teachers with which they are affiliated, may be granted leaves of absences for the purpose of accepting these positions. This leave shall be granted under general leave provisions without salary, without salary advancement, without teacher retirement, and without all fringe benefits for a maximum of two (2) years. Intent to return to work or to extend the leave to the second year, if applicable, must be submitted by March 1 of each year prior to the next fall opening of school. Failure to submit a letter of intent by the March 1 date shall result in the termination of employment.

(6) The Board agrees to provide paid annual leave of absence to one (1) elected officer of the Union to engage in Union activities directly related to the Union's duties as the certified representative of the employees covered by this Agreement.

All costs associated with such leave shall be forwarded by the Union to the Board in advance on a quarterly basis. The costs shall include the salary as provided for on the appropriate salary schedule, the required contribution by the Board to the state teacher retirement system, an amount equal to the Board's contribution for the full cost of health and dental insurance, and any other costs normally associated with the Board's financial responsibility to an individual employee, including, but not limited to, unemployment compensation insurance, worker's compensation insurance, and so forth.

The employee so released shall continue to be an employee of the Board and shall advance annually on the appropriate step of the salary schedule.

In both (5) and (6), there is only a slight subsidy to the unions and no iron-clad agreement to return the teachers to their former position. In addition, example (6) spells out the required union contribution in detail.

As is evident, school boards frequently absorb some of the costs of released time granted to teachers who serve as union officers. Inasmuch as the NEA and the AFT are wealthy unions, the justification seems to be that the subsidy generates goodwill toward the school board. There is little empirical support for this conclusion. When the concession was first made, the union officer(s) who benefited may have had more positive attitudes toward the board, but over time the subsidy to them is merely taken for granted and generates no appreciable goodwill toward the board.

6

Union Rights in Negotiations

School boards probably make more mistakes relating to the process of negotiations than they do with other bargaining topics. One reason for this is that boards tend to include their statutory obligations in the contracts, thereby giving the union contractual as well as statutory remedies for the same alleged violation of a contract. In addition, the negotiation procedures enumerated in the contract frequently include matters that should be resolved unilaterally by each party; for example, each party should decide for itself whether and when it will keep minutes of the meetings, as well as how the authority to negotiate is structured within its own bargaining team. As will be evident, the issues that must be resolved jointly are typically resolved informally at the bargaining table; if and when they are not, it is usually because one or both parties are not negotiating in good faith.

I. Negotiating Procedures

Negotiating procedures raise a host of practical issues. Where will negotiations take place? When will the parties negotiate, and how long will the negotiating sessions last? Who decides the order of items to be negotiated? How many members of the negotiating team will there be? Will the negotiations be open to others or restricted to members of the negotiating teams?

Despite the importance of these issues, it is generally a mistake to negotiate contractual language to deal with them. Under bargaining statutes, the parties are required to negotiate "in good faith"; what this requirement entails has been clarified in an enormous number of legal cases that govern the conduct of the parties. For example, most school district negotiations take place in the district administration building because the data needed during negotiations is usually found there; also, these offices have the office machines and caucus rooms needed for productive negotiations. Nevertheless, if a teacher union refused to negotiate in the district office, as sometimes happens, the district's negotiating team would be required to negotiate on a neutral site or accept some rotation of negotiations between sites preferred by the parties. In practice, most experienced negotiators in the private sector understand the rules governing negotiating procedures and have no difficulty in reaching agreement on them. When it comes to teacher union contracts, however, negotiations on negotiating procedures are a common occurrence, generally to the district's detriment because it is disadvantageous for the district to include its statutory obligations in the contract. As noted above, doing so enables the union to pursue contractual remedies for alleged violations of statutory rights. This is a huge procedural negative from the district's point of view.

Discussion of examples

The following example contains multiple problems of two types. Not only does the language include various statutory provisions, but it also contains provisions that each party should resolve on its own before negotiating.

(1) A. It is agreed by both parties that during the period of negotiations between the Association and the District all proceedings shall be closed to both employees and the public. Both parties agree that oral and written communications to employees and the public shall not contain specific references to proposals and counterproposals made at the table without prior notification of the other party. When an impasse is reached, the parties are released from these communications restrictions.

B. Each party may maintain its own minutes unless otherwise agreed upon.

C. Each party may have present at negotiating sessions not more than two (2) persons acting as chief negotiators. If a chief negotiator for either party is other than an employee, the party must certify before the commencement of negotiations that the chief negotiator acts as authorized spokesperson. The District's chief negotiator shall not transfer authority except in case of emergency. All members of the Association's negotiating team are authorized to make, accept, or reject proposals or counterproposals presented at a negotiating meeting.

D. Negotiations shall take place at mutually agreeable times and places, normally during the workday. Except as allowed elsewhere in this

Agreement, members of the Association bargaining team shall be Association members. Members of the Association's bargaining team shall be responsible for notifying their immediate supervisors of meeting times and dates and requesting release time no later than the beginning of the workday following the scheduling of the meeting. In cases of emergency or hardship, an employee's request to attend the negotiations meeting may be refused and the meeting will be rescheduled as soon as possible.

E. The final Agreement made between the parties shall be reduced in writing and initially distributed to District and Association negotiators for approval.

Example (1) includes the following provisions that simply restate the legal obligations and legal rights of the parties. Experienced board negotiators would not include any of them in a contract:

- "Negotiations shall take place at mutually agreeable times and places[.]"
- "The final Agreement . . . shall be reduced in writing[.]"
- "Each party may maintain its own minutes unless otherwise agreed upon."

The following issues should be resolved by each party without negotiations:

- The number of "chief negotiators." Sometimes one or both parties prefer to have different individuals act as their chief negotiator on certain issues.
- Whether the chief negotiators can transfer their authority, whatever the extent of this authority happens to be.
- Who is authorized to make, accept, or reject proposals.
- Whether members of the union negotiating team must be union members. (Incidentally, this provision makes no sense whatsoever, since it would preclude the local union from utilizing the services of an NEA or AFT field representative.)

In example (2), every sentence restates a legal obligation or deals with an issue that is best handled through procedures that the parties agree to during negotiations on the successor contract. In any event, district negotiators should avoid protracted negotiations over negotiation procedures.

(2) The parties agree that they will make a good-faith effort to resolve matters to their mutual satisfaction and agreement. In furtherance of this objective, it is recognized that either party may, if it so desires, utilize the services of outside consultants, and may call upon professional and lay representatives to assist in negotiations.

The School Trustees and the Association mutually agree to exchange information to assist in developing constructive proposals on behalf of students, employees, administrators, and the School District. Such information shall include complete and accurate financial reports and such items as ADA (average daily attendance) figures, sources of revenue, class size, and proposed salary schedules as available.

For their mutual assistance in successfully concluding negotiations, the parties, by mutual agreement, may appoint ad hoc study committees to do research; to study and develop projects, programs, and reports; and to make findings and recommendations to the parties.

It is understood and agreed that all tentative agreements negotiated between the parties and subsequently ratified by the parties shall be set down in writing.

In example (3), items A, B, C, F, and H are legal obligations of the parties; it is a waste of time and resources to negotiate on these matters as contractual items:

(3) A. The size of each negotiating team shall be determined by each party to the negotiations except as limited by statute.
  B. Either party may, if it so desires, utilize the services of outside consultants and call upon professional and lay representatives to assist in negotiations.
  C. The parties to the negotiations shall meet at reasonable times at a mutually agreed-upon place.
  D. When an agenda for negotiations is completed and accepted by both parties, no additions may be included unless approved by both parties.
  E. The length of each meeting shall be set at the time the agenda is established; however, any meeting may be adjourned at the request of either party.
  F. A caucus may be called by either party at any time.
  G. The spokesman for each party shall be a co-chairman of the meetings.
  H. No verbatim transcripts shall be kept nor recordings made of the meetings. Each side may keep notes of the proceedings.
  I. All items agreed to are agreed to tentatively, pending final disposition of all items being negotiated.

Other provisions are problematic as well. For example, item D is unnecessary. If the parties agree on an agenda, either party can refuse to negotiate on additional items without committing an unfair labor practice. It is always their prerogative to reject any change in the agreed-upon negotiating agenda. Similarly, item E is not necessary; neither party can force the other to continue to negotiate at a negotiating session. Although it is desirable to set an approximate time for adjournment, adherence to a rigid time schedule is frequently unproductive. As for item G, it is problematic because negotiating sessions do not have "co-chairmen"; the parties are led by "chief negotiators" who have equal procedural status throughout negotiations. Since the functions of co-chairmen and chief negotiators are ordinarily different, use of the term "co-chairman" may breed confusion. Finally, there is no need to include item I in the contract; usually, the parties agree at the table that all agreements are tentative until there is agreement on the complete contract.

From the board's perspective, the recommended course of action is to remove all provisions involving negotiating procedures from the contract. Except for setting the date of negotiations for the successor contract or reopeners, there is seldom any reason to include negotiating procedures in a contract—and there are usually several reasons not to include them. Their inclusion wastes valuable time, increases the likelihood of friction between the parties, formalizes matters that are best resolved informally, and provides the union with contractual remedies for alleged unfair labor practices.

II. Information Issues

In bargaining-law states, both parties are required to provide the other with relevant information about the issues under consideration during bargaining. Normally, this works to the advantage of the union, since the union possesses less information that is useful to the school district than vice versa; unions may possess some useful information, but school board negotiators seldom try to get it. Information about union revenues, assets, and expenses are three examples. Suppose a district takes the position that its consideration of any proposal to subsidize union operations will take into consideration the union's ability to pay. If the union then refuses to provide information about its revenues, assets, and expenses, the board might be justified in refusing to bargain over the union's proposals for various taxpayer subsidies, such as released time with pay for participation on the union's negotiating team. This possibility might or might not be feasible, depending on the decisions of the state's courts and public employment relations board.

Requests for information by the union can impose hardships on the district. Suppose a union requests information about the extent of the use of sick leave in order to draft proposals on the subject. The district is not required to conduct studies or surveys, but if the information is readily available, it must be made available to the union. What frequently happens is that unions propose increases in benefits without providing any data that justifies such an increase. The district's staff must then scurry around to find data that suggests that the union's proposal is untenable. School districts should try to avoid this kind of situation; it fosters irresponsibility on the part of unions and creates unnecessary work for a district's staff.

One way to discourage this practice is to insist that the union justify its proposals before the board responds to them. If the union cannot cite any supporting data, the board should conclude that the proposal is not being made seriously. The board negotiator should emphasize the fact that it is the union's obligation to justify its own proposals; it is not up to the district to go to great lengths to amass data that may or may not support the union's proposals. In this connection, it is important to recognize that the district is not obligated to conduct surveys or undertake extensive research to answer the union's requests for information.

During negotiations, unions typically propose overbroad information clauses that include the district's statutory obligation to provide information. A district should respond by stating that it will not include its statutory obligations in the contract, since there is no need to do so. The union can always file a charge against the district for engaging in an unfair labor practice if it believes that the district is not providing information that it is legally required to provide under the bargaining law. Furthermore, by including a union's statutory right to information in the contract, the school district provides the union with contractual as well as statutory remedies for any district failure to provide information that it should provide. As noted in previous chapters, this giving the union an additional means of redress is undesirable, since, given a choice, the union will use whichever forum that it deems most advantageous. Also, it is likely that the inclusion of a contractual remedy will expand the range of information that the district must make available to the union, because arbitrators tend to be more sympathetic to union positions than are judges.

In some instances, the district may not have the answers to the questions raised by the union. In such situations, the reason is important. For instance, it may reflect an administration's failure to maintain its records in the most informative way. The board should also be aware of the public relations implications of information that the union can request. In some cases, the answers to the questions raised may embarrass the school board, school administrators, or board negotiators.

Discussion of examples

In view of the fact that the district need not include its statutory obligations to provide information to the union in the contract, the information clauses frequently found in contracts reveal a surprising lack of board sophistication on information issues.

In example (1) below, the requirement to provide "all relevant information" is extremely broad; to avoid violating the contract, the district must provide a mass of information if the union requests it:

(1) The School District shall make all relevant information available to the Association within a reasonable time after it is requested. If the School District has documents containing the information requested by the Association, these will be provided. In the event that documents containing the requested information are not available, the School District shall permit reasonable access to their files so that the Association may itself obtain the needed information.

Note also that there is no union obligation to pay for copies in example (1); since the provision is so broad, this could lead to significant expenses for the district. Also, the clause does not address the possibility that the district might request relevant information from the union.

Example (2) is somewhat unusual:

(2) The Union will be provided notice of any request for information about the members of the unit by any nonschool personnel or organization. Individual employees will be provided notices of requests for information specifically about the employee except for requests for verification of employment, employment inquiries, salary inquiries, or other inquiries by law-enforcement agencies.

Note that the clause requires every principal as well as the central office to send the union information about any inquiry concerning a unit member by any nonschool organization or person. Presumably, then, if a teacher's spouse called to find out where he or she could find the car keys, it would have to be reported to the union. This is an absurd example, perhaps, but the clause is so broadly written that it could encompass such trivial matters.

Example (3), like example (1), illustrates how districts fail to obtain contractual protection for their rights to information from the union. This failure is especially noteworthy in this case because the unions frequently have useful information on the matters listed in the provision.

(3) The Association may request and the Board shall provide any pertinent information which forms a basis for any grievance by any or all teachers as well as information concerning any action which results in the discipline, reprimand, demotion, or deduction in compensation of any or all teachers. All pertinent information in the possession of the Association shall be shared with the Board.

In Example (4), the district has agreed to provide an extensive set of documents in each school library:

(4) The District shall endeavor to maintain up-to-date copies of the following documents in each school library. If the Association or a teacher finds that any of the documents are missing or incomplete, the Association shall advise the District personnel office, which shall seek to correct the problem.
   A. The State's Compiled School Laws
   B. The Negotiated Agreement
   C. Rules and Regulations of the Department of Education
   D. School Board Policies and Regulations
   E. Professional Teaching Practices Commission Code of Ethics
   F. Student Rights and Responsibilities
   G. Teachers' Handbook
   H. Teachers' Evaluation Handbook
   I. Title I Education Regulations, Chapters 2 and 5: Education for Exceptional Children
   J. School Board Minutes
   K. All District Curriculum Guides, K–12
   L. State Special Education Handbook

This union proposal was undoubtedly outside the scope of negotiations. The union has the right to certain information, but it does not have the right to bargain over where the district keeps the listed documents. The only saving feature of the provision is that it states that the district "shall endeavor" to maintain the copies in each school—this sets a lower standard than would language stating that "the district shall maintain" copies of the documents in each school.

Example (5) suggests that the parties involved were confused about various details relating to information issues. The clause states that the district will furnish information "[i]n addition to its statutory obligation," but the additional information would be part of the information that most states' statutes already require the district to provide.

(5) In addition to its statutory obligation to furnish information in its possession, the District will furnish such other information in its possession, in response to reasonable requests by the Association, which will assist the Association in effectively representing the teachers in the collective bargaining process and in the processing of grievances. Any information personal in nature and confidential to any particular teacher, and which the District is not obligated to furnish, may not be disclosed by the District unless written prior approval of the individual concerned has been

given. The District need not perform compilation of facts or information for the purpose of responding to such Association requests.

However, in the event that the District does agree to compile facts or information in response to an Association request, the Association shall pay all extra costs incurred as a result of such compilation, including, but not limited to, labor, printing, duplicating, and distribution costs.

The main point about information issues can be summarized briefly. In the bargaining-law states, school boards have a statutory obligation to provide the union with certain information that is relevant to bargaining. The obligation is not spelled out in the statutes, but is inferred and enforced by state public employment relations boards.

Because school districts should avoid converting their statutory obligations into contractual ones, they should oppose union proposals that would result in such conversions. If a district is willing to include its statutory obligation to provide information in a contract, it should insist that the union's obligation to provide the district with information also be placed in the contract. Finally, the board should insist that the district will not be required to compile reports or conduct research in response to union requests for information, and that the union will be required to pay for nontrivial copying and other costs involved in its requests for information.

III. Matters Not Covered

Many contracts include a "matters-not-covered" clause. These clauses refer to subjects of bargaining that are not included in the contract. For instance, suppose that a district requires a doctor's certificate for sick leave of four or more days in duration. The union position may be that this is acceptable, and thus it should be included in the contract. However, the board's negotiator may object that if the provision is abused while it is in the contract, the district could not remedy the situation until the next contract goes into effect—which may be two to three years in the future. Therefore, the board refuses to include the clause in the contract, because to do so would eliminate the district's legal right to take remedial action if teachers abuse their right to take sick leave for up to three days without a doctor's certificate.

Consequently, the parties may agree to maintain existing policy on the issue, but to do so without including the policy in the contract. The district could then change the policy during the duration of the contract in order to deal with abuses, but only by bargaining over the change first. If the state bargaining law provides for protracted impasse procedures, the district should also insist upon its right to take remedial action without being subject to those impasse procedures; if the parties were to deadlock in such circumstances, the district's unilateral action would prevail. Not many contracts include such protection for the districts, but they should.

Actually, even if the contract does not refer to "matters not covered," the district might still be required to bargain over any changes in matters not covered in the contract that are within the scope of bargaining. The district should make sure that it can take remedial action promptly if there is abuse relating to matters subject to bargaining but not included in the contract.

Discussion of examples

Example (1) requires the school board to negotiate if it is merely "considering" a change in policy:

(1) A. In the event the Board of Education is considering a change in policy which would come within the scope of this Agreement, or is considering any change in District-wide educational policy which has an impact on the terms and conditions of work, the Board of Education or the Superintendent of Schools shall so notify the President of the Association. The Association shall, within ten (10) days, notify the President of the Board of Education if the Association will exercise its right to negotiate these matters. The Board and the Association shall also negotiate on any appropriation of unanticipated additional sources of public revenue which are not specifically earmarked.
   B. The Association shall also have the opportunity to present its views to the Superintendent, his/her designee, and/or the Board on other revisions of educational policy which the Association may deem desirable at a mutually convenient time.
   C. The District agrees to make every effort to prevent reduction in instructional services to students for the life of this Agreement.

"Considering" is obviously a very subjective standard. Clearly, example (1) requires the school board to negotiate if it wishes to change any matters that are not covered in the contract. In effect, the language also requires the board to negotiate on changes in matters that are outside the scope of negotiations. For example, suppose the board is considering terminating a program that is deemed ineffective; such a decision is outside the proper scope of negotiations. The union may agree that the board has the right to do this, but the union may also argue that according to the language of (1), the board must negotiate on the "impact on the terms and conditions of work," and that therefore, under the contract, any efforts to terminate the program will require negotiations. The requirement that the board negotiate over the use of any unanticipated additional sources of public revenue is also extremely unwise; this would be the case even if the contract specified some minimum amount of collected revenues as a threshold at which negotiations would have to take place. Finally, paragraph C, which commits the district to try to prevent reductions in the level of instructional services, is also outside the scope of negotiations; therefore, the board should not have included the paragraph in the contract.

Like example (1), the following example uses references to a vague standard; it also, like examples from previous sections, places the district's statutory obligations into the contract:

(2) A. Any previously adopted rule or regulation of the Board which is in conflict with a provision of this Agreement shall be superseded by the applicable provisions of this Agreement.

B. The Board agrees that if, during the period of this Agreement, it shall consider the adoption or amendment of any Board policy which shall substantially affect the working conditions of teachers, the Union shall have the right to submit its views in writing on such proposed policy change prior to the Board meeting at which the policy is to be considered, or orally at said meeting.

C. Notwithstanding the foregoing, the Board may take emergency action. Furthermore, this section shall not be construed to limit or affect the no-strike provisions of this Agreement.

In example (2), paragraph A merely restates the school board's legal obligation; even in the absence of A, the agreement would supersede board regulations and rules that conflict with the agreement. The requirement that the board allow the union input on any changes "substantially" affecting the working conditions of teachers is rather vague, since it is not clear how much change would be considered "substantial." Note, however, that the clause relieves the board of any obligation to bargain over changes on matters outside the scope of negotiations.

Example (3) is the preferred option; here, the union has clearly waived the right to negotiate during the term of the contract:

(3) During the term of this Agreement, the Association expressly waives and relinquishes the right to meet and negotiate, and agrees that the District shall not be obligated to meet and negotiate with respect to any subject or matter whether referred to or covered in this Agreement or not, even though such subject or matters may not have been within the knowledge or contemplation of either or both the District or the Association at the time they met and negotiated on and executed this Agree-

ment, and even though such subjects or matters were proposed and later withdrawn.

The language of (3) allows the board to modify any matter not covered by the agreement, whether or not the item is a term or condition of employment and whether or not it has a substantial impact on terms and conditions of employment.

IV. Severability

Severability clauses are intended to answer this question: what is the status of a contract, and/or the obligation to bargain, if sections of the contract are held to be illegal or become impossible to carry out? Most severability clauses provide that the rest of the contract shall remain in force. Quite frequently, the severability clause also provides that the parties must, upon request, bargain over a clause to replace the one that is held to be invalid.

The most common severability clause states that the rest of the contract remains in force if any provision is "declared invalid by a court of competent jurisdiction." Suppose, however, that a state district court declares a contract's agency shop clause to be invalid and the union appeals the decision. A question then arises: does the district have to bargain on the issue immediately — since the district court is a "court of competent jurisdiction" — or can it wait until the appeal is exhausted? Note that if a federal issue is involved, the appeal of a lower court's decision is likely to be resolved only after the contract itself expires. If the lower court's decision were reversed on appeal, the district might be faced with a substantial obligation that would be difficult to meet. If the district budgets for the possibility of such an obligation and the lower court decision is upheld, the union will probably try to have the unspent amounts used for teacher welfare.

The way to avoid such problems is to provide that the severability clause takes effect when a provision is held to be invalid by a court of competent jurisdiction, whether or not the holding is appealed by the union. Inasmuch as a union has the right to seek a restraining order prohibiting a district from acting in accordance with the stricken provision until the appeal is resolved, there is no reason not to include a severability clause in the contract. In view of the small chance that some provision in the contract will be held to be invalid, or that a court decision invalidating a provision will create major problems for the district, the board should not accept any severability clauses that would not allow for severability during appeal processes.

The school board is usually better off if there is no provision in the contract that would force the board to renegotiate an invalid clause. In most cases, the invalid clause provides a union benefit. Therefore, negotiations over any replacement provision will usually be subject to all of the statutory impasse procedures; this means that the negotiations are likely to drag out for a long period of time. If the negotiations involve the replacement of a union benefit, there is not much incentive for the union to agree to some outcome unless that outcome restores the benefit in some way. This is only one reason why it is preferable to avoid renegotiating if a provision is held to be illegal; any unforeseen losses can be made up in the next round of negotiations by the party disadvantaged by the ruling.

Note also that different severability clauses may apply to different sections of the contract. For example, the contract might include a salary schedule that can be reopened if state aid is greater (or less) than anticipated. Meanwhile, the rest of the contract may be covered by a different severability clause, under which the invalidation of a particular section will not trigger the need for renegotiations.

Another way for the board to deal with severability issues is to create a contractual provision under which renegotiations take place when clauses are held to be invalid, but to restrict each renegotiation process to a brief period of time, perhaps by waiving the statutory impasse procedures. The board must take several factors and possibilities into account when dealing with severability issues, but, in general, boards should avoid severability clauses that would allow for renegotiations during the term of the contract.

Discussion of examples

The following examples contain several examples of imprecise language:

(1) If any provision of this Agreement is, or shall be at any time, contrary to law, then such provision shall not be applicable or performed or enforced except to the extent permitted by law, and any substitute action shall be subject to appropriate negotiations with the Union as required by law.

Several parts of example (1) are not clear. The phrase "contrary to law" is not very explicit and should be replaced by a clearer criterion for invoking the severability provision. Presumably, a "substitute action" is an action undertaken in order to replace the stricken provision, but this should also be more explicit. Note that example (1), unlike other clauses, does not state that the parties must bargain if the district takes any action within the scope of bargaining to replace a stricken provision. After all, the district might be content to do nothing about a replacement clause. Suppose, given this, that the board does nothing to replace a stricken provision—is this lack of action considered a "substitute action"? Furthermore, example (1) merely states that the action is subject to negotiations, but it is not clear whether either party has the right to initiate negotiations over the replacement clause. For example, if the contract includes a zipper clause—which typically denies parties the right to renew negotiations before a contract expires—does either party have the right to negotiate over the replacement for the stricken provision? One would have to review the contract to answer this question.

Note how the examples in this section differ with respect to negotiations over replacement clauses. Example (1) states only that "any substitute action shall be subject to appropriate negotiations," leaving open the possibility that there will not be any substitute action. In contrast, example (2) requires immediate negotiations upon the request of either the board or the union, even if the district has not done anything to replace the invalid provision:

> (2) In the event any section or part of a section is proved to be in violation of the law, the balance of the Agreement remains valid and upon the request of either the Board or the Association the parties shall enter into immediate negotiations for the purpose of attempting to arrive at a mutually satisfactory replacement for such provision.

When a provision is declared invalid, the question is whether the rest of the contract should be declared invalid. As noted above, this issue is usually resolved by stating in the contract that all other provisions remain in force if one provision is held to be invalid. Examples (3) and (4) below merely state that the other provisions in the contract remain in effect; unlike examples (1) and (2), these examples say nothing about negotiations over a replacement clause:

> (3) If any provision of this Agreement or any application of this Agreement to any employee or group of employees is held to be contrary to law, then such provision or application shall not be deemed valid and subsisting, except to the extent permitted by law, but all other provisions or applications shall continue in full force and effect.

> (4) Should any part hereof or any provisions herein contained be rendered or declared invalid by reason of any existing or subsequently enacted legislation or by decree of a court of competent jurisdiction, such invalidation of such part or portion of this Agreement shall not invalidate the remaining portions hereof and they shall remain in full force and effect.

Example (3) refers to any application of this contract to any employee or group of employees, but the stricken provision might be applicable only to the union, which is different from "a group of employees." Example (4) avoids this ambiguity; if a provision is declared invalid, the rest of the contract remains in full force and effect.

In general, the best policy from the board's perspective is to avoid any obligation to negotiate over replacements for invalid provisions; such an obligation may force the district to undergo lengthy impasse procedures in order to resolve a single issue. Occasionally, the district will be the party that wants to negotiate over a replacement for a stricken provision, but a contractual provision that establishes a mutual obligation by the board and the union to do so usually benefits the union.

V. Duration and Expiration Date

Generally, multiyear contracts are advantageous to school boards for four reasons. First, the costs of negotiating multiyear contracts are much lower than the costs of negotiating a new contract each year. Second, it is easier for management to make concessions, and for the union to show gains, under multiyear contracts. Third, increases in salary and benefits that are provided "up front" tend to be more valued than increases provided later. Hence, management can often achieve a multiyear contract based upon increases that are initially quite generous while being quite conservative overall. Finally, bargaining annually usually means institutionalizing conflict as a year-round feature of school district operations.

Of course, several factors affect the feasibility of multiyear contracts: these include the stability of district revenues, the district's economic conditions, and the presence of items in the contract that must be deleted or amended as soon as possible. The expiration date is also important. Union negotiators sometimes feel that they cannot exert sufficient pressure on school boards if contracts expire in the summer, when most teachers are not available to participate in rallies, demonstrations, and other pressure tactics. In states where teachers can legally strike, the unions often prefer for the contract to expire just before school reopens in the fall; presumably, such an expiration date enhances the credibility of a strike or a threat to strike. If the contract expires at the end of a fiscal year, such as on June 30, it is more difficult for the union to mount an effective strike threat. The statutory impasse procedures also play a major role in the duration and timing of contracts.

Other things being equal, however, multiyear contracts are better than one-year contracts. One problem that does arise with multiyear contracts is the danger that one or both parties will be severely disadvantaged by something in the contract. The longer the term of the contract, the more likely it is that future circumstances (such as unanticipated increases or reductions in state aid) will lead to unforeseen consequences. For these reasons, contracts that last for three to five years should allow the parties to reopen an item during the term of the contract, but only for a limited period of time and with adequate safeguards against lengthy impasse procedures.

Where collective bargaining has taken place for several years, there should be relatively little change from one contract to the next. In a school system that runs efficiently, the changes will be mainly in the salaries and fringe benefits offered to teachers. Sometimes, however, school boards are unable or unwilling to improve this economic package. When this happens, the unions typically seek concessions on the work rules; for example, the union may request a longer preparation period. Once the board grants such concessions, it is very difficult to remove them from future contracts, even when they lead to severe inefficiencies. In years when the district's finances cannot accommodate large increases in teachers' salaries and benefits, school boards should not weaken the work rules in order to achieve labor peace.

Inexperienced board members and negotiators often underestimate the importance of both the amount of time devoted to bargaining and whether bargaining takes place long before the expiration of the contract or close to the expiration date. Thus, it is important to understand this point: collective bargaining is a union initiative intended to achieve benefits for unions and teachers. The longer that a board's negotiating team is present at the table, the more it will give away.

The date on which negotiations over a successor contract begin is very important. Boards should avoid allowing there to be long periods of time between the date that negotiations begin and the expiration date of the existing contract. Unions typically argue that a long period of time is needed in order to ensure the ability of the parties to utilize the statutory impasse procedures, but this argument is not valid. If negotiations begin two to four months before expiration, the unions are likely to begin with extravagant proposals, believing that there will be plenty of time to submit more reasonable proposals as the expiration of the contract approaches. When the union reaches an agreement long before the existing contract expires, it fosters a perception among teachers that the union has "caved in"; furthermore, the union loses credibility with the teachers when its early positions are changed drastically. Quite often, unreasonable proposals by one side lead to unreasonable proposals by the other. Furthermore, the parties tend not to be well-prepared in these early sessions. If they know that only a few weeks are available for negotiations, they are much more likely to be prepared when negotiations begin.

In most school district contracts, the opening date of bargaining is much too early. Although full-time union negotiators may insist upon an early date to impress their constituents, they often dislike the idea privately. After all, after the negotiator has handled dozens of contracts over the years, another contract is just that and nothing more. One way to get the union's agreement on a realistic date is to insist upon it while making it clear that the district is adamantly opposed to retroactive salary increases. This seems counterintuitive because opposition to retroactive pay increases appears to justify an earlier starting date for negotiations, but the key for the board here is to convince the union that the district will bargain re-alistically from the beginning. Faced with the prospect of losing some of the increases by refusing to accept a realistic future starting date, most unions will agree to a realistic starting date if the district's opposition to retroactive pay increases is credible—but it sometimes is not. Boards should emphasize that they will not accept retroactive pay increases; however, boards should not categorically oppose retroactive pay increases unless they are willing to stick to this position even at the cost of holding up a contract. Boards frequently do not appreciate the tremendous practical implications involved in maintaining a consistent, theoretical opposition to retroactive pay; they forget that such a stand requires that they must not agree to retroactive pay simply as a means to securing a contract. The upshot is that they announce their opposition to retroactive pay, but cannot withstand the pressure when their opposition to retroactive pay is the only issue holding up an agreement.

Discussion of examples

In example (1), the contract expires on June 30, 1999; negotiations shall commence by November 30, 1998. This means that negotiations over the successor contract will begin seven months before the expiration of the existing contract:

(1) This Agreement shall become effective as of July 1, 1997 and remain in effect to and including June 30, 1999 except as otherwise provided herein. This Agreement shall be renewed thereafter in accordance with the statutes unless either party hereto shall give written notice during the period October 1, 1998 through October 31, 1998 to the other party of its desire to modify, amend, or terminate the Agreement. Negotiations shall commence by November 30, 1998.

There is very little chance that any important agreements will be reached during the first five to six months of this period; the union negotiator has nothing to lose by waiting for the district to improve its offer. And as noted above, if by some chance the parties reached agreement on significant items five or six months before the contract's expiration date, teachers would criticize the union negotiating team for not hanging tough in order to wrest additional concessions from the board.

Examples (2) and (3) differ on what sometimes turns out to be a critical point—the actual expiration date of the contract:

(2) This Agreement shall be effective from July 1, 1995, except as otherwise specifically stated herein, and shall remain in full force and effect up to

and including June 30, 1998. In the 1997–1998 school year, each party may agree to reopen negotiations on one Article of their choosing excluding Article V, Teacher Compensation.

(3) The provisions of this Agreement will be effective as of July 1, 1996 and will continue and remain in full force and effect until June 30, 1998, or until a successor Agreement is ratified.

Example (2) provides that the contract shall be in effect until June 30, 1998, whereas example (3) provides that the contract will be in effect until June 30, 1998, "or until a successor Agreement is ratified." In example (2), the district would have the right to act unilaterally if by June 30, 1998 there was no agreement and the impasse procedures had been exhausted. This is not the case in example (3); the contract under this language would remain in effect until a successor agreement was ratified.

Example (4) is an effort to provide flexibility while avoiding protracted negotiations:

(4) Except as provided below, this revised Agreement shall become effective on July 1, 1995 and shall continue in effect to and including June 30, 1998, or continue in effect until a successor contract is negotiated.

The salary schedule, insurance benefits, and extra-duty pay schedule may be reopened by the Association each school year and the District shall have the right to reopen an article of its choice at that time, excepting that binding arbitration will not be subject to a reopener. The parties agree that negotiations for reopeners shall commence no later than May 15 of 1996 and 1997. The parties agree to reach agreement or bargain to impasse by May 25. If agreement is not reached by May 25 of the respective year, the parties agree that at the request of either, both will invoke the impasse procedure under the Rodda Act, but neither party shall be required to participate in more than two (2) mediation days prior to fact-finding. The District agrees to make a total of ten (10) days released time without loss of compensation available to the Association from May 15 to May 25, and the Association agrees that the foregoing fulfills all District statutory obligations concerning released time for negotiations during the 1996 and 1997 years.

The parties agree to commence negotiations on a successor agreement on a date to be selected by the Association no earlier than May 1, 1997 and no later than June 30, 1997. The parties agree to reach agreement or bargain to impasse within twenty-one (21) calendar days of the first negotiating session. If agreement is not reached on or before the twenty-first day after the initial session, the parties agree that at the request of either, both will jointly invoke the statutory impasse procedure, but neither party shall be required to participate in more than two (2) mediation sessions prior to fact-finding, or determination of impasse procedures if fact-finding is not invoked. If statutory impasse procedures are not available to the parties for any reason, the parties agree to seek mediation directly from the State Mediation and Conciliation Service or any other qualified source. The District agrees to make a total of twenty-five (25) days released time without loss of compensation available to the Association for negotiation in 1998, and the Association agrees that the foregoing fulfills all District statutory and contractual obligations concerning released time for negotiations during 1998.

The parties further agree that negotiations to establish the school calendar for each succeeding year of the contract will be held during the first full week of October. If an agreement cannot be reached at this time, the school calendar will be negotiated along with the reopener for the succeeding year.

According to statute, if the parties are allowed to reopen items but do not reach agreement on those items, their disagreement—even if it involves just one item—will be subject to the statutory impasse procedures. Because these procedures may involve mediation followed by fact-finding, they can tie up district resources and institutionalize year-round conflict in the district. To avoid this possibility, the contract in example (4) provides specific limits on the duration of the negotiations over reopeners. Such limits make it easier for the district to provide the union some flexibility in a multiyear contract. Although example (4) is rather complex, its emphasis on brief periods of negotiation with a definite termination point is worthy of consideration.

VI. Maintenance of Benefits/Past Practices

Sometimes union rights can be incorporated in the contract without any explicit reference to them. This may happen as a result of a "maintenance of benefits" or "past practice" clause, or sometimes even in their absence. For example, suppose a school district has allowed the union to hold meetings in district schools for several years without any contractual recognition of the union's right to do so. If the practice has come to be accepted—that is, taken for granted—then it is a term or condition of employment that cannot be changed without negotiating on it first. Note, however, that if the union has tried but failed to incorporate the benefit into the contract during negotiations, then it is not a "past practice" because at least one of the parties does not regard the practice as established.

Sometimes, contractual language explicitly refers to "past practices"; nevertheless, if the contract lacks such language, a practice that has been tacitly accepted by the district will still be considered as having contractual status. If the contract does not contain a zipper clause, the district could notify the union that it proposes to change the practice; the parties would then bargain over the status that will be accorded to that practice for the remaining duration of the contract.

The criteria for determining what is or is not a "past practice" should be considered carefully. Ideally, to be binding on the union and the board, a past practice must meet the following criteria:

- The party asserting the past practice must be able to prove that the other party was aware of the practice. However, it is not necessary to show that the other party thought that the practice could not be changed without negotiations.
- The practice must have happened more than once. The more frequently and the more recently the practice has occurred, the more likely it is that the practice should be considered a "past practice."
- The practice must be accepted consistently in the same set of circumstances. For example, if teachers sometimes left early on Friday without permission, and other times requested permission to do so, then there would be no past practice whereby teachers could leave early on Friday without permission.

During negotiations, the board should insist that the union identify the past practices that would be protected by a past practice clause. If the union cannot identify any such practices, there is no justification for a past practice clause. If the union does identify some past practices, board negotiators can then decide whether to accept a past practice clause. One difficulty that emerges with respect to these issues is that the past practice under consideration may exist in some, but not all, schools in the district; hence, one or more of the negotiating teams may be unaware of them.

A past practice clause can be useful to the district in certain situations. The district may wish to allow certain practices but be rightfully opposed to incorporating them in the contract; if the practices were incorporated in the contract, then the district would not be able to negotiate changes involving those practices during the term of the contract. If the past practice is not included in the contract, the district usually can open negotiations on it during the term of the contract. Thus, putting the practice in the contract usually disadvantages the district; at the same time, however, the union may be fearful of attempts to abolish or weaken the practice if it is not incorporated into the contract.

Instead of accepting an open-ended past practice clause, the board should prefer explicit guidelines specifying which past practices, if any, should be continued. If the teachers have typically been excused at noon on the day before

Christmas vacation, for example, the contract might state that "the parties agree to continue past practice concerning early dismissal time on the last work day before Christmas vacation." The contract should make clear that the only past practices accepted by the parties are those that are explicitly recognized in the contract.

Discussion of examples

Examples (1) and (2) illustrate risky maintenance of benefits clauses:

(1) Except as this Agreement shall hereinafter otherwise provide, all terms and conditions of employment applicable on the effective date of this Agreement shall continue to be so applicable during the term of this Agreement. Unless otherwise provided in this Agreement, nothing contained herein shall be interpreted and/or applied so as to eliminate, reduce, or otherwise detract from any employee's benefits existing prior to its effective date.

(2) Except as modified herein, teachers shall retain all rights, benefits, and privileges pertaining to their conditions of employment contained in the School Code at the time of the execution of this Agreement.

Subject to the foregoing paragraph, nothing contained herein shall be interpreted as interfering with the Employer's right to make, amend, revise, or delete any portion of the School Code; provided, however, that the Association shall be consulted on any changes to be made.

Unless the union and the district have agreed upon the past practices covered by the examples, there is a risk to the district in agreeing to either clause. Example (2) is slightly better from a district's point of view only because it explicitly recognizes a district right to "make, amend, revise, or delete any portion of the School Code," but insofar as maintenance of benefits is the issue, (1) and (2) are practically identical. Neither distinguishes district-wide benefits from those limited to a particular school or group of teachers; this raises the danger that a past practice in one school will be interpreted as a district-wide past practice.

Both (3) and (4) attempt to deal with the past practices by using language that seems to eliminate informal past practices altogether:

(3) If this Agreement does not contain in its written provisions benefits, privileges, or duties previously regarded as part of Board policies, said benefits, privileges, or duties shall not be binding on the School Board.

(4) Any prior or existing understanding, agreement, or practices, whether formal or informal, which are inconsistent with this Agreement are hereby superseded and terminated in their entirety.

Example (4) is slightly superior to example (3) because (4) terminates any past practices that are inconsistent with the contract. Arguably, (3) does not accomplish this, since it states only that such practices shall not be binding on the board. If the practices continue to exist, they carry over to the next contract; if the clause were deleted, the practices would be binding on the board. Note also that there is a difference between a benefit that cannot be enforced and one that no longer exists. For instance, the boards may lack the funds to pay for certain benefits, hence there may be no way to enforce their payment. Nevertheless, it would be to the union's advantage to have the benefits carried over to the successor contract. In any case, the district should not agree to a proposed past practice clause without insisting that the union specify which practices will be covered by the clause.

VII. Zipper Clause

A "zipper clause" is a provision that prohibits the parties from reopening negotiations during the term of the agreement. In the absence of a zipper clause, either party could reopen negotiations at any time. For example, suppose the board and the union agree on the salary schedules for the next three years. Suppose also that the district subsequently receives a much larger infusion of state aid than the parties had anticipated during negotiations. In this case, the union would want to reopen negotiations, and it would have the right to do so if the contract did not include a zipper clause. In effect, a zipper clause is a waiver of the parties' rights to negotiate for the duration of the contract, or for whatever period of time that the parties agree upon.

Quite often, a zipper clause explicitly permits exceptions. For example, since the district and the union often cannot be sure of the amount of state aid that the district will receive during the later years of a multiyear contract, the zipper clause of such a contract might apply to everything in the contract except the salary schedule and insurance benefits. Also, sometimes the parties cannot come to an agreement on contentious issues; with neither party willing to be locked into a disadvantageous position for several years, the solution may be to include an exception in the zipper clause that would allow the board and the union to renegotiate the item in the later years of the contract. On some occasions, the parties may agree to establish a joint committee to provide needed data on the issue; the issue can then be reopened either the next year or when the data is available.

Generally speaking, the district is better off with a comprehensive zipper clause. This is especially true in districts where a reopener involving just one item can activate the statutory impasse procedures. This is because when the parties are negotiating on only one or two issues, there are fewer opportunities for them to find a mutually acceptable quid pro quo and, thus, it is very likely that the statutory impasse procedures will be lengthy.

It must be emphasized, however, that unless the zipper clause clearly states that the parties waive the right to negotiate during the term of the agreement, it will not constitute a waiver of the union's right to negotiate. Arbitrators and the courts take the view that unless a party clearly waives its rights, it will not be considered to have waived them.

Discussion of examples

Example (1) will result in bargaining on a year-round basis:

(1) In the event the Board of Education is considering a change in policy which would come within the scope of this Agreement, or is considering any change in District-wide educational policy which has an impact on the terms and conditions of work, the Board of Education or the Superintendent of Schools shall so notify the President of the Association. The Association shall, within ten (10) days, notify the President of the Board of Education if the Association will exercise its right to negotiate these matters. The Board and the Association shall also negotiate over any appropriation of unanticipated additional sources of public revenue which are not specifically earmarked.

The Association shall also have the opportunity to present its views to the Superintendent, his/her designee, and/or the Board on other revisions of educational policy which the Association may deem desirable at a mutually convenient time.

Space limits how many undesirable features of the example above can be discussed here. In the first place, some of the language is vague; it is unclear what is meant by "a change in policy which would come within the scope of this Agreement. . . ." If the intent of using this phrase is to refer to changes in the contract, the contract should say so. The sentence then goes on to say that when the board "is considering any change in District-wide educational policy which has an impact on the terms and conditions of work," the board or superintendent must notify the president of the union; the union then has ten days to notify the board of its intention to negotiate on the matter. Given such vague language, it is only necessary for the union to show that a change could have an impact on the terms and conditions of work to trigger negotiations, even if the impact is only minor. Furthermore, it is not clear what "considering a change in policy" means. Does the "consideration" have to be official, that is, does it have to be reflected in some sort of board action, or does "consider" refer to a state of mind?

The clause also makes the mistake of designating individuals instead of parties. There is no need to refer to the "Board of Education" or the "Superintendent of Schools"; it is enough to require "the District" to notify "the Association." By the same token, there is no need to notify the "President of the Association" about the matter; again, it should simply be sufficient for the district to notify the union.

Finally, the requirement that the union and the board shall "negotiate over any appropriation of unanticipated additional sources of public revenue which are not specifically earmarked" is obviously a far cry from any sort of zipper clause. It is necessary to ask what "unanticipated" refers to here. For example, is the provision activated if the board anticipated the additional revenue but the union did not? In almost every respect, example (1) is an illustration of what school boards should avoid.

Example (2) is obviously not an adequate zipper clause, but it is a vast improvement over example (1):

(2) This Agreement shall be effective as of July 1, 1997 and shall continue in effect through June 30, 1999. This Agreement shall not be extended orally and it is expressly understood that it shall expire on the date indicated.

In addition, it is expressly understood that the following items may be opened for renegotiations:
    A.   Article XX;
    B.   One (1) Article chosen by each party, if desired;
    C.   Items of mutual agreement; and,
    D.   Conditions of employment changed by legislative action.
Reopeners shall commence between March 15, 1998 and April 1, 1998.

Sometimes there are good reasons for allowing specific items to be reopened, or giving the parties the ability to reopen negotiations over an item or two. For example, there are situations in which the union might be willing to accept a clause that the board desires, but not if doing so would lock the union into a bad situation for several years. Thus, if future district revenues are a huge question mark, it may be desirable to allow the union to reopen negotiations over salary, but not over anything else.

The parties can always reopen any items they wish by mutual agreement; thus the language in example (2)'s subsection C is redundant. The reopener that takes effect if the "[c]onditions of employment" are "changed by legislative action" is another matter. Many legislative actions create changes in the conditions of employment that do not reflect the primary purpose of the legislation. For example, suppose the legislature changes the tenure law; the purpose of this legislation may be to reduce the cost of dismissing incompetent teachers, but the legislation changes the conditions of employment. Or suppose the legislature enacts a different way to deal with disruptive students—again, this changes the conditions of employment, although that is not the purpose of the change. Furthermore, the criterion for reopening negotiations is not clear. Does the provision mean that the entire contract can be reopened after a given "legislative action"? What if the legislative enactment changes the conditions of employment, but there is no contractual provision on the conditions of employment that were changed? The language of the example poses many such questions, and the district should not have accepted it.

Examples (3) and (4) are strong zipper clauses with only minor differences. Both make it clear that the district can adopt policies or regulations that are not inconsistent with the contract—in other words, the district can adopt policies and regulations on terms and conditions of employment, as long as whatever it does is not a violation of the agreement:

(3) Unless otherwise specifically provided herein, it is agreed and understood that each party hereto voluntarily waives and relinquishes its right to meet and negotiate for the term of this Agreement. The District reserves the right to make and enforce policies, rules, and regulations not inconsistent with this Agreement, provided, however, that the District will not initiate or change any officially adopted Board policy within the scope of negotiations which was not included in this Agreement without providing the Union an opportunity to negotiate thereon.

(4) During the term of this Agreement, the Association expressly waives and relinquishes the right to meet and negotiate, and agrees that the District shall not be obligated to meet and negotiate, with respect to any subject or matter whether or not referred to or covered in this Agreement, even though such subject or matter may not have been within the knowledge or contemplation of either or both the District or the Association at the time they met and negotiated on this Agreement, and even though such subjects or matters were proposed and later withdrawn. The District reserves the right to make and enforce rules and regulations not inconsistent with this Agreement.

The last sentence in example (4) illustrates an important safeguard for the district. Quite frequently, district policies on the terms and conditions of employment are incorporated by reference into the agreement. For example, a district may have a noncontractual policy of requiring a doctor's certificate if an employee has been on sick leave for more than four days. If the district wants to reduce this number of days to three, it would have to bargain over the change first. This "incorporation by reference" protects the union against unilateral changes in those terms and conditions of employment that are not included in the contract; however, the language of example (4)'s last sentence ensures that the district can implement changes, such as in the forms used for certain purposes, as long as those changes are "not inconsistent" with the contract.

Several important issues involving union rights are discussed elsewhere in this handbook. Enough has been said here, however, to bring out the basic principles involved in negotiating these rights. Perhaps the most important of these principles is that boards should avoid reliance on the future goodwill and common sense of union leadership when bargaining over the rights of unions during negotiations. With respect to all such issues, the board should consider the worst-case scenario. How would the board be vulnerable if the union was determined to harass or intimidate the board over a successor contract or a particular issue? It is not suggested that the language of the contract should always be drafted to forestall worst-case scenarios, but as the examples show, many boards are oblivious to the negative possibilities that could emerge from their contracts. The board should always bear in mind that union leadership may change for all sorts of reasons, and that even sensible union leaders may be pressured by teachers into taking militant action or preparing to do so. The board's protection should lie not with eviscerating all union rights, but in negotiating sensible safeguards against the abuse of reasonable union rights.

7

Representation Issues

The union represents all the teachers in the bargaining unit on matters concerning the terms and conditions of employment. Generally speaking, most attention is focused on the union's role in contract negotiations, but the union's right to represent individuals in certain situations is often controversial as well. For example, does the union have the right to represent teachers in disciplinary hearings or parent/teacher conferences? Should it have the right? This chapter is devoted to examining these special situations in which the right of representation is either not clear or is especially critical.

I. Parental Complaints

Teacher union positions on parental complaints illustrate a basic inconsistency in the union approach to parents. On the one hand, the unions and the teachers they represent are supposed to give a high priority to parental involvement. On the other hand, the union seeks to protect teachers from parent complaints. The objective of facilitating parental involvement practically disappears in union proposals on parental complaints; the union's role as a representative of teachers (the education industry's "producers") takes precedence over its role as protector of public and parental interests in education. Although the union claims to be the protector of pupil learning and pupil welfare, union and teacher interests sometimes conflict with pupil interests. To be sure, the union's position is that it seeks only to ensure that teachers are treated fairly when parents complain; however, a brief look at their actual proposals—and, all too often, at actual contractual provisions—shows that the unions protect teachers by rendering it extremely difficult for parents to express their concerns or to question teacher conduct.

The union is usually the moving party in negotiating on parental complaints, and unquestionably parents sometimes act indefensibly during parent/teacher conferences. The problem is that teachers sometimes do also, but the contracts seldom seem to take this into account. In fact, the pervasive absence of adequate grievance procedures for addressing parental complaints illustrates the fact that teachers and teacher unions dominate the policies of the national PTA.[1]

Discussion of examples

Example (1) cited below illustrates several objectionable features that are sometimes proposed by unions for resolving parental complaints:

(1) In the event that the Board shall receive any written communications from persons who are not School District personnel, the teacher shall be notified within a reasonable period of time that the Board has received such communication and shall be given an opportunity to read such communications; however, the name of the person who has written such communication may be withheld by the Board. If any communication is to be included in the file, then full disclosure of its source, including the names or sources, must be given.

Information from an anonymous (unknown to the teacher) source shall not be used by the Board as the basis for disciplinary action under any circumstances.

The teacher shall have the right to make a written reply to any communications or notations of information received, as described in this section. Said reply shall be attached to the allegation or information during the entire length of time that it remains as part of the teacher's personnel file.

First, it is highly questionable whether the school board should obligate itself to notify teachers "within a reasonable period of time" of any written communication from nondistrict personnel. For example, the communication may alert district officials to a teacher's conduct that the district should observe without the teacher's knowledge. If a communication suggests that a teacher is stealing gate receipts, observing the teacher may be more desirable than alerting the teacher to the fact that the district is on the lookout for such behavior. Although use of the word "reasonable" might be construed as allowing delays in notification, school boards should generally try to avoid vulnerability to arbitral interpretations of contractual language.

It is also questionable for the district to obligate itself to reveal its sources of information. Many parents would not express their feelings if their names would be revealed to teachers. Bear in mind that under this language, disclosure is required for any communications that go into a teacher's file, even if disciplinary action is not taken or even contemplated. Interestingly enough, the unions do not restrict teachers this way when the teachers wish to complain about the administration. In such cases, the unions typically propose contractual language that would give teachers the right to initiate grievances without disclosing their names. This is a standard union proposal, even though it would be an unfair labor practice for the district to retaliate against any teacher who files a grievance. It is inconsistent for teachers, who are protected by law and a strong organization, to insist upon the right to file anonymous complaints against administrators while demanding the immediate identification of parents who express concerns.

Furthermore, when a complaint is first received, the district has no way of knowing whether the teacher's conduct is part of a pattern or not. If an anonymous complaint asserts that the teacher physically abuses children, and the district does not include the complaint in the file, it would either have to throw the complaint away or face a grievance for maintaining two files on the teacher, which is normally a violation of the district's contract.

Another problem with (1) is that under the provision, information from anonymous sources may not be used as the basis for disciplinary action "under any circumstances." If ten parents are willing to corroborate reports of abusive teacher conduct only if their anonymity is preserved, such information should be available to corroborate similar information from those parents willing to be identified.

Some union proposals provide that a parental complaint cannot be considered unless it is submitted in writing. This is indefensible; it would virtually eliminate all complaints, no matter how justified, from illiterate parents, such as some migrant farm workers. Unions also frequently propose that teachers should have the right to have a union representative present at any meeting between the teacher, a complaining parent, and a school administrator. This would be an intimidating situation for the parent, one that is not likely to foster a candid parental account of the situation.

Sometimes contracts require that the district cannot consider parental complaints unless they are submitted within a certain period of time after the behavior in question. Again, there is no need for such a restriction. The reality is that in their zeal to protect teachers, the unions propose to discard a great deal of information that could be helpful to the district. The underlying problem is that the teacher unions treat parental complaints as tantamount to a criminal complaint against teachers. There is no effort whatsoever to facilitate parental expressions of dissatisfaction or concern, such as those that a manager might receive about an employee in a restaurant, department store, or law office.

In the business world, management encourages customers to express their complaints and concerns. Unless feedback is received and acted upon, customers simply will take their business elsewhere. One might think that school districts, being a monopoly for most practical purposes, and hence not facing the problem of consumer defection, would be even more willing to facilitate the expression of consumer (in this case, parental) complaints and concerns, but this is seldom the case. Public schools often seem to operate on the theory that parental complaints can be ignored because most parents lack a viable alternative to the public schools.

In practice, school boards are subject to a difficult—perhaps insoluble—conflict of interest. Boards are legally charged with the responsibility for protecting the public interest. At the same time, they are producers of education who need to downplay or even conceal negative information about the deficiencies in their producer role. When a district's desire to hide deficiencies is combined with a union's desire to protect teachers from criticism, the result can be an environment in which parental complaints have very little impact.

School boards should not conclude from relatively low numbers of parental complaints that parents are satisfied with the way they are treated. The paucity of complaints is often due to the presence of procedural hurdles, not to the absence of causes for complaint. Most parents do not complain even when they are dissatisfied; after all, in addition to the procedural hurdles, there are questions of whether complaints would lead to any changes, and even whether complaints might lead to teacher reprisals against the children of complainants.

Example (2) implements a contractual procedure under which parent/teacher conferences would be used to deal with parental complaints:

(2) Whenever a parent brings a complaint against a teacher without first going to the teacher involved, it shall be Board policy to notify the teacher immediately of the parent's complaint. The administrator may offer the aggrieved parent his assistance in arranging a conference between the teacher and parent at a date and time acceptable to both.

If the parent/teacher conference does not resolve the problem, the administrator or his representative may then become the third party to the conference.

Example (2) raises this question: What constitutes "resolving the problem"? Is the problem resolved if the teacher or the parent still feels dissatisfied after the parent/teacher conference? Also, how much discretion should teachers have in setting a time and a place for a parent/teacher conference? One might suppose that the district would assume the responsibility for taking appropriate action that would take into account the views of both teachers and parents. However, it is not clear that this will be the case under example (2); the language describing the administrator as a "third party" suggests that the administrator lacks administrative responsibility in these situations. In any event, example (2) does not provide a way to achieve closure on parental complaints.

Example (3) is much more directive in responding to parental complaints, but it hardly constitutes a "Welcome" sign for parents:

> (3) Teachers will not be required to interrupt lessons to participate in parent/teacher conferences. Parent/teacher conferences will normally be scheduled no earlier than the day following a parental request unless an earlier time is agreed to by the teacher. Prior notice will be provided to teachers of scheduled conferences.
>
> A teacher may end a conference between the teacher and the parent(s) if the parent(s) is abusive. The teacher shall report the incident to the principal and request rescheduling of the conference with administrative participation. During this rescheduled conference or subsequently rescheduled conference(s) the teacher may request that the conference(s) be stopped and rescheduled if the parent(s) is again abusive. The administrator participant(s) will not unreasonably deny such a request.

From a public relations point of view, the district should have insisted upon additional language that allows for the possibility that teachers might sometimes conduct themselves unprofessionally during parent/teacher conferences. Parents are occasionally abusive during parent/teacher conferences, but teacher inaccessibility and inhospitability is at least as much of a problem.

With its focus on dealing with abusive behavior, example (3) demonstrates the desirability of district guidelines for the behavior of both parties during parent/teacher conferences. The guidelines should not be prescriptions, but should be sufficiently specific to deal with obnoxious behavior by either parents or teachers. It must be emphasized, however, that the absence of parental grievance procedures is a much more serious problem than protection of parents from abusive teachers.

II. Teacher Evaluation

The union role in teacher evaluation is extremely important. Typically, the union bargains over the criteria for evaluation, the identity of the evaluator, the number and duration of evaluation-related observations, the procedures governing evaluation conferences between the evaluators and teachers, the process for dealing with appeals from negative evaluations, and the regulations governing the teacher files that hold the evaluations. All of these items are very important, but our concern here is limited to provisions under which the union is explicitly involved in the evaluation procedure.

One such issue is whether teachers and/or the union should be allowed to file grievances over evaluations that teachers allege to be unfair. The board should not agree to such proposals for several reasons. Allowing teachers to invoke grievance procedures over their evaluations generates considerable controversy that can often be avoided. Unless and until the school district takes an adverse action based on negative evaluations, there is no need for teachers to challenge them. This is especially true in districts that allow teachers to append their own comments to a negative evaluation; there is no reason why any relevant evidence would be lost if the evaluation is litigated later or becomes the target of a grievance. The side effects of allowing teachers to file grievances over evaluations are also significant; if such grievances can be filed, principals and supervisors will be more reluctant to submit negative evaluations, despite the fact that there are already too few of them in most districts. The final outcome will be more grievances, and hence more time and resources devoted to controversies that would otherwise be unnecessary.

Discussion of examples

An important issue involving teacher evaluation is the right of union representation during the evaluation process. Consider the following example:

(1) A teacher shall have the right to representation in an evaluation conference.

Should teachers, upon request, have a right to have a union representative present during these conferences that follow up on the evaluatory observation of a teacher? Any such right would be counterproductive. If a teacher brings a union representative to such meetings, the district will be forced to have an experienced labor relations expert present also. What should be an informal process in which the utmost candor is highly desirable will become a highly formalized process in which district and union forces discuss matters warily and cautiously. This will happen because each side will want to avoid inadvertently saying something that would give the other party an advantage if the evaluation were to be followed up by remedial or disciplinary action. In short, example (1) would undermine teacher evaluation in most school districts.

Teachers request that union representatives be present at evaluation conferences in order to avoid negative evaluations, or to be prepared to challenge them. Principals and others who evaluate teachers would inevitably avoid critical evaluations if teachers had a right to such union representation, knowing that every such evaluation would lead to confrontations with union representatives. After all, if the union representatives were to agree with evaluators, the teachers being evaluated would question the value of union representation. Furthermore, if the union representatives were teachers in the same district, the costs to the district of their released time could be prohibitive.

Example (2) is less troublesome than (1), but it is still troublesome enough to be firmly rejected by school boards:

(2) All evaluation reports shall be made in writing and shall be based upon an observation of not less than one (1) thirty-minute session or two (2) twenty-minute sessions.

A conference between the evaluator and the teacher who has been observed shall be held within ten (10) school days after the evaluator has completed the last observation or observations, during which conference the evaluator shall discuss with the teacher the statements which are to be made on said evaluation form. A copy of said evaluation shall be given to the teacher.

Should the teacher so desire, he/she may request a second observation and evaluation under the conditions set forth in this Article; an Association representative may be present upon the teacher's request at the second conference with the evaluator.

There is no need or justification for union representatives to be present at an evaluation conference unless the teacher has valid reason to believe that the conference's participants will discuss taking action against the teacher. If union representation during these conferences is allowed, then the teacher will typically be represented by an experienced litigator who will know how to elicit innocent comments that may be used in the future to protect the teacher. The presence of a union representative will thus inhibit candid discussion of teacher performance, because all the parties at the conference will be thinking about how their remarks could be construed if any subsequent action adverse to the teacher is taken.

From the board's perspective, the most desirable outcome of negotiations is a contract that contains no contractual provision on a union role in teacher evaluation. The union will ordinarily have the right to negotiate on the number and durations of observations, the criteria for evaluating teachers, and the appeals from disciplinary actions that result from negative observations or evaluations, but it should not play a participatory role in implementing the negotiated procedures for observation and evaluation. Evaluation procedures that are fair to teachers need not involve the union; the union should become involved only when adverse action is taken on the basis of the evaluations. At that point in time, the union can contest the legitimacy of the evaluations.

III. Teacher Files

Unions pursue a two-pronged strategy with respect to teacher files. First, they negotiate detailed procedures so complex that almost any adverse materials on teacher conduct can be challenged on procedural grounds. Second, they try to require the deletion of negative materials in teacher files after the briefest possible time that the school district will accept.

These tendencies must be resisted. To see why, consider a union proposal under which negative material would be deleted after it has been in the teacher's file for two years, if there were no more instances of the negative behavior cited in the material. If the union proposal is accepted, it may become difficult, if not impossible, to detect undesirable patterns of teacher conduct. Suppose a teacher is accused of sexually harassing a student. It could be significant that a similar accusation had been made against the teacher four years ago, even if that accusation was not upheld; perhaps that charge was not upheld simply because no reliable witness testified. If the record of the prior incident had been removed from the file, an important bit of evidence concerning the present case would have been lost. It must be emphasized that the school district is not trying to convict the teacher of a crime; it is only trying to determine if there is sufficient evidence to justify action to protect the pupils in its care. It is not appropriate to apply the standards of evidence applicable in criminal cases to employment decisions.

Bear in mind that the teacher has the right to respond to negative comments in his or her file in a timely fashion. As long as the district does not act upon allegations of unprofessional conduct, the teacher is not likely to be harmed by leaving the adverse material in the file. Granted, district officials reviewing the file may be negatively influenced by the adverse material, but the risks posed by this possibility are outweighed by the danger of deleting material that may be relevant at some future date.

The fact is that most administrators are reluctant to include adverse material in teacher files. To do so often leads to conflicts that the administrators prefer to avoid. In most districts, the danger is not that administrators will cram the files with unjustified negative comments; it is that they avoid negative comments altogether. Sometimes, for example, they decline to include negative information because it would make it more difficult to get rid of difficult or incompetent teachers who would not be able to transfer or obtain a position elsewhere if a negative evaluation was in their files. In any case, it does not make sense to allow grievances over a report that may never trigger any action against a teacher.

Discussion of examples

Example (1) reflects union attention to detail with respect to employment file issues:

(1) A. Definition and Scope
    1. The term "file" as used herein shall mean the accumulated record of employment which is maintained by the Personnel Office. Hereinafter this file shall be called the teacher's personnel file. All other records of service by teachers shall be considered as informal and without effect upon the teacher's employment status.
    2. All personnel files belong to the School District. Each teacher's personnel file shall contain the following minimum items of information:
        (a) all teacher evaluation reports;
        (b) copies of all contracts up to and including the continuing Contract;
        (c) tenure recommendations;
        (d) record of teaching certificate;
        (e) transcript of academic records; and
        (f) correspondence with the Personnel Office.
    3. Materials which shall be identified as having been received but not shared in totality with teachers shall include:
        (a) pre-employment credentials and communications; and
        (b) communications originating from persons who are not District personnel, as set forth in Section C, below.
    4. Any report of an observation of teaching services of a teacher shall be put in writing, shown to, and discussed with the teacher within a reasonable time after such observation and prior to inclusion in the personnel file; such report shall, in fact, be included in said file if it is to be used for discharge, demotion, or suspension of a teacher.
    5. No material shall be placed in the teacher's personnel file without notifying the teacher of said inclusion and allowing the teacher an opportunity to submit additional comments which shall become a part of that file.
  B. Right to Inspection
    Each teacher shall have the right, upon request and appointment, to review the contents of his/her own personnel file, excluding confidential information described in Section A.3, above. A representative of the Association may, at the teacher's request, accompany the teacher in this review.
  C. Replies to Complaints
    1. In the event that the Board shall receive any written communications from persons who are not District personnel, the teacher shall be notified within a reasonable period of time that the Board has received such communication and shall be given an opportunity to read such communications; however, the name of the person who has written such communication may be withheld by the Board. If

    any communication is to be included in the file, then full disclo-
sure of its source, including the names or sources, must be given.

2. Information from an anonymous (unknown to the teacher) source
shall not be used by the Board as the basis for disciplinary action
under any circumstances.

3. The teacher shall have the right to make a written reply to any
communications or notations of information received, as described in this section. Said reply shall be attached to the allegation or information during the entire length of time that it remains
as part of the teacher's personnel file.

D. Disclosure of File Outside District

    Those materials in the teacher's personnel file which are described in
Section A.3(a), above, shall not be used as the basis of any evaluation
of the teacher for the purposes of information to any individual or
agency outside the district.

    Both parties agree to comply with the provisions of the Freedom
of Information Act (FOIA).

One of the issues that the district did not handle properly concerns the notification of a teacher who receives a complaint. It is questionable whether a
school board should agree to notify the teacher "within a reasonable period of
time" of any written communication received from anyone not employed by the
district. As noted in the section on parental complaints, the district may have
good reason to have an employee placed under surveillance to ascertain
whether the teacher is engaging in questionable behavior; thus what a "reasonable period of time" is in such circumstances could be highly controversial.

Note that clause C.1 requires the board to notify the teachers of all written
communications; this presumably refers to all communications referring to the
teacher in some way. The clause applies whether the communication is favorable, unfavorable, or neither. Suppose a communication refers to a teacher, and
also to several other individuals, some of whom are employed by the district,
but some of whom are not. Notifying the teacher in such a case might lead the
teacher to alert others to pending investigations. Or suppose the district receives
a note from another school district, asking for a confidential assessment of a
teacher being considered for a promotional position; is the district obligated to
show the letter to the teacher? These possibilities suggest the problems that will
arise when school districts agree to such poorly drafted clauses.

Example (2) includes an agreement on where the personnel files will be located:

(2) An employee shall have the right, upon request, to review the contents
of his/her personnel file and to receive copies at the employee's expense
of any documents contained therein. This personnel file will be located

in the Administration Building and will be the only file used by the District to evaluate an employee. An employee shall be entitled to have a representative of the Association accompany him/her during such review, provided the employee requests the same.

This clause raises an interesting issue. To take an extreme case, some school districts in Alaska are much larger than some states. In such large school districts, should the teacher file be kept at the teacher's school, or at the central office? It should probably be kept at both locations, since the school's principal and the district's central office may both legitimately need to review the entire file.

Districts are well advised to impose a cap or limit on the costs that they will pay to provide teachers with copies of their files; (2) does this by making employees bear the costs of copying. However, note that it is very undesirable to allow a union representative to be present during evaluation reviews unless disciplinary action is anticipated.

Example (3) provides ample protection for the district:

(3) Teachers shall have reasonable access to their personnel files and the right to have copies of materials therein at a cost not to exceed the actual cost to the district.

By not specifying the union's rights to examine the files, the location of the files, or any restrictions on what may be placed in the files, the district can accommodate the union on these matters to the extent that the district deems feasible, while retaining the right to change the regulations if there is a need to do so. In particular, example (3)'s refusal to specify a participatory role for the union in maintaining teacher files is a major improvement over examples (1) and (2).

IV. Disciplinary Hearings

Many contracts provide that if and when the school district requests that a teacher be present at a hearing, and there is reason to believe that the hearing may lead to disciplinary action, the teacher has the right to have union representation at the hearing. The disciplinary action under consideration does not have to be a loss of pay or benefits; it may simply be a reprimand or warning. However, since a reprimand or warning could affect a teacher's chances to get tenure or a promotion, unions seek the right to represent teachers, if requested, at any hearing that might culminate in disciplinary action. Even if the hearing is for the purpose of ascertaining whether disciplinary action is called for, a teacher often has the right to have union representation. This tends to formalize the hearing, but from the union and teachers' points of view, teachers should not take the risks associated with the absence of knowledgeable representation at such hearings. Obviously, it becomes necessary to arrive at an agreement establishing both how much notice of such hearings the district must give a teacher and union, and also the nature of the proceedings.

Discussion of examples

From the union point of view, example (1) below is not astutely drafted. It would not authorize union representation at meetings that simply consider whether disciplinary action is called for; only teachers who are being "formally disciplined" would have the right to union representation.

(1) A teacher shall be entitled to have present the building Association representative or co-faculty member when he/she is being formally disciplined for any infraction of rules or delinquency in professional performance.

The following example treats the number of supervisors, rather than the purpose of the meeting, as the criterion for determining when the employee has a right to union representation:

(2) Whenever any member of the bargaining unit is at any meeting concerning observations or ratings with more than one supervisor, the individual shall be entitled to have a representative of the Association present to advise him/her during such meeting or interview.

Suppose, for example, that two different supervisors observed a teacher and are present at the follow-up meetings. Even with this number of supervisors, there is still no reason to have a union representative present unless the meeting is intended to or may reasonably result in disciplinary action.

Example (3) provides for union representation only in cases involving transfer or dismissal:

(3) Whenever the Administration requests a meeting to discuss the continuation of that employee in his/her position or employment, he/she shall be given prior notice of the reasons for such meeting or interview, a listing of the people who will be in attendance, and shall, upon his/her request, be entitled to have a representative of the Association or legal counsel present to advise him/her and represent him/her during such a meeting or interview.

Given its wording, (3) would not be applicable if the purpose of a meeting was to discuss a possible warning or reprimand. If one accepts the idea of union representation at disciplinary hearings, example (3) would not be satisfactory, for it leaves out disciplinary hearings short of dismissal. This is because it uses a nondisciplinary criterion of "continuation . . . in his/her position or employment" to determine when there is a right of representation. This criterion appears to authorize union representation when transfers are contemplated, but that may not have been the intent of the provision.

Example (4) is also not specifically applicable to all meetings that may result in disciplinary action:

(4) When any professional employee is required to appear before the Board or any administrator for purposes of intensive staff development, probation, or reprimand, the professional employee shall be given reasonable prior notice of the reasons for such meeting and shall be entitled to have a representative of the Association present to advise and represent the professional employee during such meeting.

The phrase "intensive staff development" is probably intended to describe meetings in which an employee is told to improve or be dismissed. Conceptually, however, the purpose of "intensive staff development" is not necessarily disciplinary action, hence the language in (4) actually goes beyond what is required to provide representation in cases that involve disciplinary action.

Sometimes the right to representation is combined with a right of teachers to terminate disciplinary meetings if at such meetings they lack representation. Consider the following example:

(5) The employee has the right at any time to terminate a conference or hearing in which he/she has no representation in order to secure timely representation.

Example (5) is poorly drafted. If the district has notified the teacher that disciplinary action may result from the meeting, the teacher should arrange for union representation before the meeting. Allowing an employee to terminate a conference "at any time" provides employees with too much authority to terminate conferences without justification.

Example (6) is also poorly drafted, since it authorizes union representation whenever the teacher "feels" that disciplinary action may result. This is tantamount to allowing union representation at any conference between the teacher and a school administrator.

(6) Whenever any professional bargaining-unit member is required to appear before the Superintendent, Board, and any committee or member thereof, and loss of pay or discipline could result from such appearance,

he/she shall be afforded the right to have a Union representative and/or legal counsel present. Meetings between a principal and a bargaining-unit member should be encouraged for a variety of reasons. However, if in the process of a meeting, the bargaining-unit member feels that it definitely becomes a matter relative to discipline and/or a possible loss of pay, he/she shall be afforded the opportunity to have a Union representative present. The bargaining-unit member shall additionally have the right to confer privately with the principal in order to assess the nature of the appearance before the Superintendent, Board, and any committee or member thereof.

The issues relating to representation at disciplinary hearings can be resolved in the following way. If the district has reason to believe that disciplinary action may result, it should notify the teacher beforehand so that the teacher can arrange for representation; otherwise, there should be no right to representation simply because the teacher feels the need for it. The problem that arises is how to deal with situations in which an unanticipated possibility of disciplinary action emerges during a hearing. In this situation, the teacher should be informed immediately of the possibility so that the teacher can exercise his or her right to representation if the teacher desires to do so.

8

Grievance Procedures

Rights that cannot be enforced are not very helpful. For this reason, the grievance procedure is always one of the most important items in a collective bargaining agreement. Its importance is derived from the fact that it spells out the procedure by which the union and/or the teachers it represents can enforce a claim that the school district has violated their rights under the contract.

Grievance procedures vary enormously, not only in their details but in their implications for the contract and school board/union relations. Whereas most contractual issues involve a small number of subsidiary issues (perhaps five to ten), grievance procedures raise scores of issues that can affect the parties to the contract; indeed, the following discussion takes up only the most important issues that arise in negotiating grievance procedures. Board members and administrators who do not understand these issues can expect to pay a heavy price for their failure to do so.

To clarify the issues, two grievance procedures are presented in full below. As we shall see, the examples share several provisions, almost word-for-word in some cases; however, they differ in that each example covers some issues that are absent in the other, and they also differ in their treatment of some issues, such as the definition of "grievance."

Examples

The first example is a model disseminated by a state education association; it shows what the unions try to accomplish while negotiating grievance procedures:

(1) A. Definitions
1. Grievance
A "grievance" is a claim by a teacher or the Association based upon the interpretation, application, or violation of this Agreement, Board policies, or administrative decisions and practices affecting a teacher or a group of teachers.
2. Aggrieved Person
An "aggrieved person" is the person, persons, or Association making the claim.
3. Party in Interest
A "party in interest" is the person or persons making the claim and any person, including the Association or the Board, who might be required to take action—or against whom action might be taken—in order to resolve the claim.
B. Purpose
The purpose of this procedure is to secure, at the lowest possible level, equitable solutions to the problems which may from time to time arise affecting teachers. Both parties agree that these proceedings will be kept as informal and confidential as may be appropriate at any level of the procedure.
C. Procedure
1. Time Limits
The number of days indicated at each level should be considered as a maximum and every effort should be made to expedite the process. The time limits specified may, however, be extended by mutual agreement.
2. Year-End Grievances
In the event a grievance is filed at such time that it cannot be processed through all the steps in this grievance procedure by the end of the school year, and, if left unresolved until the beginning of the following school year, could result in irreparable harm to a party in interest, the time limits set forth herein shall be reduced so that the grievance procedure may be exhausted prior to the end of the school year or as soon thereafter as is practicable.
3. Level One—Principal or Immediate Superior
A teacher with a grievance shall first discuss it with his/her principal or immediate superior, either directly or through the Association's designated representative, with the objective of resolving the matter informally.
4. Level Two—Superintendent
If the aggrieved person is not satisfied with the disposition of his grievance at Level One, or if no decision has been rendered within

five (5) school days after the presentation of the grievance, he/she may file the grievance in writing with the Association within five (5) school days after the decision at Level One or ten (10) school days after the grievance was presented, whichever is sooner. Within five (5) school days after receiving the written grievance, the Association shall refer it to the Superintendent of Schools.

5. Level Three—Arbitration

    (a) If the aggrieved person is not satisfied with the disposition of his/her grievance at Level Two, or if no decision has been rendered within ten (10) school days after the grievance was delivered to the Superintendent, he/she may, within five (5) school days after a decision by the Superintendent or fifteen (15) school days after the grievance was delivered to the Superintendent, whichever is sooner, request in writing that the Association submit the grievance to arbitration. If the Association determines that the grievance is meritorious, it may submit the grievance to arbitration within fifteen (15) school days after receipt of a request by the aggrieved person.

    (b) Within ten (10) school days after such written notice of submission to arbitration, the Board and the Association shall attempt to agree upon a mutually acceptable arbitrator and shall obtain a commitment from said arbitrator to serve. If the parties are unable to agree upon an arbitrator or to obtain such a commitment within the specified period, a request for a list of arbitrators may be made to the American Arbitration Association by either party. The parties shall then be bound by the rules and procedures of the American Arbitration Association.

    (c) The arbitrator's decision shall be in writing, shall be submitted to the Board and the Association, and shall be final and binding on the parties.

    (d) In the event that the arbitrability of a grievance is at issue between the parties, jurisdiction to resolve the issue shall rest solely with the arbitrator selected in accordance with the provisions of Section C.5(b) of this Article.

    (e) The costs for the services of the arbitrator, including per diem expenses (if any), actual and necessary travel, subsistence expenses, and the cost of the hearing room, shall be borne equally by the Board and the Association. Any other expenses incurred shall be paid by the party incurring same.

D. Rights of Teachers to Representation

  1. Teacher and Association

Any aggrieved person may be represented at all stages of the grievance procedure by himself/herself or, at his/her option, by a representative(s) selected or approved by the Association. When a teacher is not represented by the Association, the Association shall have the right to be present and to state its views at all stages of the grievance procedure.

2. Reprisals

No reprisals of any kind shall be taken by the Board or by any member of the Administration against any party in interest, representative, member of the Association, or other participant in the grievance procedure by reason of such participation.

E. Miscellaneous

1. Group Grievance

If, in the judgment of the Association, a grievance affects a group or class of teachers, the Association may submit such grievance in writing to the Superintendent directly and the processing of such grievance shall be commenced at Level Two. The Association may process such a grievance through all levels of the grievance procedure even though the aggrieved person does not wish to do so.

2. Written Decisions

Decisions rendered at Level One which are unsatisfactory to the aggrieved person, and all decisions rendered at Levels Two and Three of the grievance procedure, shall be in writing, setting forth the decision and the reasons therefore, and shall be transmitted promptly to all parties in interest and to the Association. Decisions rendered at Level Three shall be in accordance with the procedures set forth in Section C.5(c) of this Article.

3. Separate Grievance File

All documents, communications, and records dealing with the processing of a grievance shall be filed in a separate grievance file and shall not be kept in the personnel file of any of the participants.

4. Forms

Forms for filing grievances, serving notices, taking appeals, making reports and recommendations, and other necessary documents shall be prepared jointly by the Superintendent and the Association and given appropriate distribution so as to facilitate operation of the grievance procedure.

5. Meetings and Hearings

All meetings and hearings under this procedure shall not be conducted in public and shall include only such parties in interest and their designated or selected representatives heretofore referred to in this Article.

The second example is from an actual contract that protects management rights effectively.

(2) A. Definitions
    1. A "grievance" is a claim by an employee that there has been a violation, misinterpretation, or misapplication of one or more provisions of this Agreement, thus personally and adversely affecting the employee.
    2. A "grievant" is a unit member who files a grievance in accordance with these provisions. The Association shall have the right to initiate not more than two (2) grievances each fiscal year in addition to any grievances on Association rights specifically designated in this Agreement.
    3. A "day" shall be any day on which a majority of members of the bargaining unit are required to perform assigned duties. However, at the option of the grievant, a grievance based upon an act or condition occurring within the last fifteen (15) days of the school year may be filed in writing before the end of the first week of the beginning of the regular fall semester.
    B. Purpose
    1. The purpose of this procedure is to secure, at the lowest possible administrative level, equitable solutions to the problems which may from time to time arise with respect to this Agreement. Before filing a written grievance, the grievant shall attempt to resolve his/her problem by an informal conference with his/her immediate supervisor.
    2. Nothing contained herein shall be construed as limiting the right of any employee having a grievance to discuss the matter informally with the appropriate member of the Administration, and to have the grievance adjusted without intervention by the Association, provided that the adjustment is consistent with the terms of the Agreement and the Association has been given a copy of the grievance, if submitted in writing at Level One, and an opportunity to state its views prior to the District decision on the grievance.
    3. Since it is important that grievances be processed as rapidly as possible, the time limit specified at each level shall be considered to be a maximum and every effort shall be made to expedite the process. The time limits may, however, be extended by mutual written agreement. Failure to observe designated time limits without securing mutual agreement extending such limits shall result in a waiver of level consideration and shall give the grievant the right to proceed to the next higher level. Failure of the grievant to

adhere to submission deadlines shall mean that the grievant accepts the latest decision and waives any right to further appeal.

C. Procedures—Level One

1. In all cases a grievance must be filed in writing within ten (10) days after the aggrieved person knew, or reasonably should have known, about the occurrence giving rise to the grievance.

2. The aggrieved person shall first present the grievance, in writing, to his/her principal. The written grievance shall include:

   (a) the specific provision(s) of this Agreement that is (are) alleged to have been violated;

   (b) how said provision(s) have been violated;

   (c) the date(s) on which said violation allegedly occurred;

   (d) the specific remedy sought by the grievant.

3. Within ten (10) days after the receipt of the written grievance by the principal, he/she shall meet with the aggrieved person and a representative of the Association (if requested by the aggrieved person) in an effort to resolve it. Any proposed resolution by the principal shall be communicated to the Association within five (5) days after said meeting whenever the grievant proceeds without Association representation. The Association shall have three (3) days in which to file a response.

4. The written disposition by the principal shall be rendered within five (5) days after said meeting if there was Association representation at the meeting, or within five (5) days after the Association response if there was no Association representation at the meeting.

D. Procedures—Level Two

1. Within ten (10) days after receipt of the decision at Level One, the aggrieved person may appeal such decision by filing the grievance in writing with the Superintendent and stating the reason why the decision at Level One was unsatisfactory.

2. Within ten (10) days after the receipt of the written grievance by the Superintendent, he/she shall meet with the aggrieved person and a representative of the Association (if requested by the aggrieved person) in an effort to resolve it. A proposed resolution shall be communicated to the Association within five (5) days after the hearing whenever the grievant proceeds without Association representation, and the Association will have three (3) days in which to file a response. The written disposition by the Superintendent shall be rendered within ten (10) days after said meeting if there was Association representation at the meeting or within ten (10) days after the Association response if there was no Association representation at the meeting.

E. Procedures—Level Three

1. If the aggrieved person is not satisfied with the disposition of his/her grievance at Level Two, he/she may, within ten (10) days after a decision by the Superintendent, request in writing that the Association submit his/her grievance to arbitration in accordance with the rules and procedures delineated in this Article. The Association, by written notice to the Superintendent may, within ten (10) days after receipt of the request from the aggrieved person, submit the grievance to arbitration. If any question arises as to the arbitrability of the grievance, such question shall be ruled upon by the arbitrator prior to hearing the merits of the grievance. The decision of the arbitrator as to the arbitrability of a grievance shall be binding.

2. Within ten (10) days of the Association's submission of the grievance to arbitration, submission of the grievance shall be made to the American Arbitration Association. The parties shall be bound by the rules and procedures of the American Arbitration Association in the selection of an arbitrator and the arbitrator shall proceed under the Voluntary Labor Arbitration Rules of said Association.

3. The arbitrator's decision shall be in writing and set forth his/her findings of fact, reasoning, and conclusions on the issues submitted. The arbitrator will be without power or authority to amend, add to, or subtract from this Agreement, but shall be restricted to a decision as to whether the Agreement has been violated and the relief, if any, to which the grievant is entitled. The arbitrator's findings shall be advisory only with respect to all grievances.

4. All costs for the services of the arbitrator, including, but not limited to, per diem expenses, his/her travel and subsistence expenses, and the cost of any hearing room, shall be borne equally by the District and the Association. All other costs shall be borne by the party incurring them. Either party may request a court reporter to record the arbitration hearing, with the costs to be paid by the requesting party. If the arbitrator requests a court reporter, the costs therefor shall be borne equally by the District and the Association.

F. Rights of Employees to Representation

The grievant has the right to have a representative present at Level One or higher steps of the grievance procedure. The grievant must, however, be present at each step of the procedure. If the grievant is unable to be present due to absence from duty caused by illness, injury, or other emergency, the processing of the grievance shall resume within ten (10) days after the employee returns to duty.

G. Miscellaneous

1. The parties shall make a good-faith effort to process group grievances jointly, provided, however, that the District reserves the right to separate grievances which are, in its judgment, based upon different facts or contractual considerations.

2. The filing of a grievance does not relieve the employee of his/her duty to conform to the direction of his/her supervisor.

3. Every effort will be made to schedule meetings for the processing of grievances at times which will not interfere with the regular work of the participants. However, when it is necessary for a representative designated by the Association to attend a grievance meeting during the day, such representative shall, upon District approval which shall not be unreasonably withheld, be released for a reasonable period of time without loss of pay in order to permit participation in the meeting. Any teacher who is required to appear in meetings or hearings as a witness shall be accorded the same right.

4. In the course of investigation of any grievance, the grievant's representative shall report to the site administrator's office and shall identify himself/herself and state the purpose of the visit upon arrival.

5. Time limits for appeal at each level shall begin the day following receipt of written decision.

6. No reprisal of any kind shall be taken by the District or the Association against any aggrieved person or other participant in the grievance procedure by reason of such lawful participation.

7. All documents, communications, and records dealing with the processing of a grievance shall be filed in a separate grievance file and shall not be kept in the personnel file of any of the participants. Access to the grievance file shall be limited to the grievant and authorized Association and District personnel.

8. Forms for filing grievances, serving notices, taking appeals, making reports and recommendations, and other necessary documents shall be prepared by the District after consultation with the Association and given appropriate distribution so as to facilitate operation of the grievance procedure.

9. Any grievance involving District judgment or based upon an alleged abuse of District judgment may be based only upon a claim that such judgment was not exercised in good faith.

10. Appropriately posted and dated District notices shall be considered as binding all teachers and the Association with knowledge of the contents of said notices.

I. Definition of Grievance

The definition of "grievance" should clarify the circumstances under which a teacher can file a grievance. This is extremely important, especially if the grievance procedure culminates in binding arbitration. School boards should try to negotiate a definition that would allow the filing of grievances only in cases of violations of the contract. This does not mean that boards should not pay any attention to noncontractual grievances, but that such noncontractual grievances should be considered outside of the contractual grievance procedure.

Quite frequently, board policies on the terms and conditions of employment are not explicitly incorporated into the contract. Consequently, the definition of "grievance" may include the following clause: "Board policies on the terms and conditions of employment not included in this Agreement shall be subject to the grievance procedure." In the absence of such language, the union will try to include all such policies in the contract in order to preserve the union's ability to file grievances with respect to the issues involved in those policies.

To see why some board policies on matters subject to bargaining are not included in the contract, consider a district that has a very liberal policy on sick leave: teachers can be absent on sick leave for five consecutive days without having to get a doctor's certificate of illness. The union naturally would like to include the policy in the contract, but the district might legitimately refuse to do so, reasoning that it is willing to adopt a generous policy only because it has the right to change the policy if it is abused. If the policy were included in the contract, the district would be deprived of its protection on the issue. The outcome under such circumstances may be an agreement to leave the policy "as is" outside of the contract, so that the district can change it during the term of the contract after negotiating with the union.

At the same time, it would be disastrous to allow teachers to file grievances over their dissatisfaction with *any* board policy. For instance, dissatisfaction with curriculum policies should not be grievable; curriculum issues are outside the scope of negotiations, and violation of policies concerning these issues would not, to use the language of (2), "personally and adversely" affect the grievant.

Both examples define "grievance" at their respective A.1 sections. Note that the definition in example (1) does not limit what is grievable, whereas example (2) defines a grievance as an employee's claim "that there has been a violation, misinterpretation, or misapplication of one or more provisions of this Agreement" that "personally and adversely" affects the employee. These requirements are not present in (1).

The vagueness of example (1) should also be noted; for instance, what does the reference to "practices" at A.1 mean? Without clarification, "practices" could apply to known or unknown practices; consistent or inconsistent practices; building, department, or district-wide practices; practices of an individual administrator; or all of the above.

II. Who Can File a Grievance?

When considering a contract's provisions involving who can file a grievance, there are three important issues:

1. Can the union file a grievance on behalf of an employee without the employee's consent?
2. How are grievances that apply to two or more employees handled?
3. Is the grievant entitled to carry the grievance to arbitration, or is this right restricted to the union?

Unions try to negotiate an independent right to file grievances, which would apply even if an employee did not give consent or were opposed to union intervention. To support this position, the unions argue that what may be good for one teacher may be bad for other teachers covered by the contract. Furthermore, they note, the contract is between the union and the school board; it seems illogical that the union, as one of the parties to the contract, cannot process a claim stating that the contract is being violated.

The problem is that allowing a union to file grievances without teacher consent creates a risk that the union will file a large number of grievances over matters that teachers are not concerned about. For example, in contested elections for union office, incumbent union officers may file several grievances to persuade teachers that the incumbents are aggressively defending teacher interests. Also, unions sometimes file a plethora of grievances during contract negotiations to intimidate management.

Example (2) resolves this problem at A.2, by allowing the union to file grievances over matters in which the union's rights are at issue. For example, if the union has negotiated the right to maintain a bulletin board in each school, the union could file a grievance if the principal refused to permit use of a board. Also, by allowing the union to initiate only two teacher grievances, the district is protected against a flurry of grievances filed for tactical reasons. (Note that while the contract theoretically allows the union to file an unlimited number of grievances over "Association rights," in practice, grievances involving union rights do not affect teachers directly and may not affect them at all, hence the union is very unlikely to file such grievances for tactical reasons.) Finally, under (2), a "grievant" must be an employee who files a grievance in accordance with the grievance procedure; this differs markedly from (1), in which the definition of "aggrieved person" specifically allows the union to play that role.

III. Group Grievances

Frequently, two or more teachers will file grievances over the same issue. If this is the case—and it is a big "if"—it would be wasteful to hold separate hearings over each grievance; presumably, all the parties have reason to find some way to avoid this outcome.

Example (1) resolves this issue at E.1, by according the union a unilateral right to determine what qualifies as a group grievance. Example (1) also authorizes the union to initiate group grievances directly to the superintendent—skipping the first level of the grievance procedure hierarchy—and to process the grievance through arbitration even if no teacher wishes to do so. This is quite different from example (2), in which the district reserves the right (at G.1) to decide when multiple grievances are really dependent upon the same set of facts and contractual considerations. However, under the language of (2), the parties agree to apply the outcome of any grievance procedure to grievances that are essentially the same with respect to all relevant factors. Then, if the district refuses to treat similar grievances consistently, the union would file a grievance over the district's failure to do so; the issue would then be whether the district was justified in deciding that the grievances were essentially different.

One problem with allowing the union to file group grievances on its own initiative is that the filing of grievances often becomes politicized, either to bring pressure on school management, to gain publicity, or as part of an internal union conflict. No union officer wants to appear reluctant to support grievances. For this reason, school boards should insist upon adequate safeguards against union rights to file grievances in the absence of teacher grievants. Example (2) recognizes the possibility of group grievances but reserves to the district the right to separate grievances. If the district failed to act in good faith on this issue, the union would undoubtedly try to eliminate the district's discretion on the issue in the next contract.

IV. Purpose of the Grievance Procedure

The "purpose" section of the grievance procedure (located in section B in both examples) can affect arbitral and judicial decisions on whether a grievance is arbitrable and whether it should be sustained. For this reason, districts should avoid expansive statements of purpose. The most that they should accept is a provision stating that the purpose of the grievance procedure is to resolve claims that the district has violated, misinterpreted, or misapplied the contract in some way.

In example (1), the "Purpose" clause specifies that anything "affecting teachers" is grievable; in (2), it is clear that the purpose is to resolve disputes over the agreement at the lowest possible level. Note that (2) requires an effort to resolve the matter informally, whereas there is no such requirement in example (1). The language in example (2)'s purpose clause is adequate only because "grievance" and "grievant" are defined very tightly.

V. Time Limits

"Day" is not defined in example (1), but example (2) does define it at A.3. This definition can be important in determining whether the parties have complied with the time limits spelled out in the procedure. As in judicial proceedings, claims must be submitted within a specified period of time. These limits pertain to the amount of time that the union has in which to file grievances and to respond to the district's decisions at various stages of the procedure. Generally, unions want either no time limits or limits of an extended duration; the school district usually prefers that these time limits be brief. The more that grievances are delayed, the more difficult it is to ascertain the facts of the situation. Also, generally speaking, time limits are longer as the administrative level of the appeal rises, since the higher the level, the more likely it is that the grievance will have district-wide consequences.

Note that example (1) does not place any time limits on the grievant to initiate his or her grievance, while imposing strict time limits on the district's time to respond. It is highly desirable for a contract to include reasonable time limits for the presentation of grievances to the school district; otherwise, there is a risk that the union will accumulate a set of grievances to be submitted at a time when the union can cite those grievances to pressure the school board into making concessions. More importantly, the longer that the initiation of a grievance is delayed, the more likely it is that relevant witnesses will not be available or will forget crucial facts about the situation giving rise to the grievance. Setting time limits that require prompt initiation of grievances can help alleviate this problem.

Year-end grievances illustrate the importance of time limits. If grievances are carried over from June to September, key individuals may have left district employment, and thus be unavailable to testify at grievance hearings. Example (2) allows grievants to postpone year-end grievances until the first week of the fall semester (this is specified at A.3). This requirement is too permissive; such postponements should be allowed only when the time limits at the end of the school year would handicap the grievant, and only when everyone involved in the grievance will be available in the fall.

An important issue that is sometimes related to time limits is the teacher's obligation to know of district policies. Private sector contracts often provide that once a grievant knew (or should have known) about an act or condition, he or she has three days in which to file a grievance over that act or condition; districts should include such an obligation in their contracts with the teacher unions. Use of the phrase "should have known" is essential. Otherwise, grievants would be able to delay the filing of their grievances on the grounds that they did not *actually* know the facts giving rise to their grievances; this would allow grievants to submit grievances long after the emergence of those facts or conditions that gave rise to the grievance.

Note that a "should have known" obligation is also important independently of its relation to the issue of time limits, because it allows the district to enforce rules that teachers should know, rather than only those rules that teachers do know. Suppose that a district has a policy under which teachers must sign out if they leave the building, and that the district has posted this policy on bulletin boards in every school. Suppose also that in this district, a teacher leaves his or her school without signing out, and during this time an accident injures the teacher's students. If the district takes disciplinary action against the teacher, the teacher may file a grievance asserting that he or she did not know of the requirement, and that the disciplinary action is therefore unfair. In example (1), the grievance might be sustained for this reason; however, this would not happen in a district using example (2). Not only does (2) contain a "should have known" provision at C.1, but it also contains a provision stating that "[a]ppropriately posted and dated District notices shall be considered as binding all teachers and the Association with knowledge of the contents of said notices." Given these provisions in example (2), the teacher's grievance would not be sustained, because it is based on the teacher's lack of knowledge about the district's well-publicized rule.

VI. Required Information

To resolve grievances expeditiously, school administrators must know the contractual provision allegedly violated, how and when it was violated, and the remedy sought by the grievant. Example (1) does not require the grievant to provide any of this information, thus leaving district administrators uninformed on these matters. When grievants are required to provide this information at the outset, they will often realize that they do not have a sustainable grievance. Furthermore, when there are no information requirements, grievants sometimes change the basis of their grievance when they discover that the grievance has no basis as initially submitted. Changing the basis of the grievance would, thus, be allowed in example (1), but not in example (2).

This difference in information requirements applies to more than the initial filing of a grievance; note also that in (1), the school district may not have any idea about the reasons why its rejection of the grievance was not acceptable to a grievant who decides to appeal. This problem does not occur in (2), which has strict information requirements for appeals to higher levels of authority. The appropriate analogy here is to judicial appellate proceedings: appellate courts must be informed of the reasons why lower court decisions were unacceptable to appellants in order to have an informed basis for assessing the merits of the appeal.

VII. Levels of Appeal

Both examples include a process by which grievants dissatisfied with the rulings of a lower administrative level can appeal to the district superintendent; however, the differences between these processes are significant. In (1), the grievant must file an appeal with the union, which then files it with the superintendent. Although the language of (1) is mandatory ("the Association shall refer it to the Superintendent of Schools"), in practice the union controls the appeal process. If it believes that an appeal to the superintendent would be futile, for whatever reason, it can discourage the grievant from pursuing the grievance. If the union decides to pursue the grievance, it may be able to strengthen the appeal in various ways.

Inasmuch as (2) requires a complete statement of the grievance at the outset, these considerations are not applicable to example (2). Furthermore, example (2) does not require the grievant to appeal to the superintendent through the union. In many contracts, the union has both the right to be informed of the superintendent's decision and an opportunity to state its views before the superintendent responds to a grievance. This is acceptable when the union does not represent the grievant.

In the early years of teacher bargaining, unions and teachers were eager to tell their side of grievances to the school board; their thought was that school boards would often overrule the arbitrary decisions of district administrators. Furthermore, school board members themselves thought that they would lose control of the grievance procedure if grievance appeals went from the superintendent to arbitration. Although this point of view is held less frequently today, many contracts still require an appeal to the school board as the step before arbitration (or, more generally, before the terminal point of the procedure).

Fortunately, neither example makes an appeal to the school board a step in the grievance procedure; there should be no need for such an appeal. First, if a grievance involves a policy issue, any competent superintendent will check with his board before making a decision on the grievance. Requiring an appeal to the board reflects a presupposition that there will be differences of opinion between the board and the superintendent often enough to justify the delay and additional cost of treating the school board as a step in the grievance procedure. In practice, such systematic differences of opinion do not occur very often, and when they do, it is usually because some or all of the board members have been elected as a result of union support.

Second, from a management point of view, giving the board an appellate role is contrary to the way school districts are supposed to be run. Boards are supposed to be policymaking bodies, and school administrators are supposed to carry out the policies adopted by their school boards, with contracts serving as the school board's policies on the terms and conditions of teacher employment. Ideally, there should be a sharp distinction between those who make policies and those who implement them. Hence, school administrators should not be policymakers. When a contract does not clearly specify board policy regarding an issue, the superintendent should elicit the reactions of board members before making a decision over that issue, so that the board can retain its policymaking prerogative. With respect to the appellate process during grievance procedures, retaining this separation of function would require minimizing the school board's role in the implementation of board policies.

Finally, grievance hearings can require a considerable amount of time. Even if the grievance depends on the interpretation of a contractual provision, considerable testimony may be necessary to show how the provision was interpreted by the parties in the past. If boards must consider several time-consuming grievances, they may not have sufficient time to consider anything else. In addition, political factors may render it very difficult for school boards to observe the confidentiality of the grievance procedure.

All things considered, there is no reason to expose a school board to the risk of being bogged down in a plethora of grievance appeals. This would be true even apart from the likelihood that school board grievance hearings may be politicized by picketing and demonstrations by teachers. Even in small districts in which the distinction between "policymaking" and "administration" is difficult—if not impossible—to maintain, school boards should avoid being treated as a level in grievance proceedings that culminate in arbitration.

VIII. Reprisals

Teacher contracts often include a no-reprisal clause, as do both examples here (at D.2 in example (1), and at G.6 in example (2)). Notwithstanding, it is inadvisable for the board to include such a clause. First of all, protection against reprisals is ordinarily included in the collective bargaining statutes. Including a no-reprisal clause in the contract gives teachers the erroneous impression that the union has secured protection for teachers who utilize the grievance procedure. The clause also implies that the school board would engage in reprisals in the absence of the contractual no-reprisal clause. The inclusion of such clauses is another example of the tendency of school boards to include statutory teacher protections in the contract, under the erroneous view that doing so "does not give the union anything it doesn't have already."

IX. Right to Representation

Example (1) specifies at D.1 that the grievant must be represented by either the grievant personally or someone approved by the union. Although union representation is the grievant's option in both (1) and (2), the grievant in (1) must use union-approved representation in meetings above the level of the principal or immediate supervisor.

X. Separate Grievance File

Both examples treat the issue of grievance files in very similar ways, through the use of a provision that is standard in school district collective bargaining contracts. Note, however, that example (2) also explicitly limits access to the file to the grievant and "authorized Association and District personnel." Disagreements requiring arbitration may result from this language, however, since the identities of the "authorized" parties are not clear.

XI. Meetings and Hearings

Generally speaking, grievance hearings are limited to grievants, witnesses, the people presenting the arguments for the district and the union, and the arbitrator(s). The language in example (1), however, which allows only "parties in interest and their designated representatives" to attend, is too strong. A "party in interest" is the grievant and "any person . . . who might be required to take action—or against whom action might be taken—in order to resolve the claim."

Note also that in (2), the union as well as the district must try to schedule grievance hearings at times that do not interfere with "the regular work of the participants." This is more desirable than contractual language specifying that the parties should schedule grievance hearings at times that "do not interfere with instructional time," since the latter language would allow the scheduling of grievance procedures during teachers' non-instructional worktime. Ideally, the contract would only allow hearings to be scheduled "at times that do not interfere with the work of the participants."

XII. Costs

It is customary, as both examples provide, for the parties to split the costs of the arbitrator but pay for their own expenses incurred in presenting their cases. Occasionally, contracts require the losing side to pay the full costs of the arbitrator, but this is probably not a good idea for most school districts. The unions have personnel who are uniquely experienced in grievance matters, whereas most school districts do not. Districts utilizing inexperienced personnel should avoid a "loser pays all" approach.

XIII. Additional Differences

One of the most important differences between the examples is that (1) provides for "binding" arbitration, whereas in (2), arbitration is only "advisory." Because this issue raises so many other basic policy issues, the discussion of it is deferred to the following chapter. Some of the other significant differences between (1) and (2) are as follows:

- In (1), the grievance forms are prepared "jointly" by the board and the union; in (2), the district prepares the grievance forms after consultation with the union. The difference is extremely important; in (2), the district can require grievants to provide the information needed to assess the merits of the grievance at all stages of the grievance procedure.
- In (2), a grievance based upon an alleged abuse of district judgment must be based upon a claim that judgment was not exercised in good faith; (1) has no such provision. Obviously, the language in (2) is much more advantageous to the district.
- In (2), employees are explicitly directed to obey orders from their administrators pending the resolution of their grievances; (1) does not include this management safeguard. Although employees would normally be required to obey orders during the grievance procedure, placing an explicit requirement specifying this in the contract is desirable.

9

Arbitration of Grievances

In most teacher contracts, arbitration is the terminal point of the grievance procedure. Basically, arbitration is a procedure whereby an impartial third party makes a decision in a labor dispute; however, the effect of the decision varies with the kind of arbitration agreed to in the contract. Arbitration may be "voluntary" (the parties have agreed to it) or "involuntary" (it is imposed upon the parties by law). Arbitration may also be "advisory" (the arbitral decision is recommended) or "binding" (the parties are bound by the decision). Binding arbitration is sometimes further divided into two additional categories: "final" (the parties cannot appeal the decision to the courts), and "binding but not final" (the arbitral decision is binding but can be appealed to the courts).

Essentially, there are two kinds of disputes which may be subject to arbitration. One type is "interest disputes," that is, disputes over what the terms of a labor contract should be. If an employer and union were at an impasse over salaries for the coming year, and they agreed or were required by law to turn the dispute over to an arbitrator, this would be an interest dispute. Suppose, however, that the employer and union already have a contract covering salaries, but a dispute arises over what an employee should be paid pursuant to that contract. If the employee files a grievance alleging that he or she was not paid in accordance with the contract, and if the grievance is ultimately carried to arbitration, we have a "rights arbitration," that is, an arbitration over the meaning, interpretation, and/or application of a labor contract.

Although used in certain situations, interest arbitration is not particularly widespread in the private sector. One criticism of such arbitration is that it "chills" the bargaining process: if the parties know that their dispute might be resolved by an arbitrator, they will not make as many concessions as they would otherwise, since arbitrators are often expected to make some concessions to both sides. If, therefore, management has already offered as many concessions to the union as it can before going to arbitration, the only way the arbitrator can give the union more is to award concessions to the union that management cannot reasonably accept. To overcome this problem, some observers urge the adoption of "final offer arbitration" in interest disputes. In this process, the arbitrator is limited to choosing between the final offers of the employer or the union. This procedure is supposed to keep either party from submitting extreme proposals to the arbitrator, since doing so would lead to a heavy risk that the arbitrator will select the final offer of the other party.

There are many other variations and nuances of interest arbitration, but it encounters one major problem in the public sector that does not apply to its use in the private sector. Permitting third parties that are not accountable to the electorate to resolve the terms and conditions of public employment is widely regarded as inconsistent with our system of government. According to advocates of this view, public employment policies, like public policies generally, should be made by officials who are accountable to the public. Significantly, however, many people who regard binding arbitration of interest disputes as an unwise and invalid delegation of public authority nevertheless support binding arbitration of grievances (i.e., rights arbitration) in the public sector. The following discussion, however, suggests that if binding arbitration of interest disputes would be an unwise and possibly illegal delegation of public authority, so would binding arbitration of grievances. Let us see why this is so.

In the private sector, grievance arbitration is a means of resolving conflict over the meaning, interpretation, and application of the terms of a contract between private parties. Obviously, such disagreements concerning contractual terms arise in the public sector as well. In the public sector, however, the disagreement is also a disagreement over a public law or a policy having the force of law.

As in the private sector, the grievance procedure is the focal point of public sector contract administration. The terminal point of this procedure frequently raises contentious issues. For example, public employers frequently object to grievance arbitration, accepting it only if the arbitration is advisory. On the other hand, public employee unions typically object to advisory arbitration; in their view, advisory arbitration allows the employer to decide unilaterally whether or not the contract has been violated. Some union negotiators actually prefer a contract without a contractual grievance procedure to one with a procedure that provides for advisory arbitration.

Even under advisory arbitration, however, a school board does not necessarily make the final decision on whether it has violated its contract, since a union can still go to court to remedy an alleged violation. However, this can be costly, and it is the time and expense required to do this, rather than the legal rights of the parties, that underlies the union argument that the school board is the effective terminal point under advisory arbitration. At one time or another, most citizens have waived their rights in a dispute because of the time and money that would be required to enforce them. Undeniably, such situations exist and it makes sense to avoid them as much as is reasonably possible; thus, the union argument may be correct as a practical matter. However, it is a mistake to treat the union's need to pay the costs of litigating claims of contract violations as equivalent to the absence of any legal right to such litigation.

About 95 percent of private sector contracts provide for binding arbitration as the terminal point of the grievance procedure. Generally speaking, teacher union labor contracts are characterized by more variation on this issue. Although binding arbitration is common, and is certainly increasing in the public sector, there are also many teacher union contracts that provide for advisory arbitration, no arbitration, or even no grievance procedure at all. Binding arbitration is more common among the larger school boards, but all sorts of variations exist among boards of every size.

Several factors underlie this greater variation in public education. The private sector is covered by a single federal law, the National Labor Relations Act, whereas public education is governed by a multiplicity of state laws that differ widely in their treatment of grievance procedures. Some require such procedures to be included in teacher union contracts, some specifically authorize—but do not mandate—binding arbitration of grievances, and so on.

Timing is also a factor. Binding arbitration was the exception, not the rule, in the first contracts that were negotiated after a bargaining law was enacted in a state. Over time, more school boards agreed to binding arbitration, and it became more difficult for others to hold out against it. Even so, many school boards continue to oppose binding arbitration, hence there is more variation on the issue in public education than in the private sector.

In retrospect, it appears that many school boards that accepted binding arbitration of grievances in teacher union contracts did so as a result of their uncritical acceptance of the rationale for grievance arbitration in the private sector. According to this rationale, the arbitrator does not establish or create the terms of the contract; that is the joint responsibility of the employer and the union during bargaining. The arbitrator's task is to apply the terms of the contract to a given set of facts, in order to decide whether or not the employer has violated the contract. Quite frequently, in fact, private sector labor contracts explicitly limit the arbitrator by including language such as the following: "The function of the arbitrator shall be to determine controversies involving the interpretation, application, or alleged violation of specific provisions of this Agreement, and he shall have no power to: add to, subtract from, or modify any of the terms of this Agreement, or any other terms made supplemental hereto; to arbitrate any matter not specifically provided for by this Agreement; or to enter any new provisions into this Agreement."

Shifting this to the context of teacher union contracts, the unions emphasized that a collective bargaining contract is public policy, agreed to by the appropriate school board. They contended that an arbitrator ruling upon an alleged violation of the contract would not be making or formulating policy, but would merely be deciding whether the school board has acted consistently with the policies in the contract. As more and more states enacted bargaining laws, there was increasing acceptance of this rationale for binding arbitration of grievances in teacher union contracts.

Both sides, however, ignored one argument against this rationale, and while it is understandable why unions ignored this argument, the general failure of school district management to consider it has been unfortunate. In the private sector, management usually accepts binding arbitration in exchange for a no-strike clause. Prior to grievance arbitration, private sector unions had no contractually specified way to remedy alleged violations of a contract. Quite often, their only recourse was a "grievance strike," that is, a strike during the term of a contract initiated to force management to cease and desist its alleged contractual violations.

With a great deal of encouragement from the U.S. Supreme Court, management's acceptance of binding arbitration of grievances became the quid pro quo for the union's agreement not to strike during the term of the contract. This quid pro quo, however, was not as advantageous to public sector employers as it was to private sector employers, because in most states, strikes by public employees were already prohibited by statute or judicial decision. For this reason, if public employers agreed to binding arbitration of grievances in exchange for a no-strike agreement from the union, they would be giving the quid when they already had the quo. Undeniably, it was to management's advantage to have the union's contractual agreement to a no-strike clause, but the private sector's trade-off was clearly questionable, simply on bargaining grounds, when applied to the public sector. For the most part, however, public employers did not press the issue. Theoretically, public sector unions might have made, or been asked to make, other concessions to justify binding arbitration, but this did not happen very often.

In any event, many school boards were (and are) very uneasy about accepting binding arbitration. It was almost as if they knew something was wrong with the practice, but could not articulate their objections. Over and over again, they were beaten down by the argument that the arbitrator would only be deciding whether the board had violated its own policies, that is, the policies that the board agreed to by ratifying the contract. The unions also emphasized the argument that binding arbitration was needed so that the public employer would not have the final word on its own malfeasance. Permitting one party to a contract to be the judge of whether it has violated the contract is unfair: the teacher unions have emphasized this argument since the inception of collective bargaining for teacher union contracts. Furthermore, in order to get binding arbitration, they were usually willing to accept contract language which restricted arbitrators, sometimes even more than was typical in the private sector.

Despite the wide acceptance of binding arbitration in the private sector, and despite union acceptance (at least initially) of restrictions upon the authority of arbitrators, there is something deeply troublesome about the argument for binding arbitration in the public sector. Why would a public employer act against itself, that is, why would it try to violate its own policies, while the union would try to uphold the employer's policy? It is almost as if a policeman were urging a violation of the law while a culprit demanded that the law be enforced. As paradoxical as this would be, it is very similar to the outcome of binding arbitration in public education: the teacher union contends that the school board is violating its own policies while the school board denies paternity of the policy it allegedly adopted.

A simple example may help to clarify the issue. Suppose a school board agrees contractually to give salary-schedule credit for "five years of prior teaching experience." Let us assume that in the pre-bargaining years, the board had always interpreted and applied the phrase "prior teaching experience" as if it meant "public school teaching experience." Assume also that contractual language provides that the contract supersedes any past practice that conflicts or is inconsistent with the contract. Subsequently, the union files a grievance based upon the board's refusal to grant a teacher five years of experience credit for the years that the teacher taught in a private school. The union's argument would be that by refusing to grant the five years of prior service credit for teaching in a private school, the board is violating its own policy. True enough, the contract does not distinguish between public school and private school experience; the board is violating contractual policy by refusing to give the teacher credit for teaching in a private school.

From an arbitrator's point of view, the resolution would be clear: the teacher would get the disputed credit. From a public policy standpoint, however, the matter is not so simple. Perhaps the board should have had a more astute negotiator, or perhaps the board was careless. Regardless, a binding arbitral award granting prior service credit for private school teaching experience would establish a public policy—namely, granting credit for such experience—to which the public employer is opposed. It is fallacious to argue that in this case the arbitrator is merely "interpreting" the contract: the arbitrator is formulating policy. In the absence of binding arbitration, the board would not be forced to follow a policy that the arbitrator adopts. Furthermore, the board could resolve any inconsistencies or ambiguities by adopting the policy it desires, instead of being forced to adopt one promulgated by the arbitrator.

Note also that since a grievance may arise as soon as the contract is ratified, an arbitrator's decision may bind the board to an unwanted policy for years. It may also happen that dozens or even hundreds of teachers will benefit from an unwanted policy for this period of time. Surely, then, the arbitrator is establishing board policy in this situation. However, one may still wish to argue that there are situations in which binding arbitration only involves interpretation or application of the contract. Suppose that a board established a policy in the contract that it did not fully understand; had the policy been fully understood, the board would not have adopted it. One could argue that an arbitrator who enforces this policy does not establish the policy; he only states the consequences of what the board has established. Even under the latter interpretation, however, it is clear that binding arbitration of grievances can result in public policies that are not desired by the community's duly chosen representatives who are responsible for those policies. Under our normal democratic political processes, the board at no time would have had to pay for the private school experience of its teachers.

Thus, either our normal democratic political processes take precedence over public sector bargaining, or public sector bargaining takes precedence over our normal democratic political processes. Which process, then, is to prevail? Clearly, the analysis above demonstrates that school boards have a valid reason for opposing, or at least limiting, binding arbitration of grievances. Needless to say, the teacher unions are unlikely to concede at the bargaining table that the analysis above has any merit at all, but they have not as yet challenged it in any public forum or publication.

10

Contemporary Union Initiatives

This chapter briefly reviews two union initiatives that school boards are likely to face in the near future, if they have not been faced with them already. Because of the length and complexity of these union initiatives, it is impractical to analyze them in detail, but this should not be cause for ignoring their emergence and implications. By the year 2000, school boards employing over half the nation's teachers will probably be confronted by union proposals relating to the National Board for Professional Teaching Standards (NBPTS) and/or peer review. Significantly, legislation promoting peer review and NBPTS certification was the main feature of California governor Grey Davis's $100 million education reform proposal submitted to the California legislature in January of 1999. The fact that previous union proposals elsewhere have not dealt with these topics should not lead school management to neglect the issues arising from union proposals on these topics.

I. The National Board for Professional Teaching Standards

The NEA and the AFT are making a determined effort to persuade legislatures and school boards to support teachers seeking certification by the NBPTS. The NBPTS is a board, created and controlled by the NEA and the AFT, which certifies teachers as having attained a superior level of skill and knowledge in their professional work. The unions propose that school boards pay the expenses of teachers seeking NBPTS certification, and also propose that the boards pay teachers who are certified $3,000 to $10,000 more per year on the salary schedule. An effort is also being made to enact state legislation that would provide expense reimbursement or stipends for teachers who apply for or pass NBPTS procedures; this effort has been successful in some states.

There are both theoretical and practical reasons to doubt whether the NBPTS does—or will—identify outstanding teachers. The NEA and the AFT control the board; two-thirds of the board's governing body must be members of the NEA or the AFT, and most of the governing board's members play prominent roles in their unions. It is extremely difficult for unions to insist upon high standards of teacher skill and knowledge because the unions must respond to what a majority of their members want, and the majority of any union seldom supports standards that cannot be met by most union members.

The NEA and the AFT contend that NBPTS certification is analogous to the medical specialty boards, such as the American College of Surgeons, or to the state boards that certify public accountants. In these occupations, certification by an occupational board is not required to practice the profession; candidates for NBPTS certification, like accountants seeking to become certified public accountants, are already certified to practice their professions. Unfortunately, NBPTS procedures and standards are not remotely close to the level of expertise required for board certification in medicine and accounting.[1]

Furthermore, school boards should bear in mind that once they provide stipends for teachers certified by the NBPTS: the unions will negotiate to increase the stipends; more teachers will apply for and receive NBPTS certification; and it will be extremely difficult for the school board to reverse or even halt its expenditures for teachers who seek or have received NBPTS certification. For these reasons, school boards and legislators should avoid minor concessions that position the unions to ratchet up board expenditures for NBPTS certification.

Discussion of examples

The three examples below illustrate the most common patterns in contractual provisions relating to NBPTS certification. Example (1) provides for district reimbursement of the fee teachers must pay to undertake the NBPTS certification process; the application fee for the 1999–2000 examination was $2,000:

(1) Teachers who complete the certification process of the National Board for Professional Teaching Standards (NBPTS) shall be reimbursed by the District for the costs of the certification application fee.

Example (2) pays a stipend for NBPTS certification based on a percentage of the teacher's salary, while example (3) pays one based on a flat amount. Undoubtedly, (3) will turn out to be less expensive than (2) in the long run, especially if and when large numbers of teachers are board-certified.

(2) Teachers who have been certified by the National Board for Professional Teaching Standards (NBPTS) shall receive a fifteen (15) percent increase in their regular salary, exclusive of any stipends for extracurricular activities.

(3) Teachers certified by the National Board for Professional Teaching Standards (NBPTS) shall be paid an additional $3,000 in 1997–98 and 1998–99, and an additional $4,000 in 1999–2000.

The recommended course of action for the board is to provide no stipend for teachers certified by the NBPTS or for teachers preparing to be tested for NBPTS certification. This policy should be followed unless and until the NBPTS procedures and standards are examined and approved by qualified authorities who are not employed by or beholden to the teacher unions in any way.

II. Peer Review

In recent years, the NEA and the AFT have aggressively promoted "peer review." Essentially, peer review is a process in which teachers that the union identifies as superior are released from their classroom duties for a year or more to help new teachers. In some instances, peer review is also utilized to assist tenured teachers whose competence has been questioned for one reason or another.

Peer review programs are very expensive and have yet to demonstrate any tangible benefits for anyone other than the teachers who are paid $3,000 to $6,000 more than their regular salary to leave the classroom for a year or two. Because the procedure weakens the authority of principals to evaluate teachers, peer review runs contrary to most education reform recommendations. It should also be noted that in the school districts that have led the way with respect to peer review programs, the NEA and AFT affiliates have negotiated contracts that are extremely favorable to the unions. Peer review strengthens the unions because the unions decide, or at least have a veto power over, which teachers receive the higher salaries associated with serving as a "consulting teacher" in peer review programs.

In any case, school districts confronted by union proposals on peer review should ask the following questions:

- What are the objectives of peer review?
- What are the criteria to measure progress toward the objectives?
- What will be the total costs of the program?

- How long will it take to decide whether peer review is a cost-effective way of improving instruction?
- Is a proposal to have members of the bargaining unit observe and/or evaluate other members within the scope of negotiations?
- Will consulting teachers be evaluated on how effectively they serve in this capacity? If they will be, how and by whom will such evaluation be carried out? If the consulting teachers are not to be evaluated for service in this capacity, doesn't the proposal for peer review avoid individual accountability for a very important personnel function?
- To whom will teachers appeal if they wish to challenge the recommendations of peer reviewers?
- What provisions are or would be in place to protect the rights of nonunion teachers, antiunion teachers, or teachers who are critical of incumbent union leadership?
- How are consulting teachers to be appointed?
- How will challenges to union officers who are consulting teachers receive a fair hearing?
- Does peer review replace the tenure hearings provided by the state tenure law? If not, isn't the process merely another hurdle that the district must overcome to dismiss incompetent teachers?
- Will teachers who are not rehired as a result of peer review be eligible to teach elsewhere? Since they nearly always are, how can peer review be considered a step toward professional status? (Note that if such teachers are not eligible to be rehired, then dismissal from employment as a result of peer review would be tantamount to a statewide ban on employment as a teacher—an indefensible outcome. The teachers and/or administrators in a school district should not have the power to decide that a particular teacher cannot teach anywhere in the state.)
- Are there any costs of peer review to the union? To the peer reviewers?[2]

As my recent study of peer review, *Teachers Evaluating Teachers,* points out, it is "unlikely that any union can provide adequate answers to the questions listed, but adequacy is in the eye of the beholder. Generally speaking, it would . . . be inadvisable to agree to a joint committee to study proposals for peer review. Such joint committees usually prolong bargaining. Peer review is a union proposal; unless and until the union can make a persuasive case for it in some form, the district should not accept it. Instead, the district negotiators should counter with proposals that enable school management to dismiss incompetent teachers without the all-out opposition of the union."[3]

It is not feasible to include here examples of contractual language on peer review, because peer review plans in the leading peer review districts are lengthy, complex provisions that are unintelligible without knowledge of the rest of the contract as well as the arrangements that are incorporated by reference in the contract. At a minimum, these plans cover the following matters:

- The governance of peer review programs
- Who is subject to review
- The role of the principal in peer review schools
- The role of consulting teachers
- How consulting teachers are selected and assigned
- The qualifications of consulting teachers
- The ratio of teaching interns to consulting teachers
- The terms and conditions of employment for consulting teachers
- The procedure for appeals of peer review evaluations and decisions
- The forms used in observing and evaluating teachers who are subject to peer review
- The duration and possible termination of the peer review program
- The implications of peer review for other contractual provisions, such as teacher observations and evaluations
- The implications of peer review for the union's duty of fair representation

Some of the above topics include several subtopics that require extended discussion in their own right. Readers who wish to review the contractual language of peer review provisions and the detailed peer review plans in the leading peer review districts should see *Teachers Evaluating Teachers.*

11

Beyond Collective Bargaining

Collective bargaining is an adversarial process. Proposals such as "win-win bargaining," which emphasize cooperative negotiating techniques, are often intended to persuade school boards that the process is not adversarial; these proposals are either naive or part of a strategy to take advantage of an unsuspecting adversary. Understandably, frustrated school boards often wonder if there is a better, less adversarial way of resolving employment issues.

The answer to this question is yes and no. In theory and in practice, systems of individual representation have demonstrated their superiority over collective bargaining in many fields, including education.[1] However, it is not likely that such a system can be implemented in states that have enacted collective bargaining laws for teachers. Collective bargaining facilitates unionization; unionization leads to powerful organizations that have a huge vested interest in maintaining collective bargaining and in blocking any change toward other systems of employee representation. Nevertheless, a brief discussion of alternative systems should be helpful in all states, regardless of their systems of employee representation for teachers.

At the outset, a few basic facts about unions must be kept in mind. One is that private sector unionization has been declining steadily in the U.S. since 1953, when 36 percent of the private sector labor force was unionized.[2] In 1999, only 9 percent was unionized, and the percentage is expected to drop even further in the immediate future. In another year or two, perhaps only 7 percent of private sector workers will be unionized; this is the same percentage that prevailed in 1900.

Several developments help to explain the decline of union membership in the private sector. First, a large, if indeterminate, number of private firms cannot afford the inefficiencies associated with unionization and collective bargaining; in many competitive markets, these inefficiencies lead to intolerable burdens on firm viability. The fact that unionization tends to depress profits and weaken the value of stock in unionized companies is another factor in the decline of private sector unions; more and more employees recognize that their individual welfare is partly dependent on company welfare, and that company welfare is threatened by unionization.

Second, private sector employers have frequently provided the benefits that unionization claims to provide. These companies have adopted policies and disseminated company publications that foster worker satisfaction with their companies and their jobs. Company publications emphasize the importance and economic role of profits in enabling firms to obtain the plants, equipment, tools, and people essential for growth and survival in a competitive industry. This weakens union efforts to portray profits as synonymous with greed or wrongdoing of some kind. In addition, by emphasizing the importance of meeting the needs of customers, and by supporting and participating in community programs, many companies demonstrate that profits are not their only concern.

Finally, union membership has also fallen in the private sector because many companies have established management policies that assure employees of fair treatment, not only with respect to grievances, but also with respect to opportunities for advancement within the company. The unions tend to belittle these company efforts, but there is a sound economic reason for them. Ordinarily, companies have invested a great deal in training their employees. Just as companies would not deliberately waste or throw away their physical capital, they have good reason not to waste or lose their human capital; actions that lead valuable employees to leave the company do not make good business sense. Thus, although it is true that some company supervisors and managers do not always act fairly toward the employees under their supervision, companies often establish appeal procedures that provide safeguards against this eventuality. This is not to say that private sector employers never act unfairly; the point is that the risks of such action are frequently too low to persuade most private sector employees that they need a union.

In this connection, note that racial, religious, and gender discrimination in employment have been against the law throughout the nation since the passage of the Civil Rights Act of 1964. Employees can receive assistance from local, state, and/or national governmental agencies, as well as from a variety of nongovernmental organizations, to challenge employer discrimination along these lines. In education, tenure laws often provide protection against the arbitrary dismissal of teachers, further weakening the need for union protection.

Public education, however, like public employment generally in the United States, presents a very different picture of union strength than does the private sector. The percentage of teachers in unions increased from less than 1 percent in 1960 to an estimated 65 percent in 1999. Clearly, however, a substantial number of U.S. teachers reject collective bargaining, and this has been the case for several years. In Missouri, Texas, and Georgia, the leading nonunion teacher organizations enroll more members than the state affiliates of the NEA or the AFT, and even in states in which the teacher unions enroll more members than the nonunion organizations, union membership includes many teachers who joined the union only because they would otherwise be required to pay agency fees that are almost as costly as union dues. These teachers join because the monetary difference between the dues and agency fees is not worth the time and trouble associated with refusing to join the union.

The point to bear in mind is that teacher unions are vendors of representational services; teachers are the consumers. When a teacher union enters the scene, teachers have to decide whether union services are worth the costs; these costs include accepting the union as an intermediary between the teachers and the school board. As school boards act more wisely, more and more teachers are deciding that the benefits of union representation and membership are not worth these costs.

If this is the case, one might suppose that teachers would ordinarily reject union representation, and so they often would if not for cost factors. There are enormous personal costs involved in running a campaign to end union representation. In the bargaining-law states, there must be a campaign to persuade a sizable group of teachers (usually at least 30 percent of the teachers in a district) to request a representation election. If this petition meets the legal requirements to initiate such an election, the teachers must then conduct a campaign against an incumbent union that relies on teacher dues for its revenues. Such campaigns are highly one-sided affairs. The teachers seeking decertification of the union must pay for their campaign from their personal resources, while their union opposition has access to practically unlimited resources, including several full-time union staff to prepare flyers, operate telephone banks, contact media, and perform the other tasks inherent in a campaign of this kind.

A campaign to end union representation can involve a host of legal issues. For example, the incumbent union might challenge the adequacy of the petition, dispute the validity or timeliness of its signatures, allege that the petitioners used unfair labor practices in obtaining the signatures, or question the arrangements for the election. A frequent union tactic is to file lawsuits over these issues, knowing that the petitioners will be unable to pay for the legal services needed to fight the union charges in court. Sometimes the teacher unions also threaten to sue teachers individually in order to intimidate them.

This huge disparity in resources explains why the teacher unions are able to prevent decertification and a return to individual representation. Unions argue that teachers must believe that union services are worth the dues; otherwise, teachers would resign from the union and/or exercise their legal rights to decertify the union. In practice, however, the teacher unions sometimes go to court specifically to prevent members from resigning immediately; obviously, members who wish to resign are not going to spend thousands of dollars in legal fees to uphold their right to resign in January instead of June. Such intimidation is cost-effective for the union, but places an intolerable burden on individual teachers who wish to resign immediately—and, as noted before, in most situations, resignation is the only practical way for individual teachers to influence union policies.

School boards in states without a collective bargaining law are still in a position to institute a system of individual representation that meets teacher needs without unionization. This window of opportunity will not necessarily be available for a long period of time; the NEA and the AFT are making strenuous efforts to enact bargaining laws in states that have not done so.

In the bargaining-law states, repeal of the bargaining laws in the near future is very unlikely. The NEA and the AFT constitute core constituencies of the Democratic Party at the local, state, and national levels. It is, therefore, extremely unlikely that any state legislative chamber controlled by Democrats would vote to repeal a state bargaining law. Because the teacher unions can usually persuade at least a few Republicans in closely contested districts to support union objectives, repealing a state's bargaining law would require solid Republican majorities in both houses of a state's legislature, as well as a Republican governor. Such dominance of state politics does not happen often.

The best strategy is not to try to repeal the bargaining law; it is to offer teachers an alternative system of representation. Opposing such a choice would be problematic for the unions, since it would be difficult for them to argue that the teachers cannot choose their system of representation wisely. At the present time, teachers must choose between collective bargaining or no representation, but it is possible to draft legislation that provides teachers with other choices.

Whatever state is under discussion, however, everyone should understand that unionization has experienced an enormous and probably irreversible decline in the private sector. The unions flourish in public education only because individual teachers do not have the resources to compete against affluent teacher unions in decertification campaigns, and because public education is a government monopoly. Like most other representatives of monopolies, the teacher unions adamantly oppose any changes that might lead to reform, but their power to prevent such changes is waning as we enter the new millenium.

Appendix A

A Glossary of Collective Bargaining Terms

advisory arbitration—*See* **arbitration.**

agency fees (fair-share fees)—Payments to a union by nonunion employees as a condition of employment; these should equal the prorated costs of collective bargaining, contract administration, and grievance processing.

agency shop clause—A provision in an agreement which requires that all employees in the bargaining unit who do not join the employee organization must pay a representation fee to help defray the union's expenses as exclusive representative. These fees must be based solely upon the union's expenditures for collective bargaining, grievance processing, and contract administration; all other union expenditures are not chargeable to agency fee payers.

agreement—A written agreement between an employer (or an association of employers) and an employee organization (or organizations), usually for a definite term, defining conditions of employment, rights of employees and the employee organization, and procedures to be followed in settling disputes or handling issues that arise during the life of the agreement. *See also* **collective bargaining.**

American Arbitration Association (AAA)—A private non-profit organization established to promote arbitration as a method of settling commercial and labor disputes. The AAA provides lists of qualified arbitrators to employee organizations and employers on request, and provides legal and technical assistance to arbitrators.

American Federation of Labor-Congress of Industrial Organizations (AFL-CIO)—A federation of approximately eighty-five autonomous national and international unions created by the merger of the American Federation of Labor (AFL) and the Congress of Industrial Organizations (CIO) in December of 1955. More than 80 percent of union members in the United States are members of unions affiliated with the AFL-CIO. Use of the initials AFL-CIO after the name of a union indicates that the union is an AFL-CIO affiliate.

American Federation of Teachers (AFT)—The second-largest teacher union in the U.S.

anti-union animus—A hostile attitude toward the union reflected in an employment decision, taken without a legitimate business motive, which discriminates against an employee because of union activity.

arbitration—A dispute resolution procedure in which an impartial third party renders a decision on an issue submitted by the parties.
> **advisory arbitration**—A form of arbitration in which the parties are not obligated to accept the terms of settlement recommended by the arbitrator.
> **binding arbitration**—A form of arbitration, used to resolve grievance or bargaining impasses, in which the parties are obligated to follow the terms of settlement recommended by the arbitrator; this is distinguished from advisory arbitration.
> **grievance arbitration (rights arbitration)**—A contractually agreed-upon procedure for the settlement of grievances, usually involving interpretation and application of the collective bargaining agreement or past practices by an impartial third party.
> **interest arbitration**—A form of arbitration used to resolve the terms and conditions of employment (but *not* used to settle questions of rights under an existing contract).

arbitrator—An impartial third party to whom disputing parties submit their differences for decision (award). An ad hoc arbitrator is one selected to act in a specific case or a limited group of cases. A permanent arbitrator is one selected to serve for the life of the agreement or for a stipulated term, hearing all disputes that arise during this period.

authorization card—A statement signed by an employee designating an employee organization to act as his/her representative in collective bargaining. An employee's signature on an authorization card does not necessarily mean that he/she is a member of the organization but rather indicates that the employee supports the organization as his/her bargaining agent.

bad-faith bargaining—Bargaining motivated not by a sincere desire to reach agreement, but rather by a desire to weaken the other party or to embarrass its leadership.

bargaining unit (negotiating unit)—A group of positions that has been recognized by the employer or certified by a state labor relations board as constituting an appropriate unit for the purposes of collective bargaining.

binding arbitration—*See* **arbitration.**

business unionism—A union emphasis on higher wages and better working conditions through collective bargaining rather than by political action or radical reform of society. The term has been widely used to characterize the objectives of the trade union movement in the U.S.

cap (on cost of benefits)—A provision which places a dollar or percentage limitation on an employer's liability to fund the increased costs of a particular benefit. Caps are useful tools to help employers contain rising health benefit costs.

card-check—A procedure whereby signed employee authorization cards are checked against an acceptable list of employees in a prospective bargaining unit to determine if the organization has majority status.

caucus—In collective negotiations, a recess from bilateral deliberations at the bargaining table for the purpose of discussing bargaining issues away from the other party in negotiations.

certification—A determination by a state labor relations agency that a particular employee organization is the choice of a majority of the employees in an appropriate bargaining unit, and hence the exclusive bargaining representative of all the employees in that unit. The determination usually follows a secret ballot election of the employees in a bargaining unit.

check-off—*See* **payroll deduction of dues.**

collective bargaining—A process whereby employees as a group and their employers make offers and counteroffers in good faith on the terms and conditions of employment, for the purpose of reaching a mutually acceptable agreement and the execution of a written document incorporating any such agreement if requested by either party. Also, a process whereby a representative of the employees and their employer jointly determine the employees' conditions of employment.

collective bargaining agreement—The document incorporating the results of the negotiations between the parties; a written instrument setting forth the terms and conditions of employment, grievance resolution procedures, and any other accords resulting from collective bargaining. Also known as the "contract" or "agreement."

collective negotiations—*See* **collective bargaining.**

community of interest—A factor to be considered in determining whether employees should be grouped together as an appropriate bargaining unit. A common worksite, similar training and pay, and common supervision are some of the criteria used to determine whether employees share a community of interest.

company union—An employee organization that is organized, financed, or dominated by the employer and is thus suspected of being an agent of the employer rather than of the employees. The term also survives as a derogatory charge leveled against an employee organization accused of being ineffectual.

concerted activity—Usually means a strike, but refers to any kind of job action by a group of employees that is intended to pressure the employer to settle quickly.

confidential employee—An employee whose work responsibilities or knowledge would make his/her membership in any appropriate negotiations unit incompatible with his/her official duties. To be considered a "confidential employee," the job's actual ongoing functions must lead to knowledge of the employer's bargaining strategy and negotiating positions.

consent election—A secret ballot election, conducted by agreement between an employer and one or more employee organizations, by which employees in a proposed bargaining unit vote to decide which, if any, employee organization is desired as their bargaining representative.

consultation—The process through which the employer seeks the opinions and suggestions of employees and employee organizations in the formulation and implementation of policies. The employer maintains its management prerogatives and makes the final decisions.

contempt of court—A judicial response to an action that obstructs or tends to obstruct administration of justice by a court. In labor disputes, failure to obey an injunction, or a court order enforcing the cease and desist order of an administrative agency, may lead to contempt action that can result in a fine, imprisonment, or both.

contract administration—The condition of working under, interpreting, and applying the terms of the collective bargaining agreement.

contract bar—A contractual provision that protects the union during the life of an agreement by limiting the filing of representation petitions to a specified "open period."

contracting out—The practice of hiring a company or third party to perform services (as opposed to using existing employees).

counterproposal—An offer made by either party in collective bargaining negotiations in response to a proposal by the other party.

decertification—A procedure for removing an employee organization from its role as the certified bargaining representative. This process begins after a petition is filed with the state labor relations board alleging that the organization no longer represents a majority of the employees.

discrimination—The shortened form for "differential treatment of union and nonunion employees in regard to hire or tenure of employment as a means of encouraging or discouraging membership in a labor organization." Such discrimination is an unfair labor practice under federal and state labor laws. The term also refers to the refusal to hire, promote, or admit a person to union membership because of race, creed, color, sex, or national origin.

dual unionism—A charge (usually punishable by the union) leveled at a union member or officer who seeks or accepts membership or a position in a rival union, or otherwise attempts to undermine a union by helping its rival.

due process—The procedural protections that are enjoyed by government employees in their relationships with their various governments.

duty of fair representation—The union's duty to represent all members of a bargaining unit equally, regardless of their union membership status.

duty to bargain—*See* **unfair labor practice.**

Education Policy Institute (EPI)—A policy organization based in Washington, D.C. that publishes a wide variety of materials on teacher union issues.

election—A proceeding in which members of an appropriate bargaining unit cast secret ballots to determine which, if any, employee organization is to become the unit's exclusive bargaining representative.

exclusive representative (majority representative)—The employee organization certified to represent the employees in an appropriate bargaining unit. The exclusive representative is designated as the agent for collective bargaining and grievance processing for all employees in the unit, both members and nonmembers. No other union is permitted to represent the employees, and individual employees in the bargaining unit are not free to negotiate their own contracts.

fact-finding—An impasse resolution process that is more formal than mediation. Factfinders hold quasi-judicial hearings in which both parties present evidence to support their bargaining positions. Based on the information presented, factfinders issue nonbinding recommendations for a settlement.

free riders—A derogatory term applied to persons who share in the benefits resulting from the activities of an employee organization, but who are not members of the organization and do not pay it dues.

fringe benefits—Generally, the supplements to wages or salaries received by employees at a cost to employers. The term encompasses a host of practices (paid vacations, pensions, health and insurance plans, etc.) that usually add to something more than a "fringe," and is sometimes applied to a practice that may constitute a dubious "benefit" to workers. No agreement prevails as to the list of practices that should be called "fringe benefits." Other terms often substituted for "fringe benefits" include "wage extras," "hidden payroll," "nonwage labor costs," and "supplementary wage practices." The Bureau of Labor Statistics uses the phrase "selected supplementary compensation or remuneration practices" in place of "fringe benefits" for survey purposes.

good-faith bargaining—The requirement that an employer and employee organization meet at reasonable times to negotiate in good faith, with an intent to reach an agreement with respect to wages, hours, and other terms and conditions of employment. Good-faith bargaining does not require an employer or union to agree to a proposal or to make a concession, but each party must maintain an open mind and a willingness to be persuaded by the other party.

grievance—A complaint by an employee or a union, usually arising over a question of the interpretation or application of the collective bargaining agreement.

grievance arbitration—*See* **arbitration.**

grievance procedure—The procedure outlined in the collective bargaining agreement which authorizes employees to appeal managerial decisions. Grievance procedures generally establish who may file a grievance, what may be grieved, how the grievance will be processed, and how it will be resolved.

group grievance—A grievance in which two or more employees assert the same alleged violation of their rights.

hard bargaining—Bargaining that minimizes the interests of the other party while avoiding charges of an unfair labor practice.

hold harmless clause—A clause that protects one of the parties, usually the union, against liability in case a specific provision in the contract results in liability to third parties.

impasse—A point at which either or both parties in negotiations determine that no further progress toward settlement can be made through direct negotiation. This also refers to the state of negotiations that exists after mediation, fact-finding, and post-fact-finding negotiations have failed to result in an agreement.

injunction—An order restraining individuals or groups from committing acts which may do irreparable harm. There are two types of injunctions: temporary restraining orders, which are issued for a limited time and prior to a complete hearing; and permanent injunctions, which are issued after a full hearing and remain in force until such time as the conditions which gave rise to their issuance have been changed.

interest arbitration—*See* **arbitration.**

interest dispute—A dispute over what *should be* a term or condition of employment; this is distinguished from a dispute over the rights which *are* in an existing contract.

job action—A term for any concerted effort by employees to exert pressure on management during negotiations by using tactics which adversely affect the quality and/or the quantity of their work performance.

joint committee—A committee composed of representatives of both the employer and the union.

just cause—A standard denoting a variety of due process safeguards, such as the rights to notice and a hearing, which are used to ensure that discipline has been imposed in an appropriate manner and for sufficient reasons.

labor organization—Any organization, employee representative, committee, or plan in which employees participate and which exists for the purpose, in whole or in part, of dealing with employers with respect to terms or conditions of employment.

lockout—An employer action that prohibits employees from working.

maintenance of membership clause—A clause prohibiting union members from resigning their union membership except during specified window periods.

management prerogative—A term for the areas in which employers have the right to make unilateral determinations. These rights are often expressly reserved to employers in statutes, agreements, or memoranda of understanding.

management-rights clause—A contractual provision specifying areas or issues over which the employer retains control.

mediation—A process in which a neutral third party assists parties in a bargaining dispute to come to a voluntary agreement by suggesting possible areas of compromise, bringing a different point of view to the table, clarifying issues, and using other techniques designed to bring the parties closer together and narrow their disagreements.

merit pay—The linking of the salaries of individual employees to an evaluation of their performance. As a form of compensation, merit pay is an issue that is, by mandate, negotiable in the bargaining-law states.

minority union—A union that continues to maintain its identity, and in which a minority of employees continue their membership, even though the union does not have exclusive bargaining rights. A minority union lacks these rights because it has not been able to win the support of a majority of the employees in a particular unit.

National Education Association (NEA)—The largest teacher union in the U.S.

National Labor Relations Act (NLRA)—A federal statute enacted in 1935 that protects the rights of private sector employees to organize and bargain collectively.

National Labor Relations Board (NLRB)—The federal agency responsible for administering the NLRA.

National Right to Work Legal Defense Foundation (NRTWLDF)—A foundation based in Northern Virginia that represents, without charge, employees seeking redress against union abuses. The NRTWLDF is the main litigator in cases alleging that union agency fee charges are excessive.

negotiations—*See* **collective bargaining.**

neutral—An individual who acts as conciliator, mediator, factfinder, or arbitrator; alternatively, any disinterested third party who intervenes in negotiation disputes in order to facilitate a settlement. Also referred to as an "impartial third party."

no-reprisal clause—A clause prohibiting one or both parties from retaliating for actions taken during negotiations.

no-strike clause—A provision in a collective bargaining contract in which the union promises that during the life of the contract, the employees will not engage in strikes, slowdowns, or other job actions.

open period—A period prior to the expiration of a contract in which employees may try to decertify the exclusive representative.

organizational security—Provisions in collective bargaining agreements that provide the union various protections, such as rules of employment mandating union membership, the payment of dues or representation fees, and arrangement of the employer's collection of those monies.

past practice clause—Existing practices, sanctioned by use and acceptance, that are not explicitly included in the collective bargaining agreement (except, perhaps, by reference to their continuance), but which cannot be changed except through collective bargaining.

payroll deduction of dues—A practice whereby the employer, by agreement with the employee organization (upon written authorization from each employee where required by law or agreement), regularly withholds organizational dues from employees' salary payments and transmits these funds to the organization. Payroll deduction of dues is a common practice and is not dependent upon the existence of a formal organizational security clause. The arrangement may also provide for deductions of initiation fees and assessments.

permanent arbitrator—An arbitrator who is appointed for a specified period of time to hear all grievance arbitrations during that time. A permanent arbitrator has no tenure in his position and serves at the pleasure of the parties.

picketing—The patrolling of the entrance to an establishment by union members. The goal of picketing may be to persuade other workers to stop work or to publicize the existence of a dispute. Picketing may also be used to pressure an employer to agree to certain contract terms, to settle a grievance, or to cease and desist from alleged unfair labor practices.

progressive discipline—A process in which increasingly severe penalties are imposed on an employee when lesser discipline fails to correct the employee's behavior.

protected activity—Those activities, involving the exercise of rights under labor relations statutes, which are specifically allowed. Generally speaking, public employees have the right to form, join, and assist any employee organization (or to refrain from any such activity) freely and without fear of penalty or reprisal.

raiding—Term applied to an organization's attempt to enroll members belonging to another organization, or employees already covered by a collective agreement negotiated by another organization, with the intent to usurp the latter organization's bargaining relationship. A "no-raiding agreement" is a written pledge signed by two or more employee organizations to abstain from raiding, and is applicable only to signatory organizations.

ratification—Formal approval of a newly negotiated agreement by a vote of the organization members affected.

recognition—The acceptance by an employer of an employee organization as the representative of employees in an appropriate bargaining unit. Recognition usually follows an election in which the majority of employees have selected an organization to represent them. Under certain conditions, employers may also voluntarily recognize an organization without an election or official certification.

reduction in force (RIF)—An elimination of staff positions; in an education context, this is often as the result of a decline in enrollment.

released time—Time off from work, with or without pay, to conduct union business or for other specified purposes.

reopener clause—A provision in a collective bargaining agreement stating the time or the circumstances under which negotiations can be requested prior to the expiration of the contract. Reopeners are usually restricted to specific issues and not used for the contract as a whole.

representation proceeding—A procedure for the purpose of determining the representative of employees, if any, in an appropriate collective bargaining unit. This proceeding may also be used to settle a question or controversy concerning the representation of employees for the purpose of collective negotiations.

right-to-work law—Legislation which prohibits any requirement that an employee join or pay fees to an organization in order to get or keep a job.

scab—A derogatory term for an employee who refuses to go out on strike with his co-workers, or an employee who is hired to replace a striking employee.

scope of negotiations (scope of bargaining)—The range of subjects over which employers and unions must bargain if requested to do so by the other party.

severability clause—A clause that upholds the validity of a contract despite the invalidity of one or more provisions in it.

showing of interest—A presentation of evidence that a certain number of the employees in the proposed bargaining unit wish to be represented by the petitioner for the purposes of collective bargaining.

slowdown—A concerted effort to pressure an employer into making concessions by working at rates that are slower than normal work responsibilities.

statutory benefits—Employment benefits that are provided by statute, rather than by the collective bargaining agreement.

strike—A concerted work stoppage by employees, resulting from a bargaining impasse or some other conflict between employer and employee.

supervisor—A person, employed by management, who has the power to hire, discharge, discipline, or to effectively recommend the same. In most states, supervisors may not be included in a collective bargaining unit that negotiates for nonsupervisory personnel.

surface bargaining—Lack of intent to reach an agreement; superficial negotiating. Surface bargaining constitutes a refusal to bargain and is an unfair labor practice.

sweetheart agreement—A collective agreement that is exceptionally favorable to a particular employer in comparison with other contracts, which implies that more favorable conditions of employment, from the perspective of employees, could be obtained under a legitimate collective bargaining relationship.

terms and conditions of employment—Generally speaking, this refers to wages, hours, working conditions, and fringe benefits. Terms and conditions of employment constitute mandatory topics of negotiations, and are those matters which intimately and directly affect the work and welfare of employees and on which negotiated agreement would not significantly interfere with the exercise of inherent managerial prerogatives.

unfair labor practice—A practice on the part of either union or management which violates the provisions of the state or federal bargaining statutes. Examples of union violations include: (1) causing an employer to discriminate against an employee on the basis of that employee's membership in a union; (2) refusing to bargain collectively with an employer; (3) interfering in an employer's exercise of its rights under the statute; and (4) failing to fairly represent all members of the bargaining unit. Examples of management violations include: (1) controlling or interfering with unions; (2) discriminating against workers for their union support or activity; (3) retaliating against workers for complaining to an administrative agency; and (4) refusing to bargain collectively with the exclusive representative.

union security—*See* **organizational security.**

UniServ director—The National Education Association's term for its union representatives or business agents.

unit clarification or modification—A change in the composition of the bargaining unit. Unit clarification is a procedure for eliminating or adding certain employees to an existing bargaining unit. Accretion is the assimilation of employees into an existing unit. Consolidation is a means for overcoming fragmentation of a unit by combining existing units into one comprehensive unit.

unit determination—A procedure by which a labor relations agency determines the appropriateness of including or excluding employees in certain positions from the bargaining unit. Unit determination criteria are frequently established by statute and provide guidelines to the agency in judging what positions to include or exclude from the bargaining unit.

unit determination criteria—Factors established for guidance in creating bargaining units. These include "community of interest" (the existence of common aspects of employment), "efficiency of operation" (the employer's capacity to function in view of the inclusion of certain employees in the same unit), the bargaining history of the parties (the manner in which the parties have previously functioned), and the preferences of the employees.

walkout—A concerted abandonment of work and/or the workplace as an effort to achieve concessions from the employer, protest a policy, or demonstrate support for a group or cause.

whipsawing—The tactic of negotiating with one employer at a time, using each negotiated gain as a lever against other employers in the same industry or geographic area.

win-win bargaining—Bargaining procedures that emphasize cooperative techniques as a way to achieve agreements that are beneficial to both employers and unions.

work stoppage—A temporary halt to work, initiated by workers or the employer, in the form of a strike or lockout. This term was adopted by the Bureau of Labor Statistics to replace "strikes and lockouts." In aggregate figures, "work stoppages" usually means "strikes and lockouts"; applied to a single stoppage, it usually means "strike or lockout" unless it is clear that it can only be one of the two. These difficulties in terminology arise largely from the inability of the Bureau of Labor Statistics (and, often, the parties themselves) to distinguish between strikes and lockouts; drawing this distinction in particular cases can be difficult because the party initiating the work stoppage is not always evident.

work to rule—A job action in which employees adhere to the letter of a labor contract in an effort to pressure employers into concessions of one kind or another.

zipper clause—A provision in a collective bargaining agreement that explicitly states that the written agreement is the complete agreement of the parties and that anything not contained therein is not agreed to unless put into writing and signed by both parties following the date of the agreement. The zipper clause is intended to prevent either party from demanding renewed negotiations during the life of the contract.

Appendix B

References

Basic Patterns in Union Contracts. 13th ed. Washington, DC: Bureau of National Affairs, 1992.
A good summary of how various issues are treated in private sector labor contracts.

Edwards, Harry T., R. Theodore Clark, Jr., and Charles B. Craver. *Labor Relations Law in the Public Sector: Cases and Materials*. 4th ed. Charlottesville, VA: Lexis Law Publishing, 1991.
The best analysis of the legal issues growing out of public sector bargaining.

Geisert, Gene, and Myron Lieberman. *Teacher Union Bargaining*. Chicago: Precept Press, 1994.
An analysis of the most important issues that must be faced in collective bargaining with teacher unions.

Haar, Charlene K. *The PTA: The Untold Story*. Forthcoming.
The first detailed analysis of how teacher union contracts affect parents.

Lieberman, Myron, ed. *Bargaining: Before, During, and After*. Chicago: Teach 'Em, 1979.
A how-to manual on bargaining with teacher unions. Covers bargaining-policy issues, subjects of bargaining, strategy and tactics in teacher bargaining, and school board/union relations. A glossary of labor relations terminology and the rules of the American Arbitration Association are also included.

Lieberman, Myron. *Public Education: An Autopsy*. Cambridge, MA: Harvard University Press, 1993.

This book presents the case for a competitive education industry, and why it will materialize.

Lieberman, Myron. *Teachers Evaluating Teachers: Peer Review and the New Unionism*. New Brunswick, NJ: Transaction Publishers, 1998.

Critically analyzes the theory and practice of peer review in K–12 education.

Lieberman, Myron. *The Teacher Unions*. New York: Free Press, 1997.

The most comprehensive analysis of the NEA and the AFT—their policies, revenues, membership, bargaining objectives, political operations, influence, and much more.

Strassman, Esther, Curt Wary, Norman Cluley, and Kathleen Vogt. *The Negotiations Advisor*. Trenton, NJ: New Jersey School Boards Association. Updated annually.

Although geared to New Jersey law and judicial decisions, this is a very useful publication for school board members in any state that has enacted a bargaining law.

Notes

Chapter 2. School Board/Union Relations

1. The following discussion of management rights is adapted from Joseph Herman, "Strategy and Tactics in Negotiating with School Employee Unions," in Myron Lieberman, ed., *Bargaining: Before, During, and After* (Chicago: Teach 'Em, 1979), 115–20.
2. Unfortunately, state judicial opinions since 1975 have narrowed management rights in California considerably.
3. See Myron Lieberman, *The Teacher Unions* (New York: Free Press, 1997), 225–28.

Chapter 3. Organizational Security

1. See Myron Lieberman, *The Teacher Unions* (New York: Free Press, 1997), 147–71.
2. *Lehnert v. Ferris Faculty Association,* 111 S.Ct. 1950 (1991).
3. See Lieberman, *The Teacher Unions,* 172–90.

Chapter 4. Union Rights

1. See Myron Lieberman, *The Teacher Unions* (New York: Free Press, 1997), 109–23.

Chapter 7. Representation Issues

1. For a detailed discussion of this point, see Charlene K. Haar, *The PTA: The Untold Story,* forthcoming.

Chapter 10. Contemporary Union Initiatives

1. For a detailed analysis of the NBPTS, and of various problems associated with it, see Myron Lieberman, "Take the $25 Million and Run," *Government Union Review* 11 (Winter 1990): 1–23; and Danielle Duane Wilcox, "The National Board for Professional Teaching Standards: Can It Live Up to Its Promise?" in Marcie Kanstoroom and Chester E. Finn, Jr., eds., *Better Teachers, Better Schools* (Washington, DC: Thomas B. Fordham Foundation, 1999), 163–97.
2. This list is adapted from Myron Lieberman, *Teachers Evaluating Teachers* (New Brunswick, NJ: Transaction Publishers, 1998), 97–98.
3. Ibid., 98.

Chapter 11. Beyond Collective Bargaining

1. For evidence and an explanation of this issue, see Leo Troy, *Beyond Unions and Collective Bargaining* (Armonk, NY: M. E. Sharpe, in press).
2. Ibid.

Index

Accountability, 30, 180

Advisory arbitration, 177, 179, 180, 196. *See also* Arbitration

Agency fees, 5, 57, 61, 63–69, 71–72, 193, 195

Agenda: of negotiations, 124; of school board meetings, 93, 94

Agreements, 195. *See also* Collective bargaining agreements; Teacher union contracts

American Arbitration Association (AAA), 195–96

American Federation of Labor-Congress of Industrial Organizations (AFL-CIO), 196

American Federation of Teachers (AFT), 11, 12, 27, 59, 69, 101, 187, 196; and the National Board for Professional Teaching Standards (NBPTS), 185–86; and released time for union officers, 117, 120; and unionization, 193, 194

Announcements, 91

Anti-union animus, 103, 196

Arbitration, 9, 196; and grievances, 52, 170, 171, 174, 175, 179–84. *See also* Advisory arbitration; Binding arbitration

Arbitrators, 181–82, 183–84, 196

Authorization card, 196–97

Authorization form, 58, 62, 69, 70

Bad faith, 15–16; bargaining, 197

Bargaining. *See* Collective bargaining; Negotiations

Bargaining laws, 29, 121, 125, 129, 194

Bargaining unit, 12–14, 49, 197

Binding arbitration, 169, 177, 179, 181–84 passim, 196. *See also* Arbitration

Bulletin boards, 86–89

Bureau of Labor Statistics, 200, 207

Business unionism, 197

California, 33, 185

Cap: on benefits, 197

Card-check, 197

Caucus, 197

Censorship, 84, 86, 87

Certification: National Board for Professional Teaching Standards (NBPTS), 185–87; union, 193–94, 197. *See also* Decertification, union

Check-off. *See* Payroll deduction of dues

Civil Rights Act of 1964, 192

Collective bargaining, 1, 14, 64, 136, 191, 197–98; alternatives to, 191, 194; and public education, 8, 51, 192–93; and state laws, 8–9, 14, 57; and statutory benefits, 51–55. *See also* Negotiations

About the Author

Myron Lieberman is a senior research scholar of the Social Philosophy and Policy Center and is chairman of the Education Policy Institute. He was educated at the University of Minnesota and the University of Illinois and has taught at the University of Pennsylvania, Ohio University, the University of Southern California, and the City University of New York. He has served as a consultant to six state legislative bodies and several national organizations on questions of collective bargaining, as an expert witness, and as a chief negotiator or consultant in collective bargaining in numerous school districts.

Dr. Lieberman is the author of sixteen books on education policy, including *Public Education: An Autopsy* (1993), *The Teacher Unions* (1997), and *Teachers Evaluating Teachers: Peer Review and the New Unionism* (1998).